GEORGE FREDERIC WATTS

VOL. II

THE ANNALS OF AN ARTIST'S LIFE

H. H. H. Cameron, photographer.   Emery Walker Ph. sc.

G. F. Watts

1888

GEORGE FREDERIC WATTS

VOLUME II

THE ANNALS OF AN ARTIST'S LIFE

BY

M. S. WATTS

HODDER & STOUGHTON
NEW YORK
GEORGE H. DORAN COMPANY

COPYRIGHT

ILLUSTRATIONS

	FACE PAGE
G. F. Watts at Work on "Physical Energy" (1888) .	*Frontispiece*
In the Garden at Little Holland House, Melbury Road .	85
Garden Doorway, Limnerslease	209
Limnerslease on the South Side	218
A Limnerslease Workshop	271
In the Barn Garden	284
G. F. Watts at Work upon the Statue of Lord Tennyson (August 1903)	305
G. F. Watts at Limnerslease (November 1903). An Instantaneous Photograph	315
G. F. Watts (1904). Unfinished	319
The Studio, Little Holland House, Melbury Road . .	324

ERRATA

Page 20, line 18, *for* Evelene *read* Eveleen.
„ 39, line 3 from bottom, *for* Thorneycroft *read* Thornycroft.
„ 40, top line, *for* Thorneycroft *read* Thornycroft.
„ 64, line 5 from bottom, *for* Sinaiitic *read* Sinaitic.
„ 85, line 3 from bottom, *for* Aitcheson *read* Aitchison.
„ 135, line 7 from bottom, *for* Colleone *read* Colleoni.
„ 219, line 4 from bottom, *for* Pilgrim's *read* Pilgrims'.
„ 234, line 8, *for* Leon *read* Léon.
„ 299, lines 21-22, for *Afterwards* read *After*.

CHAPTER XI

The mesmeric influence possessed by individuals must be possessed by artistic productions.

Without this quality they will be cold, and not breathing, will not live always. Those who live by breath a great work hypnotises—a work in which there is life speaking to life.

G. F. WATTS.

CHAPTER XI

In the spring of the year 1880, Mr. Rickards was asked to show his whole collection of Signor's pictures; and he sent some fifty-six in all to the Manchester Institution. Thus, for the first time, the public saw and were able to judge of a considerable portion of the work of his life. Almost seven years before, in writing to Mr. Rickards, Signor had given him as his opinion that works of art, of a certain class, could only be understood when collected and exhibited together. He wrote thus :—

"I agree with the writer in the *Globe* that contest is healthy, and creates and fosters energy and eagerness, so up to a certain point may be productive of vigour; but, whilst appreciation of art is of the character that distinguishes it at present, such competition only leads to business speculation, just as activity in trade very often only tends to encourage adulteration. I believe the critic wrote, as critics but too often write, without considering more than one aspect of the case. Anyhow, I have come to a very different conclusion, and feel very strongly that the best way to create interest in a more solemn and serious character of art would be to get together a sufficient number of pictures of the class, and exhibit them all together."

He held that "unripe judgment and hasty criticism must be the unfortunate result of exhibitions open only for a short time, and of works wholly heterogeneous."

Sir Coutts and Lady Lindsay had been to see Mr. Rickards's collection, and had told Signor that they were immensely struck by the value given to the work. They had, in fact, come back as he writes, "converted to the opinion that an artist's pictures should be seen together."

Nevertheless, when the idea of showing the pictures publicly was first mooted, he shrank from the ordeal, and Mr. Rickards tried to reassure him by sending him an extract from the *Academy*, where some years before a very appreciative notice of the collection had appeared. The writer had said : "Collectors do not often limit themselves to the works of a single master, nor, among modern painters at least, are there many who can be said to claim such exclusive worship. The experiment has, however, been tried with the best results in the case of Mr. Rickards, where the talents of a living painter are represented with a fulness that could scarcely be matched elsewhere." With his thanks for this article Signor writes :—

"I should indeed be difficult to please if the notice did not satisfy me, but I fear it is from too friendly a hand. I confess I dread the result of your experiment,—of the effect on the public of so many pictures by the same hand, challenging criticism under conditions of light, etc., not contemplated by the workman.

"I dread this unfavourable result less on my own account than on yours, for I think it would give you great pain to have your old friends mauled by adverse criticism. As for myself, such things have happened to me many a time and oft; but, though I am not without my due share of an artist's sensitiveness, the contemplation of the wide distance on which I have always fixed my eyes enables me to estimate the present at its real value, and not to take for rocks the ordinary stepping stones of daily life.

"I hope you are well; I am not good for much myself, and have done very little work.

"Pray have the light of the exhibition room lowered as much as possible, the more the better. It requires a hundred years to bring a picture that aims at grave effects to its proper tone; until after that lapse of time it should not be exposed to strong light."

On the close of the exhibition at the Manchester Institution, Mr. Rickards wrote: "From all quarters I continue to receive accounts of the educational work they (the pictures) have succeeded in accomplishing."

The effect of the experiment—indirect as it may have been—was to suggest to Sir Coutts Lindsay the idea of forming at the Grosvenor

Gallery a winter exhibition of what came to be called the Watts Collection.

Signor was now being urged once more to use his pen in the *Nineteenth Century*; this time on the subject of the so-called lesser arts, held by him to be of vital importance to great art. "The work of a good craftsman was," he said, "as necessary to the life of a fine art as the root is to the tree." Art without this root is nothing but an exotic. He wrote: "Environed by mechanical works and trusting to machinery, the powers of observation have almost ceased to be, to the majority, a human characteristic. The most deadly foe to art is machinery, because standing in opposition to sense of beauty of form and arrangement. The rudest handwork is never without unconscious beauty, never without a something that belongs to the life."

Lady Marion Alford had asked him to write upon the School of Needlework, established lately at South Kensington, and Mr. Knowles proposed that an article on this revival should be written.

I find a letter from Lady Marion's daughter-in-law, Lady Brownlow, asking him to help this cause by writing a letter for publication. Mrs. Percy Wyndham had also added her petition. To her he replies: "Why do you all persist in believing me capable of all kinds of things? I haven't an idea; at this moment no one can feel more like a fool! I wish you were in town to talk the matter over with me, ever so little;

however, I hope you are well and enjoying the country." And again, later, answering a letter of Mrs. Wyndham's, he says :—

"MY DEAR MRS. WYNDHAM—Exactly !— what you want are some eloquent, some burning words that will create a rush into the work.

"Doubtless I ought, any one ought, to be able to say something in a matter so important, and that I really feel so much as part and parcel of a great subject, but I can only say my say in a most prosaic manner, and have no gift of persuasion. What is wanted is something from Ruskin, or Morris, or perhaps best of all Burne-Jones. I have already set down something of what I would say if speaking on the matter, and will show it to you when you come to town ; but I do not think you will find anything in it. Perhaps even I have found myself, Balaam-like, called upon to say one thing, and somewhat prophesying in another direction, but I shall look forward to some talk over the subject.— Meantime believe me to be affectionately yours,
"G. F. WATTS."

The paper appeared in the form of a letter in the *Nineteenth Century* for March 1881. "Needlework," he wrote, "which has existed since the days of Penelope, is worthy on its own account of vigorous efforts to preserve its vitality. As one of the best means of carrying taste into household surroundings it cannot be too highly prized. As affording honourable employment for many whose conditions must be a source of great pain to all but the most thoughtless, it takes a place among the important considerations of the time." He did not enter into the scheme with undue hope, for he wrote : " It can hardly be expected that an age that sets so little store by the charm of beauty for its own sake, and fails to perceive practical value of art of any kind, will take much interest in your school, until its practical value can be demonstrated and generally felt, and this will take time." On this theme at another time he wrote : " I have often been sadly obliged to conclude that the most thoughtful prophets of this age care little about Art, and have come with great regret to believe that Art in its noblest form is an extinct expression of mind and action. There exists something like a distinct idea that pleasure in outward beauty of form, and colour, and arrangement is opposed to the practical. Whether it is an advantage to lose any natural gifts may at least be doubted." The letter Signor wrote satisfied Lady Marion Alford, who writes to tell him she has been congratulated by several persons competent to give an opinion, and she adds : " Your praise is most valuable, and your advice to the women who work most excellent."

Again in January 1883, in the *Nineteenth Century*, Signor published an article on " Dress." Of this in a letter of the date February 6, 1883, Lady Airlie writes to him : " I have read your article on dress. You speak from a loftier standpoint than other critics, and leave behind you the jargon of schools. The charm of your article to me is, that it is your own voice speaking, it is some of the gathered thoughts of a lifetime, it is not an article you have invented, but yourself, and the teaching of your life."

In writing to friends at this date, allusions are made to some suggestions that he should devote the iron studio to hanging the many pictures he had already completed; and that the "Iron-pot," or "Tin-tabernacle," as his correspondents variously called it, should be used as a temporary gallery for his pictures, and that to this, once a week, the public should be admitted. From this proposition he began to realise that the addition of such a gallery to his own house would be a convenience to him, and might be of interest to those who cared for his work. Having lost his friend Mr. Frederick Cockerell, by his too early death, he asked a brother Academician, Mr. George Aitchison, to undertake the work of designing a gallery, and by May 1881 it was built, and the pictures placed.

He very much disliked having his own work on the walls of his working studio; but he had found how liable to damage pictures were when standing on the floor turned with their faces to the wall. After the opening of this newly-built gallery upon Saturday and Sunday afternoons, he was pleased to find that visitors came in considerable numbers, and that of these, many strangers to him wrote to thank for the privilege. To Mr. Rickards he says :—

"I hope you will come to town this summer (1881); my pictures now are hung and make rather an imposing show, at least in respect of number; but it is distressing to me to see how many are unfinished. I must undertake no more new things, for it will not do to leave an accumulation of incomplete things behind me. 'Hugh Lupus,' too, is in a dreadful state—cut to pieces! I found, when it was nearly done, a radical defect; and, though everybody protested against a change, I decided upon something like doing it all over again, preferring rather to leave the thing undone than let it go less good than I could make it."

In the winter of 1881-82, at the Grosvenor Gallery, a collection of some two hundred of Signor's pictures were exhibited. It was called a "bold, not to say audacious experiment of Sir Coutts Lindsay's," but nevertheless criticism was generally favourable, and the work of forty years, carried on unremittingly and with entire consistency from the first year to the last, was brought to the notice of the public for the first time in London.

He had many kind letters of congratulation, and on the evening after the private view Mr. William Graham, so well known both as a collector of pictures and for his delightful personality, expressed the pleasure this exhibition afforded him, saying :—

GEORGE FREDERIC WATTS

"I cannot allow the day to pass without a few lines to express the great pleasure I, and indeed I should say we, have had in our visit to the Grosvenor.

"It scarcely needed that, or any other evidence to sustain the admiration with which your work has always inspired me; but I must confess a new astonishment at the grandeur of it when presented *en masse*, as it is on these walls, and at the abundance of your productive power which the collection manifests.

"That such an exhibition must tend to raise not only your own reputation, but to exalt the British school in the estimation of all capable judges, and especially amongst the accomplished artists of the Continent, there can be no doubt; and it certainly strikes me on the whole that the present exhibition is the most remarkable and the most successful one the Grosvenor has yet accomplished."

Lord Lytton a week or two later sent him the following letter:—

"KNEBWORTH PARK,
"STEVENAGE,
"21*st January* 1882.

"DEAR MR. WATTS—I cannot repress the wish to give some expression, though it be but a note of exclamation, to the grateful and delighted feelings with which during this last week I have been wandering amongst the trophies of your noble life which are now collected at the Grosvenor. They are indeed a

GEORGE FREDERIC WATTS

splendid assemblage of great achievements in those *Hohe Regionen, wo die reine Formen wohnen*, all of them stamped with the authentic birthmark of Genius.

"My sensations in contemplating them all together were to me those of a traveller who suddenly finds himself, on awaking, in the midst of some far land—the birthplace of rare fruits and flowers, or precious ores and gems, of which till then he had seen only isolated specimens, scattered here and there about the world, and some of them in incongruous company.

"I have ventured to address this 'note of admiration' to you because, even had you been able to attend the dinner to which I was asked, I should have had no opportunity of seeing you there; being myself prevented from attending it by unavoidable engagements. But I confess I have learned, without much regret, that it is not to be; for eating and drinking appear to me grotesquely inappropriate modes (not improved, but the reverse, by the commonly accompanying postprandial oratory) of expressing admiration for a man's genius or gratitude for his work. Mine for yours are, I confess, not quite free from the chauvinism of an old-fashioned satisfaction in the reflection that the genius and its work are those of an Englishman.—Yours, dear Mr. Watts, very truly, LYTTON."

GEORGE FREDERIC WATTS

To him Mr. Watts replies :—
"*January 29th*, 1882.
"Little Holland House.

"Dear Lord Lytton—I am touched to sadness by your letter; how can all this be merited by any efforts of mine? I haunt the footsteps of the great dead, those who, while they ennoble their birth-land, enrich the world and ennoble humanity itself. From my childhood I have had a longing to be of that band, but I dare not think it is for me; and praise such as yours, and from such as you, seems somehow more distinctly to show me what is not, by showing me what your own genius presents to you as mine. It is you who complete the strain if I strike the chord. The dread of being a deceiver, even without the intention, is more distressing to me than the want of general sympathy (through which I have hitherto worked) has ever proved. I would rather be under-estimated. You, the Poet and Artist, for they are identical, will, I know, understand me although I express myself clumsily.

"I have got into great disgrace by declining to accept the dinner. All my instincts recoiled from the thing, and it is a great satisfaction to me to find that you approve.

"I want to have your sympathy. I shall want the sympathy of those whom I most admire and respect, for life now is all down hill with me, and I have my best to do.

"To be accounted a worthy son of that great

England first (for among the very first it is in so many things) has ever been my aspiration. I have, as I said, lived too much with the spirits of the great to be in error as to the achievement. . . . I am afraid I have meandered about a good deal and not been very clear, but I think you will pick out my meaning.—Yours most sincerely and gratefully, G. F. WATTS."

The dinner alluded to in these letters was proposed to be held in his honour on January 25, at the Grosvenor Gallery. The report of this reached him at Brighton, the Committee being obliged to find out what support would be given to their proposal before consulting his wishes. The idea proved to be more distasteful to him than even his best friends had suspected. He wrote off at once to Sir Coutts Lindsay to ask him as Chairman of the Committee to put an immediate veto upon the scheme. And so to him at Brighton came letters from his friends full of repentance, each humbly begging to be freed from the charge of having been a prime mover. Mr. Burne-Jones writes :—

"Alas, it is nobody's fault in particular; many of us wanted to feast you in a cosy and unostentatious way, and the number of people who wanted to join in the manifestations grew and grew. It would have been a great success. But now it is over. We all felt you had a bit misapprehended the matter as regards the Grosvenor Gallery; it was not a Grosvenor

GEORGE FREDERIC WATTS

Gallery affair, it was to be held there because your pictures are there. Now we'll talk of it no more. I don't know who told you I was the originator of the idea. I had no more than others the claim of that distinction, but of course, whatever part I took, I am sorry enough now, sorry to have vexed instead of pleasing you, such being the innocent purpose. I will run round to see you when you come back.—Your affectionate NED."

Sir Coutts told him that probably a hundred of his friends would have been present: "Amongst politicians, Gladstone and Harcourt; and Leighton, Millais, Poynter, and other Academicians were acting in this matter through the Committee."

A friend and brother Academician, Mr. H. T. Wells, wrote at this time :—

"THORPE LODGE,
"CAMPDEN HILL, W.

"MY DEAR WATTS—I must send you just a line to say how sad I am at having to give up all hope of being near you on the 25th, because of a mere private dinner engagement which I had accepted twenty-four hours before I heard from Mr. Hallé.

"I am to dine with the Mr. Aird who is the owner of so many of Calderon's recent works, and as I could not be present at a large dinner given to R.A.'s and A.R.A.'s some two months ago, because of my attendance upon poor Street, he has now secured me upon a second chance. I must go since I have said 'Yes,' but my heart will be with you, my dear Watts. I would have given much to join in the cheer for you in the midst of the noble collection of your works. Sincerely and heartily I congratulate you on your bared life, which calls for all our respect and admiration at the 'Grosvenor.'

"The harmony of it is even more than I had counted upon, who, as you know, have had the privilege of seeing the separate works in progress and completion during the last twenty-two years. Except a few of the Holland House pictures, all, or nearly all, I found to be old friends.

"There is one exception, and that is a most notable one—the portrait of Sir Charles Dilke. I cannot think how I missed seeing it. I knew you were painting it, and I was often in your studio at that time; and yet now it comes upon me as a novelty. It is surely one of your very, very best! And how well the paint keeps in all the works! The 'quality' has become in many instances absolutely precious. An almost posthumous glory will be upon you because of this gathering together of your works.

"I hope you are recruiting your health just now. I called at Little Holland House this afternoon and learned that you are at Brighton, so I'll hope this will be forwarded to you.—Yours very truly, HENRY T. WELLS."

GEORGE FREDERIC WATTS

The reply is as follows:—

"*Jan.* 15*th*, 1882,
"29 Lewes Crescent, Brighton.

"My dear Wells—Your letter gave me very sincere pleasure, in the first place for the friendliness of its tone, and secondly for the opinion it expresses of the collection at the Grosvenor Gallery. I know what an acute and honest critic you are and value the flattering things you say more than I can say.

"I have received an amount of praise which has greatly surprised me, which I am not accustomed to, and which indeed I feel less comfortable under than I did under comparative neglect.

"With respect to the dinner, your letter and another received by an earlier post were the first intimations I had of the proposal. I have written to Sir Coutts to say the thing can by no means be. I distinctly though very gratefully decline the invitation, which I wonder the friends whose names I see forming the Committee could for a moment have thought I would entertain the idea of accepting.—Yours very sincerely, G. F. Watts."

Other honours now followed. The Vice-Chancellor of Cambridge wrote on April 28 to ask him to allow his name to be proposed to the Senate as a "recipient of the honorary degree of LL.D. in recognition of your distinguished services to art." At this time it had been arranged that the Duke of Devonshire should give him sittings for two portraits, one for the University and one to be presented by the University to the Duke, who was their Chancellor. The distaste for anything like publicity, together with a very distinct sense that such work as his should not be appraised by contemporary opinion, and the dislike he felt to taking a place from which he would one day have to climb down, made him at once write to intimate that an acceptance was impossible to him. The Vice-Chancellor replies : " I cannot express to you what a deep feeling of disappointment there was in the University, that we could not have the opportunity of expressing our appreciation of all that you had done for art in this generation, and of the noble and disinterested way in which you had pursued it for its own sake. I have ventured to ask the Duke to overcome your objections."

The tragedy in the Phœnix Park took place soon after the sittings had begun, and the Duke's heroic bearing under such annihilating sorrow made a lasting impression upon my husband. The University, in deference to their Chancellor's bereavement, wished to postpone the conferring of honorary degrees for another year, but the Duke would not allow this.

Two years before, Dean Liddell, at that time Vice-Chancellor of Oxford, had written to Signor, saying : " Will you come and be made D.C.L. at our commemoration, arraying yourself in the

GEORGE FREDERIC WATTS

scarlet and crimson robe in which Reynolds delighted to paint himself, and in which your President is now depicting himself for the Florence Gallery?' And the following day he writes further :—

"*May 26th*, 1880.

"DEAR MR. WATTS—I must plead guilty to having proposed your name, together with that of Mr. Millais, to the Council; but the offer of the degree comes from them, not from me. I am sure all the world, especially the judicious part of it, will endorse our judgment, and say we shall be honoured by enrolling you among our honorary members. If you really from any private reason would rather postpone your visit, of course I will not press it. But you will see from this morning's *Times* that some leaky member of Council has betrayed our secret. I really shall like to do what you would like best; but I cannot consent to withdraw your name on any public grounds.—Believe me to be yours very truly, H. G. LIDDELL."

The letter from Mr. Watts between these two seems not to have been preserved, but the reference the Dean makes to his objection on "public grounds" may safely be understood to mean that he had suggested that the University might come to regret having chosen to confer upon him its honours. The offer was again renewed, the Dean and Mrs. Liddell having overcome his reluctance. The Chancellor and

GEORGE FREDERIC WATTS

Vice-Chancellor on behalf of Cambridge also prevailed, and the honour of LL.D. of this University was given to him on June 13, the D.C.L. on the next day at Oxford.

Canon Scott Holland once told me that he made Signor's acquaintance at Oxford on the day that he was taking his degree. The noise and hubbub that the undergraduates were making rather distressed him on Signor's account, and he made some sort of apology for Oxford, adding that this was quite barbarian; but Signor answered very heartily, as if he rather enjoyed it, and said, "Oh, we must be barbarian sometimes."

At the time when the collection of Signor's work was on exhibition, a poem of twelve stanzas appeared in the *Fortnightly*, the author being Mr. F. W. H. Myers, who had recently married Miss Evelene Tennant. The three first verses being generally descriptive of the painter, it is perhaps pardonable to single them out from those which describe particular pictures.

> For many a year the master wrought,
>   And wisdom deepened slow with years;
> Guest-chambers of his inmost thought
>   Were filled with shapes too stern for tears;
> Yet Joy was there, and murmuring Love,
>   And Youth that hears with hastened breath,
> But, throned in peace all these above,
>   The unrevealing eyes of Death.
>
> Faces there were which won him yet,
>   Fair daughters of an iron age;
> In iron truth portrayed he set
>   Warrior and statesman, bard and sage.

GEORGE FREDERIC WATTS

From hidden deeps their past he drew,
    The ancestral bent of stock and stem ;
More of their hearts than yet they knew
    Thro' their own gaze looked out on them.

Yet oftenest in the past he walked,
    With god or hero long gone by,
Oft, like his pictured Genius, talked
    With rainbow forms that span the sky :
Thereto his soul hath listed long,
    When silent voices spake in air,
Hath mirrored many an old-world song
    Remote and mystic, sad and fair.

I am also tempted to add to these, the last stanza, which expresses the mystic after-effect of the pictures upon the mind of the poet as he pondered upon the mind of the painter, while passing by familiar ways, on a January night, amid the stir of life in the nineteenth century.

Then as he walked, like one who dreamed,
    Thro' silent highways silver-hoar,
More wonderful that city seemed,
    And he diviner than before :
A voice was calling, All is well ;
    Clear in the vault Selene shone,
And over Plato's homestead fell
    A shadow of the Parthenon.

CHAPTER XII

The future of the greatest Art will be to suggest spiritual ideals: appeals to that gift which man alone possesses—imagination.

G. F. WATTS.

CHAPTER XII

AT the International Exhibition in Paris some nine pictures of Signor's were exhibited. They had been carefully chosen by Sir Frederic Leighton as representative. It so happened that an American lady, Miss Mary Gertrude Mead,[1] on a visit to Paris thus made acquaintance with his work for the first time, and finding herself much impressed by it, was led when in London to go to the Gallery at Little Holland House, to make further discoveries for herself. While there she accidentally met the painter and they soon became friends. On each opportunity for further acquaintance she found herself more and more in sympathy with his aims. He, on the other hand, was surprised at her appreciation of Greek art, and her quick apprehension of the greatness of any work of that school which he was able to show her. Before she left England she had made up her mind that his pictures should be seen in America. She had many preliminary difficulties at New York, and also in opposing the objections offered by Signor, who

[1] Mrs. Edwin Abbey.

was difficult to persuade, but she was not to be daunted. To the fear he expressed that she was biassed by a personal interest in his work, she replies : " I want your pictures to come to America for the sake of the people here, and not for your sake ; I want them to come that the people may hear the voice of a great teacher, and believe me, please do believe me, many will listen, for there are many people here who are just like me, and if I ever felt sure of anything I feel sure they are hungering for a sight of such pictures as yours. Trust me, if we can get over the difficulties in sending for the pictures you will never be sorry that you lent them."

At first, in his alarm at the idea of the transatlantic voyage, he hoped that she might be contented with a series of reproductions which would at least make known the character of the design. For this purpose he had large photographs taken upon which he worked in monochrome[1] matching the tone of the photographs, and using oil colour as his medium ; certainly with very beautiful results, but not to be accepted in place of the originals.

When neither Miss Mead nor her American friends would accept the alternative, Signor finally withdrew his objections and consented to lend his collection of pictures. He nevertheless writes to her :—

"This exhibition is to me, I must confess, a

---

[1] The isochromatic plates had not then been introduced.

terrible nightmare. I cannot say that it is other than a tribulation, and you must take it as a thing done for you, a return for your affectionate sympathy. . . . The pictures are packed and go by the *Canada*, I think on the seventeenth" (September 1884). " I expect nothing but disappointment, not for myself—I do not think I am ever disappointed—but on the part of American art-lovers. I shall console myself with the thought that I do my best, and that I certainly did not and should never have thought of originating the presumptuous idea of sending works for exhibition in America. Do not take the trouble to telegraph, but write me a letter to say that they have arrived. I can wait for a letter. When they are gone, and I can do nothing more, I shall not feel impatient : what will be, will be. . . . I shall wish them safe back because I wish to present the best (carried as far as I can) to my own country ; but if they go down, or are otherwise destroyed, my regret will not be the death of me."

Before they reached New York a little worry was raised up for him by correspondents in the American Press. On the publication of a short notice of the forthcoming exhibition he was sent an intimation privately, and, judging from the offending paragraph, on what seems very insufficient grounds, that he had been represented as pointing out to the American public the merits of his own work.

To Miss Mead, to whose mind the true proportion of this small matter was clear from the first, he writes when telling her of the incident: " Merits ! " he continues, " with the ideals I have and the knowledge I have of what has been done by the great ones, how can I claim merits ! I am supposed arrogantly to point out how my pictures are to be understood and admired. Mr. X—— writes to Mrs. Barrington that I lie under the imputation of vanity and self-sufficiency. I think it is a conclusion arrived at with more haste than generosity, but as far as I am concerned it is of small importance; it touches me no more than an imputation of habitual drunkenness would. And what can it matter? As far as I am concerned, nothing; not because I am above it, but because only work can have any real influence or ought to be remembered. Whether I am vain, or whether I use words inconsiderately, or whether I am personally misinterpreted, is of no importance whatever. Beyond this I really don't care, the things I do care for being of sufficient size and brightness to shut out obscure personal considerations. . . . I have no more wish to be praised for my work than a bricklayer who builds a wall expects praise for his bricklaying. If the wall answers a good purpose that is enough; of course it should be built as well as possible—so much a matter of course that praise should not be called for."

He was about to speak to an American audience for the first time, and knew it to be a responsibility. He writes : " I am specially

GEORGE FREDERIC WATTS

interested in America, as I feel that it has the world's future in its hands. About its material magnificence I have no doubt, but I want it also to have the spiritual grandeur that shall place it in an atmosphere above all the States the world has ever seen. . . . I also do greatly wish that it may be understood that I should never have had the presumption to suggest offering my essays for exhibition in America. I do but what I am asked to do. You will find that I was not successful in getting loans, but I have sent the best belonging to me. . . .

" I greatly dislike—what is commonly done —making up the exhibition room artificially ; spectators in the dark, and light unduly concentrated on the things exhibited. But for the sake of those interested in making the matter as successful as possible (legitimately), I would suggest that none of the pictures should be hung above the level of the eye or in cross lights. My pictures cannot look what they are until they are varnished, from my habit of using very dry colours which do not shine or show their transparency till varnished. (This will be proved by passing a wet sponge over them, and this especially in the richer and darker parts.) Few or none are varnished, as few are finished, so that they require that the light should not return to the spectator's eye. Supposing the spectator stands here, X, the light should be so above or behind him that it should strike thus—

GEORGE FREDERIC WATTS

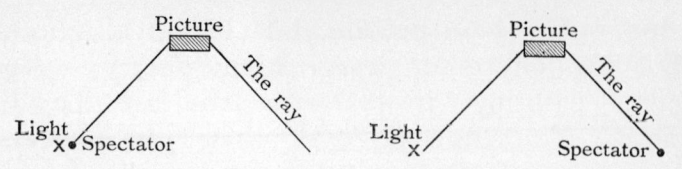

I think you will understand, a few experiments will soon make you feel the difference."

Out of a large number of letters written by Signor to Miss Mead at this time, the following seems worth quoting as characteristic of the place work held in his life.

"*Jan.* 9*th*, 1885,
"Brighton.

"Dear Fellow Traveller—I have just had your letter forwarded to me here, and send back one half sheet in return immediately; the half sheet out of your own letter. I have nothing to say, but I thank you for all the kind things you say. I am not yet very well, and feel very sad about the events and misfortunes that have befallen us;[1] they seem to make everything that concerns myself so very small, not but what I think I at all times feel the balance pretty correctly, and know that even a nation's misfortunes do not greatly affect the apparently eternal movement.

"I go on with my work, and should, I think, go on just the same amid the wreck of empires; for I know very well that the greatest possessions the world has had, and will ever have, are not the achievements of armies or even of statesman-

[1] The expedition to Khartoum for the relief of Gordon.

ship. All these become but historical ghosts, but the efforts of imagination, poetry, sculpture, painting, if really worthy are for all time. You know (I think) that I do not class my own efforts, excepting in intention, with those, but with that I have nothing to do. I try to do my work as each soldier in our little army performs his duty. So I go on, and have some new designs which I will have photographed that you may see them. I have not heard that the Museum wishes to keep my pictures longer than was projected; I don't know any particular reason for objecting. I wonder if you had the engraving from my portrait? I wanted it to be seen as an engraving, believing it would be of service to the young man—a new engraver.[1]—Yours affectionately,
"G. F. WATTS."

In another letter he continues :—

"I should be glad if (should you come across any artists or admirers of the French School) you would explain that my work is no protest against any school or method or principle whatever, excepting that one which denies that art should have any intellectual intention; that I am the first to admit my want of dexterity with the brush, and to perceive that in some cases (portraits, etc.) this is a very serious defect. Where the effort is to produce a pure abstrac-

[1] Mr. Charles Campbell, whose early death in 1887 was a real sorrow to Signor.

tion, if I had the power, I should on principle abstain from making it apparent. Of course (taking my own point of view), if the absence of it fairly suggests a want, the absence is a serious defect, but I think the distinction I point out does exist.

"In saying this to you I know that you will understand that I have no wish to influence opinion or excuse faults, nor do I want you to hold the things up to admiration; but I perceive in some of the remarks that have been under my observation an apparent notion that I set up being a reformer of art. I do nothing of the kind, and am as far as it is possible to be from condemning any method or view. Art has a very wide range over both subject and manner. That art, whose object is to present the familiar, has full claims to our admiration within its sphere, and I only object to it when it claims to be considered the only art that should be cared for. I should object to the exclusive admiration of the French School of Art, and indeed of anything else for Americans, principally because I think the vivacity of American intellect will rather lose than gain by the French element which it seems to me to have a leaning towards.

"I am sure you will feel that I say this with all respect for the vivacity we English would be all the better for possessing, and you must only repeat what I say about my views of art if the subject should come up naturally. I don't want

GEORGE FREDERIC WATTS

to preach, and I do not wish any one should preach for me."

The Exhibition at New York was popular, and the pictures excited such interest that he was asked to allow them to remain until October.

To the official request he replied : " If my pictures can help to stimulate an interest in art which, appealing rather to the intellect and finer emotions than to the senses, can never be popular, I am much too happy to be accepted as a pioneer in that direction to hesitate, and do willingly give my consent that the pictures remain in the Museum till October. That my name should find a place in the list of those Englishmen who have had the good fortune to help ever so little to strengthen the interests in the concerns and welfare of the Old Country, which I, as an Englishman, hope and trust America will always feel, is a distinction greater than I ever expected, and of which I am indeed proud."

To Miss Mead he writes on the subject as follows :—

"*Feb.* 10*th*, 1885,
"BRIGHTON.

" If you really think any good can be done by the pictures remaining so much longer, why, my great object in work, and indeed in living (notwithstanding an unusual tendency to *make mistakes*), is to do something worth doing if possible.

GEORGE FREDERIC WATTS

"It has not been given to me to influence peoples, or to shape nations, nor to speak with the persuasive or prophetic voice of the poet; but what I can, I would do; therefore you may be sure that both for this reason in the abstract and also for the great respect I have for America, and the desire to help in any way, small or great, to strengthen a thoroughly vital stream of interest and relationship between us across the sea—why, if it is thought desirable to keep the pictures longer than was intended, I shall be very unwilling to make difficulties. With respect to the going to Boston it must be a matter for consideration; there is the risk of the railway. I send you what I suppose will be a sufficient authorisation—you must use it with discretion. In order to avoid trouble with money matters, and caring nothing about money for itself, and to be free to give my undivided attention to the things I do care for, I have given up the greater part of the proceeds of years of work, reserving only what is barely enough to allow me to feel independent, living as I do in the most abstemious manner. But, as it may happen that the sources from which I draw this necessary income may fail, or that I may find myself requiring more than in my calculation seemed to be necessary, the copyrights of my pictures are property it would be very imprudent to alienate. So please, in giving the permission I place in your hands, bear this in mind. You will find people able to instruct on the subject. Many artists make a very considerable income out of the copyrights of their pictures, but these are popular men and paint pictures and subjects publishers care to engrave and publish. I have never been of these, you will not find me represented in any print-seller's windows, but still I should desire to retain the copyrights for many reasons."

The "mistakes" my husband refers to in the foregoing letter caused him much, I think unnecessary, contrition. I should not dream of referring to this small affair but that, in consequence of this incident, in more than one published account of him an undue accent has been laid upon his tendency to make mistakes from want of memory. In this instance the question was whether Mr. Watts summoned Mr. Z—— to his house and asked him to write about the pictures, or whether (as Mr. Watts had understood) Mr. Z—— intended to write about them. This only I know, that a letter from this gentleman is in my possession, written somewhat earlier in this same year 1884, in which he says, "I want to ask you the favour of being allowed to write a little paper on your recent work in painting and sculpture." This paper was for an English editor who was about to publish (as the letter explains) "a series of such articles by various hands dealing with the present work of the leading artists. They intend to lead off with yourself and have asked me to write it. I hope you have no objection."

GEORGE FREDERIC WATTS

I think, therefore, it may be conceded that the proposition in the first place came from the literary man, and that Signor's impression was not so very incorrect.

This same letter continues: "There is some danger that America may become too long occupied with craving after material success, taking undue delight in big fortunes and small inventions. So young and great a nation should have for aim the ennobling of the human race. With regard to what you say about art, I think it is less a matter for reason than for feeling. Art, as its means of utterance are visibly mechanical, is considered far more important from a material point of view than poetry, or music, which I think puts its professors and lovers wrong. It has two functions, one in common with poetry and music, to touch the finest chords in our nature, and help to keep alive what is elevated and noble, the other to represent material conditions in such wise that thereafter those who look at nature may see her with a truer and more intelligent sight. It cannot add beauty to the flower; the flower is infinitely more beautiful and perfect than any representation can be; but it can make the spectator see in the flower more than he did before. Nature's language, imperfectly understood by the many, is rendered by the Artist-translator more intelligible, and henceforth the observer has gained a finer vision. Your acquaintances who study in Paris and elsewhere,

GEORGE FREDERIC WATTS

and discover that they have lost time, simply mistake the means for the end; they will have learned enough if they endeavour to apply what they have learned. Most people have enough language to enable them to say something, if they have anything to say; it is in forgetting that art has anything to say that speech in it is made so valueless. The want of belief in Art as an agent in real civilisation is at the bottom of its failure, it has nothing real to do. Poetry retains its place, and music is perhaps rising; but architecture, painting, and sculpture are no longer expressions of purposes."

His pictures thus collected, though not travelling further than New York, were absent for a year; on their return they went to the Art Gallery at Birmingham; and before this exhibition closed they were asked for, and Signor lent them to the Nottingham Art Gallery, and some fifteen of their number to Rugby School. In consequence the Gallery at Little Holland House was not replenished till July 1888. Miss Mead was rewarded for all her efforts, made with untiring energy and tact, by what may be called the great popularity of the pictures in New York. My husband often remarked upon the modest way in which from the first she kept herself in the background—a matter so skilfully arranged by her that very few indeed knew that the exhibition was due to her initiation and to her persistent labours.

GEORGE FREDERIC WATTS

On June 25, 1885, Mr. Gladstone wrote the following letter :—

"10 DOWNING STREET,
"WHITEHALL.

"MY DEAR MR. WATTS—I have to request with the sanction of Her Majesty that you will allow yourself to be enrolled among the baronets of the United Kingdom. It gives me lively pleasure to have the means of thus doing honour to art in the person of so distinguished a representative of the noble pursuit.—I remain most faithfully yours,   W. E. GLADSTONE."

This communication was received with surprise, for although Lord Carlisle had intimated that some honour was likely to be offered, Signor was unprepared to find himself chosen out to be the first painter to whom the honour of a baronetcy was offered. He explains this to Lord Carlisle, saying : "I don't exactly know why, but I made up my mind that what was intended was the distinction of a C.B., which would really leave me where I was. I never was more surprised than by Mr. Gladstone's letter, and did immediately and by hand send him a reply in which I said that the honour was excessive and for more and many reasons beyond my acceptance. . . . I know that the compliment to art pure and simple would be of the greatest value."

In his letter to Mr. Gladstone declining the offer he says: "You, I am sure, will understand that I do not undervalue such distinctions, but

GEORGE FREDERIC WATTS

rather that I value them more than people generally do. I value them as meaning a great deal."

He had several reasons for his refusal, but the one dominant in his mind was that it was not " in keeping "—using the word in the artistic sense. His pictures were often praised for being " in keeping," and those who knew him best, knew how entirely in keeping with the elevation of his art was his life in the everyday. Seclusion had become his habit since his life had become more solitary. In the summer of 1883 the marriage took place of his adopted daughter Blanche, to Herbert Somers Cocks, and this to a certain extent accentuated his loneliness. The loss of her young and bright companionship in the winters at Brighton was great to him. No doubt his sensitiveness had been increased by the solitariness of his life, in so much that any public expression of recognition was a disturbance, almost (as in the case of the Grosvenor Gallery dinner) a vexation. What other men could receive as a pleasant encouragement, to him appeared to be nothing but an embarrassment.

I remember his telling me at this time that his neighbour, Mr. Thomas Thorneycroft, the sculptor, had sent a note to him asking him to spare a moment for the purpose of witnessing the signature of his Will. Mr. Thorneycroft was not well, and had been setting his house in order. When talking together for a few minutes afterwards, Mr. Thorneycroft remarked, "So you won't let them make you Sir George. Well, never mind, you will be Saint George anyway."

During the autumn of this year Mr. Horsley read a paper at the Church Congress called "Art Schools and Art Practice in their Relation to a Moral and Religious Life," in which he protested against the system of artistic training which necessarily involves the study from the female nude. To Signor it was a matter of regret to find himself entirely in opposition to the views of an old friend and brother Academician; but he was indignant that the professional model (whom as a whole out of long experience he could call "a distinctly moral class") should have been entirely misrepresented. He resented it further, as it implied condemnation of artists in general. He wrote to Mr. Horsley telling him what he thought, but in such a manner that the letter was received in the right spirit by his friend, who in his reply especially thanked him for the tone, which, he said, distinguished it from others he had received upon the subject.

He had written: "I beg you to believe that no one can do more justice to your intentions than I do; but I think you are quite wrong in bringing the subject forward in the Church Congress and appealing to the judgment of those who, from different direction of thought and habit, must be altogether unable to judge correctly. If it were a question of morals pure and simple it would be different, but it is not a question purely of morals, though it may appear to be so to those who know nothing about the matter. The class of the professional model affords no proof whatever by scandals, of moral degradation, and to abolish the class (unless you abolish art) would have the result of driving students into the crookedest arts to obtain models, or a less evil, though I think a great one, into seeking in Paris the means of study not to be found here.

"Unquestionably you have more than a right to conscientious opinion, and right-minded men must always respect conscientiousness ; but your appeal should be made to the members of the profession. By appealing to outsiders you create an unnecessary amount of opposition. Certainly my idea of art is not the same as yours, still I think I am as far from being indifferent to the morality of it. I even think I believe its utterances more important than you do, consequently I believe its responsibilities to be greater. I cannot imagine that any sanely-minded individual would find it necessary to re-focus his thought after looking at the Theseus or the Milo Venus before entering a drawing-room or even a church."

When asked for his opinion by a newspaper correspondent, he bore testimony to the fact that he had never seen any signs of degradation in any model ever employed by him. He had never in his experience seen the least approach to any hint of objectionable conduct or word from any member of a life school.

I have also the draft of a letter written for publication, but I believe withheld. In this he said : " Every right-minded man will sympathise with effort in every direction to purify manners and abolish abuses, but it is quite possible to divert the best intention so as to produce the worst consequences. To abolish a *métier* the very nature of which, though paradoxical as it may appear, is a guarantee against irregularities of conduct, would have the result of driving students into disreputable society and companionship in order to obtain means to study.

" Absence of the sense of proportion is one of the commonest characteristics of ardent minds, especially when called into activity on subjects that touch upon religious questions."

In combating the notion that models and students must alike suffer degradation, Signor suggests that if such evils resulted from the prosecution of these studies, professors also must be included, and remarks that here Mr. Horsley had profoundly touched the honour of his brother artists.

" These, according to him, contaminating systems and influences have been in operation for more than a century. How often during that period has the model appeared in the Police Courts on charge of immorality, drunkenness, theft, or attempted suicide — evidences of the degradation we should have a right to expect?

"Have students and professors of art given cause for scandal beyond any other class high or low? Some indeed have been eminent examples of morality and piety. John Flaxman to wit, who must have drawn and modelled from life more than most.... Immorality in the study of the beautiful and wonderful human structure (is it not written 'God made man in his own image'?) strikes those who are habituated to that study as ludicrous, just as it strikes those to whom it is strange as immoral. Such is the force of habit! Practices pursued in the light of day for a century without any appreciable evil result need not alarm the most timidly sensitive, but it might be extremely dangerous to turn the tide of an unenlightened public opinion upon such a system of study.

"It is as necessary to keep watch on and check the increase of unconscious hypocrisy consequent on the progress of our civilisation as it is necessary to watch and hold in check as much as possible the enervating tendencies arising out of our modern habits, greatly the consequence of the very progress we so much prize. These might in time make life impossible in our uncertain climate. We have no power over natural conditions, and neither in our habits of life or in our thoughts must we too much ignore them."

Upon this subject, but not to be included in the draft of this letter, he writes: "To my mind

GEORGE FREDERIC WATTS

the artist, like the poet, dealing primarily with what is beautiful, should consider himself entrusted with that mission and feel a responsibility attaches to his character and his work."

It has been said that Signor never made use of the model, but this was not the case. To the end of his life he occasionally made use of one. In earlier years a large number of studies were made from a model whom he always called " Long Mary," who sat to him, and to him only, from the early 'sixties and onwards for several years. He told me he never made use of her, or of any other model, when painting a picture. He said, " I don't want individual fact in my pictures where I represent an abstract idea. I want the general truth of nature." When speaking of this with Sir Hubert von Herkomer the Professor remarked, " Nature is in your mind as you want it." "Yes," Signor answered, "I have it in my mind, not in my eye. I want to tell you the impression she makes upon me. Art is not a presentation of Nature, it is a representation of a sensation."

When painting, Signor referred to the studies made in charcoal on brown paper from this most splendid model—noble in form and in the simplicity and innocence of her nature—a model of whom he often said that, in the flexibility of movement as well as in the magnificence of line, in his experience she had no equal. Many of the studies made from her are now in the possession of the Royal Academy and at the

GEORGE FREDERIC WATTS

British Museum, while some are preserved in the Sculpture Gallery at Compton. They inspired his work from the first half of the 'sixties to the end of his life. The pictures "Daphne," "The Judgment of Paris," "The Childhood of Zeus"—the Eve trilogy—"Dawn," "Olympus on Ida," "The Wife of Midas," are notable examples of paintings in which he referred to these studies. In his sculpture work she inspired the "Clytie" and the first "Dawn," but the muscles for the "Clytie" were carefully studied from a well-known Italian male model, of the name of Colorossi, and for this bust also a beautiful little child, not yet three years old—Margaret Burne-Jones—was laid under contribution, and was studied in her mother's arms!

During the spring of this year (1886) Signor had some correspondence and conversations with his old friends Lord Aberdare and Sir Henry Layard on the subject of the future of those pictures which, during the greater part of his life, he had regarded as devoted to the nation.

To Lord Aberdare he wrote (January 9, 1886): "I have long intended to leave my series of portraits and the best of my efforts in ideal directions to the nation, but the wish has grown upon me not to wait till I can leave them, but to give them while I live. In addition to the pleasure this would give me, there is the reason that the work I have not painted to sell—but with this destination—has accumulated till I have no small difficulty in housing it.

GEORGE FREDERIC WATTS

"When you come to town will you take some interest in the matter and pay my studio a visit to talk it over with me? There is a side of the question I do not overlook. What is bequeathed may be accepted or not, but it is awkward to refuse a gift, even though it should be of little value, therefore I want some advice. . . . It seems to me that it would be a good thing to bring all the pictures together and get public opinion as to whether they are worthy to be offered for national acceptance. I think I might manage to do this."

Both Lord Aberdare and Sir Henry Layard agreed that it was time that he should define his wishes more precisely and put the offer into a definite form.

Of this matter Lord Aberdare wrote :—

"1 Queen's Gate, S.W.,
"March 20th, 1886.

"My dear Watts—After a consultation with Layard yesterday I spoke to Lord Spencer on the subject of your offer. I mentioned to him a suggested plan, namely, to send to the National Portrait Gallery your portraits of deceased celebrities, and to retain the rest—the imaginative pictures—at the South Kensington Museum in the manner with which, Layard tells me, you have been made acquainted. I found Lord Spencer not only interested but warmly sympathetic; he objected to the division of your pictures until the whole of the portraits could be transferred together to the National Portrait Gallery, and seemed to think that a room could be found for the purpose of keeping them all together. I need not say how glad I was to find that he received your generous offer in so becoming a spirit.

"I think, therefore, you may now formally communicate your proposal to Lord Spencer as representing the Government.—Believe me, ever sincerely yours, ABERDARE."

To Signor's letter Lord Spencer replied as follows :—

"SPENCER HOUSE,
"ST. JAMES' PLACE, S.W.,
"*March* 23*rd*, 1886."

"MY DEAR MR. WATTS—As you say, I heard from two sources of your desire to present some of your works to the nation.

"I can with perfect truth assure you that I think such a gift would be of great value and importance to the country, and your munificence will be immensely appreciated. If we can at South Kensington help in carrying out your wishes we shall, I am sure, be much pleased.

"I have been so extremely busy that I have not had time to ride as far as your house, but I thought of doing so more than once. I shall certainly carry out my intention before very long.

"Meanwhile, we shall be glad to give you any information which you may desire as to our

GEORGE FREDERIC WATTS

galleries, etc., and if you would allow me I shall be glad to send Mr. Armstrong to see you.—Very truly yours, SPENCER."

In a later letter, after Lord Spencer had made the public announcement, he wrote :—

" I wish I could have expressed in more suitable terms my admiration for your works and my appreciation of your desire to give them to the nation."

The national portraits, however, had as yet no permanent home, and were at this time on loan in the Bethnal Green Museum ; so the practical result was that some six or seven pictures, two of which were portraits, were lent to the South Kensington Museum, and were there hung upon a wall above a staircase. It was on this staircase that the French art critic, Monsieur Robert de la Sizeranne, confessed to have been converted from one set of opinions to another. He wrote, in the *Revue des Deux Mondes* : " Some years ago, when I visited South Kensington Museum for the first time, I found myself by chance on the staircase leading to the Art Library, one of the least frequented corners of the vast palace. I had then the conviction that mythology was a genre, false, feeble, and superannuated. . . . I was still of this opinion when I set foot on the first step of that staircase. When I had reached the last, I no longer believed that myth was dead ; nor that to expand the

GEORGE FREDERIC WATTS

form of a fact to the impersonal, the sexless, the universal, was to take from it the ardour of sentiment, the dramatic element of life. What then had come between these two opinions? Two canvases by Watts, 'Love and Life' and 'Love and Death'—the most mysterious of the powers that dominate man. The artist had understood what resources, what life, they afforded for his abstract creations."

It is now well known that through the munificence of two patriotic men — William Henry Alexander, the donor of the National Portrait Gallery in St. Martin's Place, and Sir Henry Tate, who built the National Gallery of British Art at Millbank—the painter lived to see his gift securely housed.

The Portrait Gallery was opened on March 26, 1895, and the Tate Gallery on July 21, 1897.

I am reminded here, though it does not belong to this time, that Signor happened to say of some picture he was painting, " I think it is one I might offer to the Nation," and then added with a twinkle, " Not that the Nation cares a dump." It matters little whether in 1886 the nation cared or not. There were some units who did. I was making a drawing at the time in my studio in Bloomfield Place, Pimlico, from an adventurous little boy, aged eight, who used to pick up a few shillings, when holidays from school allowed of this, by offering himself as a model at studio doors. One day, from his perch on a high chair, he amused me by asking, " Do you know what I calls Mr. Watts ? I calls him pynter to the Nytion."

When speaking one day to a man in his studio of the amount of work he had put into a certain picture destined for the nation, Signor had remarked that no sum that could be offered to him could repay it, and his visitor answered, "The Nation is not altogether grateful, I am afraid." "That I have nothing to do with," said Signor ; " I have been right in my attempt, and the question of success, or whether I have deserved any gratitude, does not occupy me for a moment."

CHAPTER XIII

CERTAINLY it is heaven upon earth, to have a man's mind move in charity, rest in Providence, and turn upon the poles of truth.

BACON.

CHAPTER XIII

THE last years of which I have been writing are memorable to me, as soon after my father's death in 1881 we came to live in London.

This meant for me the opportunity of seeing Signor much more often, and as a humble student of art as well as one paying homage, for in the nature of things this had to be where the influence on life was of the best ; these opportunities were to me priceless. Any attempt I then made to write an impression of a visit to him—of what he said or of what he was—always fell so short of the inspiring moments they were intended to preserve, that the pages were usually torn out of the locked and sacred book, and I copied instead the words of some master in language to express what I wanted. One day James Martineau said this for me : " And above and beyond all the advantages which a higher culture gives in the mere system of communicating knowledge, must be placed that indefinable and mysterious power which a superior mind always puts forth upon an inferior; —that living and life-giving action, by which

GEORGE FREDERIC WATTS

the mental forces are strengthened and developed, and a spirit of intelligence is produced, far transcending in excellence the acquisition of any special ideas."

A few torn-out, not torn-up, pages remain, and I see that I write in 1883, "I think my fear is all gone, what I feel now is only reverence"; and I go on to speak of his genius for understanding all the little things of life. Something in him compelled his friends unasked to talk simply of their little duties and difficulties, and he never made them feel anything but glad that they had given him their confidence.

On one of these early days I can still see him vividly before me. He was standing with his back to the poor little black mantelpiece of painted wood set with Dutch tiles which had been transferred, because of his affection for it, from old Little Holland House to his new big studio, where its very unsuitableness declared that it had an interesting history. I had said something of the everyday of life, and then had spoken of life as a whole; and the answer came so simply, with the slightest possible droop of his head, as if there was weight in the thought, "Yes, standing between two Eternities."

I wrote then, "That is his charm! just the right thing said in the simplest way, and his words follow me through the day, and are a new strength." It was in October of this year that Signor allowed me to begin for study a copy of one of the portraits in his gallery, and so during the autumn and winter, with another fellow-student, now a well-known artist, Mr. J. P. Beadle, I was at work painting at Little Holland House. It was then I saw Signor every day, as he happened that winter to be spending less time at Brighton. The following winter it was different, he was much away, and I remembered as I walked from Eccleston Square (where we were then living) to my studio in Bloomfield Place, that I looked out for the ennobled faces I had passed in the street last year on coming back from my day in the gallery of Little Holland House. Now seeing only ugliness or worse, I knew my interpretation had then been different, and that the revelation of the soul behind the face was failing me. It was his gift, as an artist and as a man, to reveal the nobler undertones. Many years later a clever woman, and one whose opportunities in life put it in her power to know every one distinguished in any way, said to me, " If I don't see Mr. Watts for some time, I am the worse for it ; I believe that the earnestness of this age is in great part due to the influence of Mr. Watts and of Carlyle." The same feeling compelled me one day to say, " Oh, Signor, when I am with you I grow " ; and after we married, others said things of this kind to me in speaking of him, and that not unfrequently. I remember a friend, a minor poet, turning to me on her first visit to him to say, " Oh, Mary, I think if I lived with him I could achieve something." In his habitual attitude of endeavour to learn and seeking to know, how unconscious he remained of this effect on others!

One morning, in the spring of 1884, he had allowed me to bring a chief friend of friends to see him and to play to him. It was a February day of glorious sunshine, and the big studio was full of colour from the great canvases that stood about; and, under Geraldine Liddell's hands, the ancient little piano was uttering Beethoven and Bach. At the first pause he jumped up quickly and crossed the studio like a boy, saying, "She's full of music, she's full of music"; then to please me she hummed, with something of the sound of a violin, as she played the dear little old air of the song "My Faithful Johnnie," for which Beethoven had made an accompaniment; and how charmed he was with her doing this, and with that simple air. As a matter of course nothing appealed to him more than perfect naturalness, and he told us he had come to know that there was nothing he disliked more—especially in music—than being made aware of what he called the "professional element." There was nothing in this friend that did not spring out of her, as he quickly knew, and of her he said, "She has a great nature, and her music is an expression of it." From that time and onwards she often came and brought others—sometimes a first and second violin, sometimes a quartette; and he was very happy amongst these new friends; his heart was young and its door stood open for the new to enter as they would. From this first day onwards to the last, Geraldine Liddell held a singular place with him, and Melbury Road was renamed by her " Paradise Row."

Stimulated by the wave of appreciation from friends, and even from an outside public, for his works collected at the Grosvenor Gallery had made them better known than they had ever been, the studio seemed to hold a wealth of new designs. Of these the " Hope" has ever been one of the most popular. It and " The Dweller in the Innermost" were both under his hand during the winter and spring of 1885–86. "The Deluge" also was in the studio, and "The Dawn," and his "Olympus on Ida" was begun. Though laid up for some weeks in January and February, he had ready for the Academy "The Death of Cain," and for the Grosvenor Gallery the " Hope" and the " Soul's Prism," which he afterwards found not to be satisfactory as a title and changed to " The Dweller in the Innermost," and portraits of Lord Salisbury and of Lord Lytton.

During the last two winters I had been spending two evenings in the week at a boys' club in Whitechapel, going there with a friend who taught a rough sort of mosaic, and who had persuaded me to have a class for modelling in clay, merely to give the lads, who were chiefly shoeblacks, an interesting hour or two,

GEORGE FREDERIC WATTS

and to arouse in them the knowledge of the pleasure of making something in their leisure time. The movement now known as "The Home Arts and Industries Association," of which I and my friend were members, was young, and Signor entered keenly into my interests. He had heard much of it from its founders, Lord and Lady Brownlow, and I see by a little note I have that he had been trying to enlist the sympathy of brother artists, I think in the matter of giving designs.

"*March* 31*st*, 1886.

"My dear Mary—I am longing to know if anything promising has come out of my speaking to Mr. Walter Crane and Mr. Shields. Also I want to know something about St. Jude's School, Whitechapel—I think you go there. I have been asked for some thirteen pictures, among others the great 'Angel of Death.' Of course if they can be of service I should be glad for them to go, but I should be unwilling to risk injury to some of these pictures, which I regard as no longer mine, having given them to the Nation. Any morning after Friday that you can come I will be ready to see you soon after eleven, but bring some bit of work with you; it is long since I have seen any.

"Signor."

Such interests took me often to Little Holland House, and he sometimes came to my studio to criticise a portrait I was trying to paint of an old friend—General Frederick Cotton—who was so self-sacrificing as to sit to me. And so it was that he slipped gradually into knowing that a woman's care and companionship might make the way that still lay before him less lonely, and early in July he told me that he needed me. There was nothing professed but what was simple and befitting. He wrote: " I want you to know that I have come to feel for you the most profound and tender respect, and the most absolute trust in the qualities of your nature."

There was to be no immediate step. I was soon allowed to tell my own people, but the very natural feeling that marriage, at his age (for he was now sixty-nine), must cause some surprise and comment, made him wish that for the present nothing should be said until our plans had become more defined.

I went to stay with my brother and his wife at my old home in Scotland, as had been long arranged. The days that followed immediately were filled with an unexpected sorrow. At the entrancing age of three, the little son of the house fell from his pony, and for one month lay between life and death till the day came when hope was over.

It was a double grief to me that my letters must needs make Signor a sharer in those harassing changes, when hopes flickered up only too soon to burn low again—and this to one who could make so tender a response. " I could hardly read your letter for very pity," he wrote; "I feel with you to have suffered a personal loss." Then, being himself very unwell, and obliged to be in his room and in bed, he asked for a pencil, and drew for the desolate mother a tiny sketch. "The Angel of Death," he wrote to me, "with a child in her lap, on whose head she is placing a circlet—Death the Angel crowning Innocence."

Towards the end of October I returned, still believing that at some indefinite time we were to enter upon this new life. I found him very unwell, and most anxious that we should hurry on every arrangement for going away for the winter. His doctor, Mr. Thomas Bond, who for so many years had done his utmost to keep him well, was very insistent that the change to such a climate as Egypt would be good. Just before leaving Scotland, Signor had written to me that the first person he had taken into his confidence was Mrs. Leslie Stephen,[1] from whom he had at once received a blessing on his venture.

"She is simply delighted, and wanted to write to you instantly, so you see a big stone is laid." Later she writes to him: "Do not delay; if you don't take care I will make Leslie put on his cassock again and marry you off hand; you must get away from these cold winds." In the bundle of letters I have before me, I find one from Andrew Hichens, who,

[1] Julia Jackson, whom he had known from her earliest childhood.

since his marriage to May Prinsep, had been to Signor both a devoted son and friend.

"Monkshatch, Guildford,
"27th October.

"My dear Signor—Granny[1] has told us your great news, for which I say 'Thank God' as heartily as ever I said it in my life. You need not be told how entirely dear you are to us, and how very nearly all that concerns you touches us. Very often we have been saddened by thinking of the increasing loneliness of your life, and of the difficulty that we, always at a distance, had in doing anything to make your long hours of enforced inactivity less burdensome. And now the only way of bringing assured sunshine into your life has come to you, from the one quarter from which I can imagine it possible, and I can't say how thankful and joyful I feel about it. It is impossible for any one who loves and honours you as we do, not to rejoice and to feel happier about you than we have long been able to do. I have heard a great deal from Annie of Miss Fraser Tytler, and from the little I have seen of her myself, I should say that no other woman I know deserves or is fitted for the trust she undertakes. It is a serious, solemn, and sacred thing which she has to do, but it is one which any noble woman, sympathetic as I know she is, will feel to be a privilege and a glory, and find the

[1] Mrs. Prinsep.

truest happiness in doing worthily. Now I hope you will get well quickly, and fly south to get strength and avoid our fogs and frost. We both have colds, but May is better.—Always, dear Signor, your most affectionate

"A. K. Hichens."

He had, so he wrote to me, been making the announcement known in several directions, purposely as prosaically as possible. Sir Frederic Leighton's absence abroad prevented his writing to this chief friend till November 3rd.[1] "I am going," Signor writes, "to surprise you very much and perhaps incur disapproval. You will feel doubtless that at my time of life the thing is out of harmony." The announcement did very likely surprise and distress him, but I judge solely from the affectionate good-bye, with moistened eyes, which Sir Frederic took of his friend before we left for Egypt. Signor was too precious a friend to give into unknown and untried hands without anxiety. I understood this, and value all the more his words spoken several years later, when I happened to take my brother and his wife to make Sir Frederic's acquaintance one Sunday afternoon. With the characteristically quick sense of what would please them, he took my hand in both his, and, turning to them, said, "This is the little lady to whom we are all most deeply grateful."

[1] The letter was kindly sent to me by Sir Frederic Leighton's sister after Signor's death.

GEORGE FREDERIC WATTS

We were married very quietly, early one morning in November, from the house in Surrey my stepmother had taken after moving from Eccleston Square. My youngest brother had written from Scotland, " Let us know the day, and Ted and I will be there to give you to the Nation " ; and they were there, and on a grey, still morning we walked down a country lane to church, and from church straight to the railway station, and so to luncheon in Chester Street, alone with Mr. and Mrs. Hichens, her sister, and Miss Liddell. A few days later we were on board a P. and O. steamer and on our way to Egypt.

He caught cold whilst we were still in the colder seas, and we thought it well to land at Malta, where we spent a fortnight before going further. How he loved to feel the warmth of a southern sun once more, revelled in the colour and the pure clear line of everything against the depths of sea or sky, and felt that to have a winter home at Malta would probably lengthen his life, and in many ways help his work. Through the kindness of the Governor and Lady Simmons, everything was made easy for us, and a suitable house was found, and secured for next winter before we left for Egypt.

As our route was to be through the Suez Canal, we saw the quay at Port Said from the ship's side just far enough removed from that moving crowd of Eastern people to lose sight of its squalor and dirt. Apostles and prophets

GEORGE FREDERIC WATTS

seemed to be moving grandly to and fro, and the Holy Family to pass quietly along in the background—Mother and Child upon the ass, the father leading it—a harmony of blues and browns, as if from the brush of some great master. A group of boys played and quarrelled, and rolled each other in the dust, a tangled mass of red, and green, and orange, till a commanding figure arrived like Nemesis, with flying draperies, to scatter them with smart strokes of his staff. Here was the human being, not dressed but clothed, every line of each garment expressive of some dramatic or stately movement, the colours stained to harmonies unknown to Western eyes.

Then the ship was coaling, and as if from out the river Styx itself, the great black barges, with mysterious black-hooded beings seated within them, passed to the ship's side, and through a cloud of dust, almost as black, gave out their cargo. And of the full number of passengers on that—the (then) largest ship of the P. and O. Company—only two of us cared to look at that sight, and Signor was strengthened in his belief that pleasure in beauty is now but an exotic amongst us. We left our steamer (the *Thames*) at Suez, remaining there that night; one hour of it, never forgotten, was spent on the roof of our hotel at sunset. The Sinaiitic Range was to our left, the calm waters of the gulf before us repeating all the splendour of the heavens. We looked down at the dark silhouette of a little boat moored in the bay, in which a man standing

GEORGE FREDERIC WATTS

upright looked to us like a sculptured figure in bronze. Suddenly from a minaret near went up the cry to heaven, " God is Great, God is Great, God is Great, God is Great, I witness that there is no God but God." The figure in the boat made a gesture with the hands as of prayer, and then went prostrate before the glory.

We reached Cairo on Christmas Eve, and during the week, under the guidance of friends, often with Mr. Hamilton Aïdé, an old friend of Signor's whom he met there by chance, we saw something of old Cairo, and dreamed about in ancient dynasties at the Boulak Museum ; and, as there was no Mena House Hotel at that time, through the kindness of the Sirdar[1] we were able to stay a few days at the deserted villa just under the Pyramids built many years before by the Khedive for the use of the Empress Eugenie. The Sphinx had at once enthralled Signor ; he therefore greatly wished to stay near it, and so be able to see it under various conditions of light. New Year's Day found him, in its early hours and late, studying this riddle of the ages ; " itself a symbol of time," he said, " strong and calm, inexorable with a smile that is cruel. No words can have described, or I think ever can describe, the Sphinx. It is not beautiful in the ordinary sense, yet it has some elements of unexampled beauty. It exercises an extraordinary fascination. The line of the cheek, as seen against the sky, is surprisingly beautiful—a sweep of twenty feet, and the

[1] Sir Francis Grenfell, later Field-Marshal Lord Grenfell.

expression of the face, battered out of shape as it is, has still something indescribably impressive." He knew he had undertaken much when he set himself to paint the portrait of the Sphinx; he tried for the massiveness and the weight of this rock-hewn giant, with yet a certain delicacy, and even tenderness, both from the quality of line and from the crumbling surface of the sandstone, at the same time wishing to express what he perceived in it—an epitome of all Egyptian art, its solemnity, mystery—infinity! The line of the cheek he found so subtle that it cost him hours of labour before he could be satisfied. From the many studies made on the spot a small picture was painted. It is neither moonlight nor sunlight—the wide-eyed watcher is dark against a dark-blue sky. This little picture is now in the Gallery at Compton. Except as great monuments to the labour and skill of the workmen, the Pyramids did not impress him; he felt they came too much into competition with nature, and that compared with the Libyan Range they were small. We left this spot on January 4 for the dahabeah *Vittoria*, which we had arranged to take from Messrs. Thomas Cook and Sons; and we never regretted having placed ourselves in the hands of this firm. At that time Mr. John Cook, the senior partner, was much in Egypt. He was still catering for the army of occupation after the campaign of 1884–85, and his name was a passport to the confidence of the fellaheen. It greatly pleased my husband to

GEORGE FREDERIC WATTS

find that by just dealing he was upholding the standard of an Englishman's word.

It was now our lot to travel delightfully in our own home, our English comforts about us, our time quite our own. The owner of a dahabeah on the Nile, as every one knows who has tried it, has only one master, the wind—sometimes a very exacting master—but on the whole we were fortunate.

After the first ten days, as we went further south, a troublesome cough which caused some anxiety disappeared. Signor was able to live almost entirely on the deck, enjoying everything about us with an artist's quick perception. The sailors on board, the fellaheen on shore, had endless interest for him; and he studied the workman at the shadouf for his grand pectoral muscle, so well developed by this primitive labour. It was a delight to him that in these men he saw the long sharply defined shoulder-blade, as well as the big oblique muscle strongly marked, as he had always contended these should be, though never so found in the professional model. The fellaheen have remarkably square shoulders, from which the column of the neck rises grandly; and they have usually great length between chin and throat, giving a beautiful sense of looseness, balance, and freedom. The further south we went the deeper the bronze colour of the people became; the Berber type especially delighted him. The features gained the refinement of bronze, and the rich, warm

GEORGE FREDERIC WATTS

browns so much appealed to his sense of colour that he began to think the Western complexion was quite a mistake! Now and again he noticed amongst the Berbers the type of man chiselled upon the walls, a survival of some thousands of years. Once or twice individuals of very distinctly Greek type appeared. For instance, at Luxor a colossal Rameses had been excavated, and was being removed from the site upon which he had stood for so many centuries ; a long string of workmen towed the massive statue, and amongst these was a young man of remarkable beauty, his clothing knotted and twisted about him into a delightful arrangement of lines, the colour of it not white, but a rich low-toned ivory, and every movement of his limbs was magnificent. Between Luxor and Assouan the bronze figures working the shadouf were plentiful, and from far and near the chanted song of these men was carried to us on every puff of wind. One evening we passed close to two vessels moored side by side to the river-bank and being loaded with sugar-cane ; the men moved to a rhythmic march with song, the bare feet stamped out the measure as each bore his burden across the empty boat to the boat being laden, and the crash of the cane on the deck fell into its place in the refrain : a song of labour probably far older than the days of Joseph.

It need not be said that ancient Egypt was of absorbing interest to Signor. The more remote the dynasty, the greater the claim made on his attention. On the walls of Karnac he found one head in low relief where the artist had allowed himself greater freedom from conventionality, and he thought it worthy to be called Greek in its character. Of the restriction which seemed purposely laid upon the decorative artist in Egypt he wrote :—

"The inspiration of the artist may be a gift quite apart from his intellectual or moral greatness. Possibly the Egyptian law-giver who so restricted artistic expression had perceived in art the tendency to emasculate a nation. Sanity and balance are required to carry all great gifts to perfection. In Shelley's character, for instance, there is a loss of manly stability, the result of his ultra-artistic temperament.

"The most ancient art of the Egyptians is the most natural, indeed certain frescoes display a knowledge and dexterity not to be exceeded in the present day. A wooden figure, probably far the oldest statue in the world, has nothing archaic about it, proving that the conventionality of the later art was the result of well-considered calculation. Profoundly impressed with the comparative insignificance of daily life, the temple and the tomb received all their solicitude, and it is certain that they felt material reality would neither suggest nor harmonise with the spiritual ideas that symbolic art would be in accordance with. Probably they perceived that pleasure in exact imitation would produce the dexterity that would draw the mind from the serene altitude in harmony with tomb and temple, and that portraiture would grow up to the development of vanity."

Also, apart from its ancient history, Egypt as it is to-day (or perhaps I should say as it was in 1887) had feasts of pleasure to give to his eye and mind. He watched the Egyptians at work making a railway cutting of some depth, every spadeful of which was carried away in the primitive baskets, the work raising such a cloud of dust meanwhile that the smoke of Sodom and Gomorrah seemed there, and a solitary figure in white the wife of Lot. The expanse of serene desert, alone clothed with the colour of light, had more of divine beauty and of awe for him than a thunderstorm about a mountain peak, or a hurricane at sea. He liked nature in her reticent moods better than when she went into extremes. We passed under grand cliffs of sandstone, and he noticed how in their structural formation they had suggested to the early builder the form of the pylon and the pyramid.

He was never tired of watching the flight of the kites so continually above our dahabeah, hovering and circling with a magical sweep higher and higher, until they almost disappeared into the blue. In this, to him, was the rhythm of Nature, and for him the kites were unconsciously tracing lines of some majestic composition. But all the birds of Egypt interested him, and it pleased him to see some of these walking in and out of groups of children without fear. Once a flock of flamingoes was visible in the distance, and ibis, storks, bee-eaters, and hoopoes were common. The banks now and then were thronged with swallows, like swarming bees about a hive; and there also the weird vulture was often to be seen, several together seated in a line, looking like human beings wrapped in long cloaks—misers, perhaps, reincarnated—their lean necks stretched out in an attitude of greed.

How sad he was when our boat was dismasted at Assouan! No dahabeahs were allowed that year beyond the first cataract, the country being still disturbed; and so, with the stern turned to the sun, we began to drift down the river, and as symbols were much to him, he did not like this.

"Do you feel you have seen more than you ever did before?" he asked; "do you realise better that there is but one law that runs through all nature? The great laws of nature are all wrought one within the other—one principle is under all. The mistake has been in dividing off things into separate wholes. Here is religion, here is art, here are politics, and so on, whereas they are all one in fundamental principle—this to me is a truth that pervades and penetrates all life.

"The book of the world has been opened to us from its earliest chapters. When you have seen Greece and Egypt you have got the key-note to all that is beautiful in art."

But there were many happy days still for us upon the Nile. "The discernment of sacred truth and beauty is perpetual"; and so, when, in the perfection of the maidenhair fern in a crevice of the majestic rocks, he saw Nature's lesson of completeness, or stood moved and silent before the afterglow of an Egyptian sunset, or under the stars at night, or listening to some noble passage in the book that was being read to him, his enjoyment of it all was marked by one aspiration—"to be worthy of it."

On our journey down we invited Mr. Hamilton Aïdé to stay with us; he joined us at Luxor for a fortnight—a very pleasant guest. He read to us, and talked delightfully of the interesting men and women he had known.

After seventy days of life on the dahabeah *Vittoria* she moored at Cairo, and, very loth, we ended our happy time. Too late I regretted having no photograph of "our wooden house,"[1] inside of which we had certainly found "the golden room"; and I searched in Cairo at many photographers' shops, hoping to find a photograph of any dahabeah about the size of ours, but failed. Oddly enough, a month later, in the window of a Constantinople shop, the photograph of the *Vittoria*, with our own crew aboard her, was there for us, a present for which we thanked the fairies. By the doctor's advice Signor tried what might be gained by taking

[1] The saying runs thus: "Sometimes within a wooden house a golden room is found."

the baths of Helouan, and there for three weeks we were in the midst of the desert, which did not fail to charm him. After Helouan our next destination was Constantinople. Embarking from Alexandria we passed by Crete, saw Mount Ida capped with clouds that hid the goddesses, and coasted near the islands of Greece, all so well remembered by him in the days of his cruise in the *Gorgon* and in the *Swallow*. Our vessel put in at the Piræus, and, having some hours to spend there, we found rather unexpectedly that there was time to go up to Athens. I had some fear about seeing this wonder of the world—the Parthenon—in case I should not be able to understand its beauty; but when at a curve on the railway line it came suddenly before our eyes, this was enough; there were no further misgivings.

On our arrival at Athens we drove at once to the Acropolis, but it was the Good Friday of the Eastern Church, and we were on the point of turning away from the closed gates when a welcome gleam of Eastern colour in a carriage following ours suggested that a possible exception might be made for the Indian Princes, who, on their way to England for the Jubilee of 1887, were our fellow-travellers. So it proved; and by the courtesy of Sir Bruce Hamilton, who had the special permission, we saw the Acropolis under a peculiar effect of beauty never repeated during the three weeks spent here later. As we passed through the Greek islands the day before, the weather had been grey with mist and some rain, but now all was changed. A vision of such blue as never steeps a northern landscape! The Bay of Salamis was blue to its depths, blue poured into a cup of gold; the sky was blue, not that of a dye nor of a paint, but as if fold over fold of some ethereal web was laid over and over again to infinity. "We have got something for life," he said as we turned away. "If I could paint that, I feel it would be worth a lifetime, a lifetime of work, even if I did nothing else." He never did paint that picture, but had he not already summed up the whole sentiment of that hour in the picture he had called the "Genius of Greek Poetry"?

I thought of it then, and find I wrote that day: "He has painted those same palpitating depths of blue, and as we looked out through the pillars of the Parthenon the very breath of Nature seemed to take human shape in the air."

The next day, on our way to Constantinople, as we coasted along, the plains of Troy were clearly in sight; Mount Ida in the distance, with snow upon her, and below the Tumuli of Achilles, of Patroclus, and of Ajax, and Samothrace opposite. The *Iliad* was in his mind as he looked upon these and talked long of gods and heroes. I remember his telling me then that he saw in Homer's gods a conception of unrestrained power; their vices were the vices of men, but worse; for the reason that they had no one outside themselves to whom they could appeal as greater than themselves. The heroes of the *Iliad* were far better than their gods ; they undertook nothing without prayer to their deities for light and guidance.

For a few hours next day our boat lay in the harbour of Smyrna, where thirty years before the *Gorgon* had moored for some hours to take in provisions, and where Sir Charles Newton came on board to join the expedition. Two mornings later we anchored at Stamboul ; as an east wind was blowing with grey wet mist, the aspect of the Golden Horn had an unpleasantly familiar look for northerners. April is early enough in the year for Constantinople, and still too early for the place to which we were going—Candilli, where Mrs. Arthur Hanson had invited us to her house on the Bosphorus. The wind still swept keenly down the grey waters from the Black Sea and snowy hills, so that a few days later we thought it better to move down to Constantinople, sorry enough to make the poor exchange to an hotel in Pera. But twice during our short visit we saw the interesting and picturesque sight of the Bulgarian and Armenian peasant women coming to Mrs. Arthur Hanson with their work. For, triumphing over ill-health, and having from this cause become almost completely deaf, she was still carrying on the work for these refugee peasants begun by her years before. During the Turkish and Russian war, guided by a

GEORGE FREDERIC WATTS

Turkish Pascha whom she held in great esteem, she had gone down into the quarter of Constantinople where these poor people were crowded together—suffering from want and disease—and had undertaken to organise work for the women, all of whom were exquisite embroideresses, and, arranging for a market in Vienna, in Paris, and in London, she had enabled them to maintain their families. Twice a week they came to her, bringing their finished work, and sat in rows up and up upon her picturesque staircase, the lower steps of which were at the water's edge, for the Bosphorus was the highway, and a caïque your carriage. But from these lower steps of stone a wooden staircase branched into two separate flights, both curving upwards to the same landing on the upper floor. The sight of these stately women was something to remember when on every step they sat, some with their babies in their arms, some with last stitches still to do, all waiting a summons from the Turkish *kavass* who brought them one by one to Mrs. Hanson. The number of every pattern she gave out was entered, every bit of silk was weighed, and the colours and shades were chosen by her, besides the payments and the ledger work entailed by the undertaking. It was said that these grateful people had been known to come miles to find a spot where they could catch sight of the roof of her house, there to call down blessings upon it. A tribute paid to one whose strenuous life ended too early may be quoted here. An Attaché at the English Embassy, young and with life at its best, once said of her: "I used to go down from Thérapia whenever I felt gloomy, to be cheered up by Mrs. Hanson; her hearing lost, her fortune lost, and stricken by a mortal disease, she nevertheless always sent me away in love with life again." The war with Russia in great part destroyed the fortune of the Hansons— long the leading merchant house in Constantinople—and the ensuing anxiety and work were mainly the cause of the death of the senior partner, Mr. Arthur Hanson, while still a young man; but her courage never failed her. Of my husband, whom she had not known before, she soon said to me: "Every day he comes deeper into my heart. I looked at him to-night, and I do not know why, but the words, 'And a little child shall lead them,' suddenly came into my mind; there is that lowliness which I have always found to be the corner-stone of greatness."

In the hotel at Pera, the weather being still bad, the search had to be made for canvases, that precious time should not be wasted; and Signor began to paint again. One head was painted from nature straight off in four colours; drawn in with a brush in burnt umber, used very transparently to avoid darkening, he got the flesh tones over this entirely with Venetian red, yellow ochre, raw umber, and of course flake white.

GEORGE FREDERIC WATTS

He also painted as a commission the head of a little boy, the son of Sir Vincent Caillard, whom he found a delightful companion. The hours therefore that he was forced to spend shut up in an hotel were somewhat lightened by work. We managed, however, when he was better to see something of Constantinople, but we were not sorry to leave for the milder climate of Greece, and we arrived at Athens to find summer there before us. From our sitting-room window we looked down upon orange trees in full flower and, over this scented carpet of vivid green, to the Acropolis. An old friend, Madame Casavetti,[1] had chosen the rooms for him and made everything comfortable, and during the three weeks spent there, had his health allowed of it, she would have arranged all sorts of expeditions; but just when we might have gone to Olympia and elsewhere, he was not at all well, so we stayed at Athens, and forgot the much that was missed in the pleasure of the much that we found.

The National Museum was new to him, and of course was still unfinished; but such rooms as were completed held enough to attract him day after day. The head of Victory, a cast of which was always in his studio at home, especially enthralled him; he agreed with Sir Charles Newton that it was of the school of Pheidias, if not the work of the master's own hand. "To have done

[1] Euphrosyne Ionides, whom he had painted when she was a girl, on his return from Italy.

one such thing," he said, "is worth a lifetime! Is she not a goddess something more than human? In the neck there is the beauty of the swan, and the power of the horse, something more than a woman; and yet that something more so kept in restraint that it is felt not to be impossible."

He was pleased to find Professor Penrose working out his theories, by measurement of the Parthenon; and there at times they met, to have much talk about the truths perceived by each in Greek art.

Mr. Penrose showed Signor his discovery of the curve in the base line, and also in the cornice of the pediment. He put his hat down at the far end and told Signor to stoop to the level at the other end of the base line, where it could be seen that what appeared to the eye as a straight line was in fact a curve sufficient to hide the hat from sight. He explained that the Greeks foresaw that the lines of the pediment would have the effect of making the straight line of the cornice seem to deflect; therefore they decided to curve the cornice slightly, and, for this purpose, began with making the base line curve also. The pillars are slightly off the perpendicular, and the fluting of the diaper at the top is deeper than it is at the base. The less precise mind of the artist ventured to make the suggestion that these men, sensitive to the means of nature, felt that they must give their lines just the flexibility that would make the building rise like something growing out of the rock itself, so making it a living thing, with none of the rigidity of rule and measure.

With Shakespeare he found that " Nature is made better by no mean, but nature makes that mean "; and certainly the impression that the building grows and flowers out from the rock, and is one with its surroundings, is clear to the mind at the first glance.

" Here in Athens," he said, " one realises that great art and great nature are one. The emotional beauty of the work of Pheidias is of the class of emotion produced by great nature. A touch more would have taken away from its serenity, and lost something of that effect of sacredness that is produced in the mind. From the Parthenon I would pass without a change of feeling through a gallery of work by Titian, Tintoret, or Giorgione; Raphael perhaps less, except in the San Sisto, and even in that picture there is a coldness in the line, though the sentiment goes even more into the blue than these Greek sculptures do. Michael Angelo wanted to give a stronger emotion, and so sacrificed serenity. Greek ornament, and the character of its beauty of extreme preciseness, precluded any great variety. As every circumstance of life contributed towards making the art of the Greeks touch perfection, they were able to concentrate upon a technical completion. In the middle ages life was more like our own. The Greeks were not troubled by the complexity of a later civilisation. As a people living under most unusual conditions they produced art that could never be imitated or rivalled. I assure you that at home, as I sit before the casts I have of the Theseus and Ilissus on my studio mantelpiece, and see them lit up by every variety of light by day and by night, from different points and at different times, it seems to me that each little bit, as it shines out more clearly, must be the one upon which they had lavished all their care, and had tried to make its perfection absolute.

"In the best sculpture you have the palpitations of colour, that seem to suggest all the elements of the picture; you unconsciously see it painted. Now in later work, such as the Laocoon, this is not to be imagined; it is sculpture only."

Of the lost statue of Pallas Athene he said: "I sometimes feel as if I can see it. The fragments give one a great idea of what the Pallas Athene was, probably most spiritual and exceedingly strange."

Mr. Tricoupi was at this time Prime Minister, and, urged by Mr. Aleco Ionides, Signor painted his portrait; the sittings, interrupted by four days of illness, were besides made unusually difficult because of the interest he found in talking to his sitter. I recollect his telling me that in talking of possible changes to come in the balance of European power Mr. Tricoupi had said, "You are safe in England only so long as you have a strong navy."

They talked of Greek art, and Signor told me Mr. Tricoupi thought the Hermes unsurpassed as a statue, and he had differed from this opinion. Praxiteles, he said, could not touch Pheidias; for the reason that the mind of Pheidias was occupied with form, that which is the greatest intellectual effort : the surface—the finish—was nothing to him in comparison ; but the beauty of the work of Praxiteles is on the surface, he cared to give a face, and this to Signor's mind proved decadence. " In the work of Pheidias," he explained, " the folds mean drapery ; he was too wise to do more than say, 'This is a super-added material, loose, and adapting itself to the limbs which it encloses, as the foliage encloses the flower.' In the Hermes of Praxiteles there is evident endeavour to suggest texture, and sheen of the peculiar fabric." He added that none but the Greeks at their best time had tried to give a kind of tremulous, palpitating beauty in every line of drapery. " It is," he said, " the music of form, light, and colour."

Mr. Tricoupi expressed himself as against the attempt to revive the use of the ancient Greek language ; he thought it was a mistake, for the reason that a language was a spontaneous growth increasing with, and representing the need of races, or even of particular generations. Therefore to force a form of language on a people was unnatural, for the reason that it could not adequately express an entirely different set of conditions. The result, he thought, would be the production of grammarians rather than men of ideas.

The evening before we left Athens he

said, "The curtain is just going to fall on six months of delight." Each day there, save just the four when he was ill, had been filled with purest pleasure. The charm of such times is not to be described, it has been—it was exhaled like the scent of a flower, and that is all that can be said.

At Messina our boat was told off to tow a disabled sister ship of the same line (the *Messageries*), and all passengers were given the option of staying on board, to travel more slowly, or of removing to another *Messageries* boat ready to start at once. We, who preferred slowly coasting round Italy, were in the minority, and therefore had all the advantage of the less crowded ship; and the cruise was full of pleasure. A summer sea fog drifted about us one day, through which Corsica was suddenly revealed like opal and pearl, and then lost again. The disabled ship loomed strangely through the fog, and the two pictures "Off Corsica" and "The Sea Ghost" were painted later from the impressions of that day. After two days in Paris, spent between the Louvre and the Salon, we were once more in England on a fair June evening—England, rich, peaceful, and picturesque, the Gothic towers of Canterbury rising from amongst English elms—and he was glad to find that neither Egypt nor Greece had in any way cheapened for him the beauty of English landscape. Nor was the weather to be put to shame, for the next morning the sun rose clear of cloud behind Sir Frederic

GEORGE FREDERIC WATTS

Leighton's chimneys, and as early as he could, Signor went over there to find his friend. And now the peaceful life in art began for me. From my windows in "Paradise Row," when I awoke at dawn, I looked out upon the fresh green of the trees of the neighbouring gardens that met round our own, where song-birds and wood-pigeons were common, and the red and white hawthorns were full of flower. There was a little first breakfast together in the studio when the light was still dim, and the only sound in Melbury Road was the lamplighter's step on his way to turn out the street lights. Then, looking up from my letters, I would see Signor's light figure turning quickly from canvas to canvas, every movement full of enthusiasm and the expression of earnest endeavour. And round and about the big designs stood filling the room with an impression indescribably serene.

I should not have dared to invade him at that time but that my invitation came. I was told I was not to get up unless I liked it; but, he added, "It will be very nice if you can"; and so we were there till seven; then the real toilet for the day followed, and the real breakfast at eight. Breakfast was in a room we called the dining-room, but it was in fact the ante-room to the gallery, and with it was open to the public on Saturday and Sunday afternoons. And so we found ourselves breakfasting with some twenty pictures around us, and when I wanted to boast, I could point to my " dado of Watts portraits."

In the garden, Little Holland House, Melbury Road.

GEORGE FREDERIC WATTS

For, in fact, the dado of that dining-room was the background for his portraits of the great men of the day, his destined gift to the nation. Sometimes the gallery doors were wide open, and from the cool north breakfast-room one looked into sunlight playing upon all that the gallery held of colour and of line. But the pleasure of it was all mine, for he, more often than not, stood there sad and disappointed, saying, "I wonder how it is that I cannot do what I want."

This year of Jubilee the Queen's weather was prevailing; so, unfailingly, after breakfast the great horse and its rider rolled out from the sculpture studio into the garden, and the work on "Physical Energy" went on. Up on ladders and down below on the stage the figure in the white smock worked on tirelessly. Sometimes with hammer and chisel, for the gesso was hard as stone; sometimes modelling up, with small additions of the plaster and tow about the size of the palm of his hand, prepared and given to him by his man. If he was well, and the day fine, the working hours were stretched sometimes to sixteen. Standing and walking as much as he did, he made it a habit, when he wanted rest, not to sit down, but to lie down. In our absence abroad some necessary alterations and additions had been made in the house by Mr. Aitcheson, and he had given the drawing-room a pretty little niche which made the right place for a long divan sort of seat; and it served a double purpose, for, as Signor was slightly deaf, the niche concentrated sound, and he heard better there, and so it became his favourite corner, and he chose to spend his evening lying there, listening to reading. In all the years that I read to him I never knew him to allow his attention to flag; he never grew drowsy. The slightest mistake of mine was pointed out at once. "From almost everything I find I can learn something," he said; and this not of books alone. He lived and worked through all the daylight that was possible; kept time with the sun and the birds in summer, and went upstairs to bed at nine o'clock. As he looked at his watch I can recall his saying, "How I wish it was time to begin work again." During the months in Egypt his mind had been constantly occupied with the work awaiting him at home. Amongst his pictures he dwelt especially upon the "Love and Death" and "Time, Death, and Judgment," his wish being to bring these pictures more and more to the perfection of which his mind conceived.

I have heard Lord Tennyson speak scornfully of the book collector's mania for first editions, whilst on the contrary the first was of less value than a later edition, when the perfecting of the work had been carried further by revision, and Signor felt much the same about the value of the original picture. If the impression to be conveyed by his picture was of greater importance than usual, every line, and the character of every line, of the various parts was pondered over, sometimes during many years. On his return home, when the second version of the " Love and Death " upon a large scale was first brought out and put upon his easel, he saw that, owing to some subtle changes in line and tone, the figure of Death had neither the weight nor the slow movement he desired to give it. So day after day he thought and toiled, and I saw each fold of the garment deliberately reconsidered, a hair's-breadth of line or a breath of colour making the difference that a pause or an accentuated word would make in speaking. For instance, by raising the hand and outstretched arm a less judicial and severe impression was conveyed, and by this slight alteration the action changed from " I shall " to the more tender " I am compelled."

In building up a picture his first care in the matter of technique was that the under painting should be light. White mixed with the ochres or raw umber was what he more often used than white with terra verte. " We have sensitive spirits to deal with," he said, when telling me of a contemporary copy known to have been made upon a dark ground of the "Three Ages" by Titian at Bridgewater House. The original picture painted on a light ground is exceedingly fair and pure ; the copy is now so dark that it is difficult to see what the subject is. Instead of relying upon obtaining a certain quality of tone by a method which, when first painted, is very delightful, a quality obtained by darkening the ground with oil-colour and applying the lighter or more opaque paint over this ground, Signor preferred to use a thin wash of pure powder-colour mixed with water only, and applied it over the oil-colour when this was dry and hard. By this method he obtained the subdued tone, but avoided the danger of subsequent darkening of any of the lighter colours. This water-colour was sometimes a permanent blue, sometimes one of the umbers, laid in with a full brush, and then carefully wiped off—a process by which he managed to get such delicate tone as was required; and as it had the advantage of drying quickly, it was ready for the application of oil-colour almost directly. He preferred this to the more usual glaze of oil-colour, believing that in this water-colour medium there was less danger of future darkening. The stain of the water-colour he found to be absolutely permanent, indeed most difficult to remove if he wished to do so, and long experience had made him confident that so used —as an under glaze—it did not darken the most delicate colour laid over it. A piece of evidence to the effect that his careful preservation of the light ground had the illuminating quality he believed it to have, was given him one day by Mr. Charles Hallé, who had just been arranging and hanging the pictures on loan for exhibition at the People's Palace. While at work there, a dense fog came on, just as he and his colleague were placing two portraits, one of which was by Signor. By daylight they judged them to be fairly equal in tone, but, as this sudden darkness fell upon them, Mr. Hallé said that one portrait became invisible, while by comparison Signor's work shone out like a lamp. The light ground was doing its work, and reflecting amid the semi-darkness what rays were still active.

In his desire to preserve this purity of colour he never allowed himself to put a touch of fresh colour upon his picture until the paint beneath was absolutely dry. He liked his pictures to be exposed to the strongest sunlight. " I like them to be baked," he used to say ; and for this purpose the canvases stood about for days, or even weeks, in a glass house in the garden. Before he worked again upon them they were well sponged with lukewarm water, and rubbed over with a raw potato cut in half, the edges of the cut being carefully pared away. Even in the country it was astonishing to see by the blackening of the water how very necessary these washings were, if purity in the colour was to be obtained.

He did not think that it had been left on record that the great masters of the Renaissance were careful never to work upon paint until it was absolutely dry ; but he was sure that the climate of Italy would naturally reveal this advantage to men who were certain to seize upon it.

GEORGE FREDERIC WATTS

He detested lumps of colour left protruding from the surface, and if in one painting a certain coarseness of texture could not be avoided before the next was applied, when the colour had become sufficiently hard, these rough projections were well rubbed down with a buffalo-horn palette-knife. His method of glazing with oil-colour was, I believe, original. Perhaps it should not be called glazing, as the word conveys the idea of transparent and flowing colour, while he instead used stiff colour, and at first applied more than was required. Then with scraps of paper, purposely lying at hand on the dresser for this use, he would rub off as much of the colour as it was possible to remove, thus leaving what may be called a mere breath, but all that was wanted. For such treatment it will be understood that the paint beneath had to be perfectly hard and dry.

As years went on he asked Mr. Scott Taylor (Consulting Chemist to Messrs. Winsor and Newton) to have his colours still more stiffly ground, and many of these were sent to him in porcelain jars, to be kept under water so that there should be no evaporation from the scant proportion of linseed oil, and that the paint should remain of the right consistency and ready for his use. The colour supplied in tubes was also specially ground to the stiffness he required.

His brushes of hog's hair were worn down —even purposely rubbed down—till their bristles were short and very stiff. He also laid on touches of colour with paper stumps intended for use with charcoal and chalk.

As time went on he became better and better satisfied with this method of using stiff colour, so much so that towards the end of his life he sometimes said that he felt that he was only then beginning to know how to paint. The clear edge that he found himself able to get with some ease pleased him, for he abhorred a smear. He thought that exhibitions discouraged beautiful workmanship, as, at these, it must have less than its due effect—the result of competition with work painted to be striking.

For him, in this sensitiveness of surface and texture, there arose one of the perennially fresh springs of interest for every working day. No method was entirely satisfactory. There were ever fresh discoveries to be made, and the joy of for ever seeking made him glad to be up with the first streak of daylight. "Every day is a birthday, every moment of it is new to us," he said cheerfully; "we are born again, renewed for fresh work and endeavour."

CHAPTER XIV

ALL great art in every age represented and gave material expression to the character and scope of the thought of the time. Egyptian art did, Greek art did, Mediæval art did. They made no claims to artistic eminence, but assert the intellectual and moral value of art.

The best art deals with what is noble and beautiful, and gives us friends rather than acquaintances; dexterity will astonish and please, but can never be loved.

G. F. WATTS.

CHAPTER XIV

On his return to Little Holland House old friends and new came quickly to see him. Amongst the first to welcome him back was one of the oldest friends, though one of the youngest of men, Lord Wemyss. "My severest critic," Signor called him. There was always much banter and fun when he came, and fresh enthusiasm over an old master or a new genius. On Sunday afternoons my anxiety was often that the pleasure of welcoming too many at a time might overtire him. Considering that he went out nowhere, it was proof of the constancy of his friends that those made in Florence, or even before he went there, or those made in his Charles Street studio, so often came to find him in these last years; more especially as for some time an idea had got about that he was very inaccessible. "I look back," he said to me once, "and think how wonderfully good I have found the world. People call it a bad place; I am sure I have not found it so, I have so many good friends. I think they care for the desire after something I cannot attain to. There is not much else in me to care for."

Another day another facet would catch the light, and he said: "One of the endeavours I have made a part of life is to try to see people justly, taking temperament, character, and surroundings into consideration, and not expecting to find all the graces and virtues growing where there was nothing to nourish them. The balance of things is seldom found; great qualities are sometimes found with a certain lack of refinement, and great refinement sometimes with a weak fastidiousness. We must not expect it to be otherwise, it is the barren side of the mountain. I have been grieved by very good people failing to perceive this. They would have no patience with a character below the level of what they could admire, and so were incapable of doing justice to others. We are unfortunately always aware of contrast, while proportion is being lost sight of. A far greater thing than contrast is proportion."

With certain friends it had long been arranged with him that their visits should be at particular hours. During many years, at old Little Holland House, his friend Frederic Leighton had come almost every day. But as time went on these frequent visits became impossible. He had become President of the Academy, and had besides lavishly laid out his time and himself on duties which became the more exacting because of his high sense of what he owed to any undertaking with which his name was connected. But on all Sunday mornings when they were both at home in Kensington, Sir Frederic was in Signor's studio by nine o'clock. He never failed unless he was ill, and in that case the note of explanation never failed to come.

The two friends were generally alone together, but sometimes Signor sent for me, and then I could enjoy their brisk interchange of thought, Sir Frederic's words and ideas always flowing with the rush of a mill-race.

One morning Signor had described to him what he had just heard from Professor Jowett, who had looked through a microscope of high magnifying power, first at a thorn and then at a very fine needle point under the lens; the surface of the thorn had appeared as polished and smooth as it was in nature, while the needle point appeared as rough as a piece of metal ore. "Ah," said Sir Frederic instantly, "of course the one was a growth from within, the other an application from without;" so swiftly seizing upon the cause, the underlying truth that marks the difference between that which is and that which merely seems to be.

Differing as they did often with one another, there were many amusing little duels. Signor had perhaps mentioned the words "Principles of Form." "There are no principles of form," exclaimed Sir Frederic. "I beg your pardon," Signor asserted, "there are principles of form, and very definite they are; with colour this is not the case." "Oh, there you are wrong! Of course there are principles of colour;" and so the half of an hour passed too quickly in lively and interesting discussion, each continuing to hold to his own opinion to the end.

The discovery of beauty in amateur work was a singular pleasure to Signor. It was difficult to know sometimes why a drawing that appeared to be crude, perhaps even childish, would for some reason fire his imagination. He was often chaffed by his friends about this; and once, when he was showing Sir Frederic some work of the kind and had said, " Look at this! Now I declare *I* could not draw a line like that ! "—" No, fortunately not," Sir Frederic rapped out as he scrutinised the work of art.

Mrs. Charles Wylie had her hour on Sunday morning also, and often came to discuss grounds, recipes, and methods of the old masters; sometimes to spar over social and political questions, upon which they differed profoundly.

But on weekdays there were particular friends who more often came with the dusk, to find Signor resting on the long seat of his niche, as that corner in the little sitting-room was named.

How pleased he was when the door opened and Mr. Burne-Jones, his " dear Ned," came to sit by him, to give a whimsical turn to the face of the commonplace, as he could better than most; or, when speaking with a sort of pathetic gravity, one humorous saying followed another. Perhaps—and this time more than half in earnest—Mr. Burne-Jones would confess that he felt ashamed to walk along the street, because he was certain every person he passed knew quite well what bad work he had that day been doing.

Canon Barnett (at that time the warden of Toynbee Hall and Rector of Whitechapel) and Mrs. Barnett came many times this summer, especially as Signor was painting his portrait, his gift to Mrs. Barnett. At the first sitting he made a rapid sketch; this he continued on the second day, but, not quite satisfied with the texture of his canvas at the end of the hour, he rapidly sketched in another portrait on yellow canvas. Four days later, upon this he painted and completed the portrait now in Mrs. Barnett's possession, working from two o'clock till six. Signor's sympathies had from the first been given to churchmen who held liberal views and had the widest sympathies with the poor. Frederick Denison Maurice was well known to him, and sittings for a portrait had been practically arranged, but for some reason they were deferred, and never again did the opportunity occur. He liked to remember Mr. Maurice's answer when asked if he would accept the office of first president of the Working Man's College, and had replied, "Whatever you like, president or porter." There was a proposition, when the college was first opened, that Signor should take some share in the teaching of art, and it was a matter of great regret to him to be obliged to decline; indeed, to keep even tolerably well, his powers of usefulness (as he himself expressed it) were bounded by the walls of his studio.

GEORGE FREDERIC WATTS

The Master of Balliol, Professor Jowett, was also much with him this year. As early as 1879, at the Briary, he had begun a portrait of the Master; but he was never satisfied with the likeness, and was still anxious to carry out the undertaking, though dreading it (for it was a type of face that was immensely difficult to him to render). He now set to work again, and most patiently the Master gave innumerable sittings. He accomplished the portrait, but with very great difficulty. Professor Jowett was staying with Miss Nightingale, and brought messages and letters from her, as in old days Signor had been anxious to paint her for his national collection. The portrait was in fact begun, but she was not well at the time, and the work was interrupted and not carried further. Sir William Richmond subsequently made his fine portrait of her.

Shortly before we left for the winter the Russian painter Verestchagin came to see Signor. There was a collection of his work on exhibition at the Grosvenor Gallery, and the truth and dramatic power of these pictures had impressed Signor. One picture, a reminiscence of the Turko-Russian War, depicted a barn-like temporary hospital with its long row of beds, where over every single face was drawn the sheet as a death cloth, and its title, "All quiet at Shipka," was tragic enough. Verestchagin himself, a strong, robust soldier, was full of *bonhomie*. He went round the pictures in the studio and appeared to like them much; he suggested to Signor that the angel in the " Court of Death " should wear some distinctive badge or sign that she represented Death. Signor gave himself a little time to weigh the matter, but after a few minutes said quickly, " No, I won't," at which Verestchagin laughed heartily. Before he left he said he had come expecting to find an imitator of the Old Masters, but instead had found the most independent man he knew.

Of the younger generation at this time came one whom Signor had known from babyhood, Mr. Philip Burne-Jones, who had lately been making delightful portraits in oil-colour on a small scale. He was anxious to paint a portrait of Signor at work upon the horse. He often stayed for luncheon, so saw something of Signor at leisure, and they enjoyed many talks together. Of him he once said to a friend, " Even if Signor tells one what one does already know, he says it in a way that makes it sound more true than it ever was before." Sir Philip (to use the name now best known) on one occasion plunged straight into a difficulty for Signor. One of his pictures by misrepresentation got into the hands of a fraudulent dealer. By his prompt action in swooping suddenly down upon the misdemeanant, he managed to reduce a man of six foot and over to wax in his hand, and returned in his hansom cab triumphant and with the picture, one on which Signor set value. In future he called him his " man of business." More than once this kind friend proved himself to be a wise adviser, and when Signor wished to sell a picture, gave most practical aid.

The friends were many and delightful, and one might easily be betrayed into expanding into a volume on these alone. As my own people came to know him well, they understood my happiness, and he was soon loved by all mine. I remember when my father's sister, who, since her husband's death, had lived far more in a spiritual world than in the actual, saw him for the first time, she said to me, "I looked into his face and read all your happiness there; a serene calm, all spirit, and so beautiful."

In September of this year Signor wrote a letter and sent it both to the *Times* and *Spectator*, making a suggestion for commemorating the fiftieth anniversary of the Queen's reign by a monument raised to deeds of heroic self-sacrifice in everyday life. "The character of a nation as a people of great deeds is one, it appears to me, that should never be lost sight of. It must surely be a matter of regret when names worthy to be remembered and stories stimulating and instructive are allowed to be forgotten. The material prosperity of a nation is not an abiding possession; the deeds of its people are."

Though many people were interested and approved of the idea, the matter was not taken up generally. Mr. Passmore Edwards was inclined to give the necessary funds, but Signor was unaware of this till later. Miss Octavia

Hill and Mrs. Barrington, however, with the help of Mr. Walter Crane, undertook to decorate the Red Cross Hall at Southwark with pictures illustrating heroic incidents. Signor was glad to know of the project, but it was not his scheme. After considering the matter, he felt sure that the design for the memorial should be of the simplest character. On the tablets recording the names of those whose lives had been sacrificed, the mention should be made as briefly as possible of the act that had cost a life. He wrote at the time : " The facts it is proposed to record cannot be subject to opinion, as all art must be. No art can stand on a level with the sublime sacrifices, the memory of which it is the desire to rescue from forgetfulness. Art, which should be worthy of and demand recognition for its own sake, must not be presumptuously put forward in competition. A record of the event, date, and name is all I ever thought of or proposed. I have none of the means necessary for the carrying out of any great object. All I can attempt will amount to no more than something of the nature of a simple cutting of the first sod."

At length, in 1899, he did at his own cost build a simple cloister in St. Botolph's churchyard. Of this he wrote at the time : " Merely a covered walk, not splendid as the deeds, but unaffected as the impulse." There are now some forty-eight names placed upon this wall. They are all persons who were connected with London or within a certain radius of it. Carved into the beam supporting the roof of this covered walk are the words : " In Commemoration of Heroic Self-sacrifice."

But autumn fogs now awoke the longing for the blue skies of Malta, and early in November he was settled in the house at Sliema we had secured the winter before. Everything promised well. The big room he made his studio and its windows, which admitted a more diffused light than he had at home, pleased him much. We were within a few minutes' walk of the seashore, where Mediterranean blue-green waves came rolling in. Sometimes when a land wind blew, their crests of foam thrown back, Neptune's horses seemed to be racing towards us, and here this as a subject for a picture occurred to him ; the impression now made on his mind remained fresh, and was painted some three years later in London. On a canvas upon which Mrs. Wylie had laid in with tempera colour the little hovering figure of a cupid from Signor's design (a part of the fresco at Carlton House Terrace), he painted that sea at its bluest and greenest, to attract the little man to go a-fishing with his scarlet line. This picture is now well known as " Good Luck to your Fishing."

In the centre of his studio, which was the drawing-room of the house, there hung a huge glittering chandelier. To the unimaginative its glass drops and beads appeared to be the last thing in the world to suggest a picture. It was

GEORGE FREDERIC WATTS

French according to the taste of thirty or forty years before, and nothing more. But he had found there some suggestion of the beautiful, and from it grew the solemn and mystic figure holding the universe in hands that encircle the sphere; the picture he named "The All-pervading." And I am here reminded that Signor told me that the giant figures of the reposing continents in his picture of "Chaos" were suggested to him when looking at the cracks and stains on the dirty plaster of a wall. He saw the whole composition mentally, and carried it out years afterwards.

In his latest years "The Sower of the Systems" was suggested by curiously refracted rays of light thrown by a night-light upon the ceiling of his bedroom.

These first weeks were full of pleasures, and we sometimes wondered if we could, like Polycrates, find our ring to drop into our blue seas. The colour and light was an endless joy to Signor's eyes. For him the wall or coping of Maltese stone against the sky recalled the clear beauty of a painting by Basaiti; and Valetta, from our windows across the bay, shone like something wrought in fine old silver.

We had not been very long at Malta when Signor received a letter from Mr. William Agnew (not yet come to his honours) asking him to let him have one of the two large-sized versions of the picture of "Love and Death." Signor had been, as was his habit, intent on making the second version better than the first, and he naturally wished that his best should go to the nation. It was so with his popular picture of "Hope." Finding while it was still in the Grosvenor Gallery that it was much liked, he determined to try to repeat it, with certain changes which he believed would make it a better picture. I see in a letter to Miss Mead of 1886 that Mrs. Barrington writes : "Signor has painted a second 'Hope,' far more beautiful than the one in the Grosvenor Gallery, and one of these he intends to give to the nation." It was because he believed it to be the best that he reserved it for the nation, and in 1887 sold the first version.[1] In 1888, when his purse had been drained by the circumstances of his severe illness, an offer of two thousand guineas was received by him at Mentone for the version of "Hope" he had set aside for the nation, and which at that time was hanging in South Kensington. The offer he very naturally refused.

As regards the picture of "Love and Death," his first reply to Mr. Agnew runs thus :—

"I have just received your letter, which wandered a little for want of precise direction. I do feel greatly honoured by the wish that my picture, 'Love and Death,' should be chosen to commemorate your extremely interesting exhibition. A year ago I should have been tempted

---

[1] He allowed a small copy to be made of this picture by Cecil Schott, a young student. It was made at the request of Madame Casavetti, and was entered in the list of the pictures inherited by her children as "A copy made by Cecil Schott and worked upon by G. F. Watts."

to present it to the town of Manchester to commemorate the event, and, indeed, I had intended never again to take money for any of my later pictures of this class, but a great change in my life has necessitated a change in my views on money matters. Though I shall not any more than formerly make money my object, and shall neither paint portraits nor accept commissions, and shall present my work of a certain class and range to the nation, reason and justice present to me considerations which must not be ignored. I shall be glad to meet your wishes, but in the first place I wish to make the picture as good as the one you saw in my studio, not by making it like, for there are many alterations in colour—especially in the latter—but by carrying it further, as I think I can do, towards what I understand by real completion in the same direction. I think I am justified in believing it a representative work. It is actually the result of many years' labour, not merely by the accumulation of experience gained by constant application, but literally. I have worked constantly upon it since it was first exhibited in 1877, not in the way of making experiments upon it and alterations, but by improving its workmanship and details; this I think I can still do, so that in the future it may be among those that have a place of their own. Under these circumstances I must either have a large price for it, or it must remain till I have done with everything, when I do not think it will be sold

for a small one; of course I remember it is a second picture, but its fellow, belonging to the nation, will never be sold. Many thanks for your kind wishes. I am enjoying the light and colour, and hope to improve.—Yours sincerely,
"G. F. WATTS."

A very generous offer having been received from Mr. Agnew, Signor wrote finally :—

"DEAR MR. AGNEW—I have concluded that, as a sign of being in fellowship with the movement you and your colleagues are instituting in Manchester, the picture you desire to possess shall be placed in your hands as a gift to be bestowed as you think best. I gave you in my former letter the reasons I felt for prudence with regard to the future. I am asked to reconsider this.

"Though puzzled sometimes between giving my work or accepting the wherewithal that makes it possible to respond to the many appeals upon one's purse and inclinations to be generous, we have concluded in this case that the willingness to give of one's best is a more useful thing than a gift of money. I would only stipulate that I shall have the 'Love and Death' to work on if I please when I return, and that the choice between the two shall rest with me.—Yours truly, G. F. WATTS."

In Mr. Agnew's reply, dated December 1887, he says : "The effect of your generosity will be far-reaching ; it has already sent a thrill through the hearts of those who are best and noblest in Manchester City. Dear Mr. Watts, accept my grateful acknowledgments and the expression of my earnest belief that no words of mine can express how I feel towards you. I have not had the honour of making Mrs. Watts's personal acquaintance. Yet I ask you to permit me to offer my felicitations to her. I feel she has had no small share in this matter."

Alas, we had not found the ring to lose and to carry our misfortunes into the depths of the sea. Towards the middle of December Signor first knew that his old friend Mrs. Prinsep was very seriously ill, and on the 21st of December the black-edged letters arrived to tell him of her loss. Death seems more cold, more inexorable than ever, when the life it takes away is, as was hers, full of movement, enthusiasms, affections, and anxieties. Signor was much shaken by the news and said to me, " How sad the dismemberment of that sisterhood!—like the pages of some beautiful book torn out one by one."

He sat down at once to write to her sons and to Andrew Hichens, and then went quietly back and resumed his work, never out of harmony with any serious mood. I did not think him well next day; on the next again he told me he did not feel so, and proposed that we should take an early walk, as he thought the open air would be good for him. We went out, and during that walk he became alarmingly ill. Weeks followed of much anxiety, nursing was constant; in the midst of continued sleeplessness, partly due to an attack of eczema of such a severe kind as to be almost torture, his consideration for others through all was very striking. He always lamented the trouble he was forced to give to those about him, his nurse, his devoted housekeeper, myself, and Miss Prinsep, who was spending the winter with us. At last, by the middle of February, his doctor, despairing of improvement at Malta, advised change, and I, with his man-servant and nurse, took him by sea to Naples. We landed at Naples the next day. Though the voyage had been borne better than we could have hoped, it was a great relief when —pioneered by the Neapolitan doctor, who came on board to meet us—he was once more in bed in a comfortable room in one of the large hotels. There we found friends, Miss Ida Verner and her aunt, also Sir Henry and Lady Layard. It was soon seen that we were well advised to leave Malta, for Signor certainly now made progress, and one day he was well enough to be taken up by the lift to the roof of our hotel. It was midday, and the sun broke in full power from behind the moving clouds, so that the city glittered here and there like a jewelled breast beneath a purple mantle, and the bay was a wonder of colour. That evening, hearing that a Neapolitan artist was downstairs in the vestibule of the hotel selling little paintings made in gouache, he sent to make an appointment for a lesson in the use of this material to be given to him next day.

Accordingly, for an hour master and pupil were at work together, and he found that with gouache he could rapidly make notes of his impressions of Naples. The weather was cold, Vesuvius half covered with snow, and as he never ventured to the roof again, when he was able for it we moved up to the higher situation of the Hotel Bristol, where the view from his window was splendid; and there he stored up impressions of colour which later went on to canvas.

During the fortnight at Naples his recovery was satisfactory, and the doctor allowed us to continue our journey. We had chosen Mentone as the place most likely to suit him. After a stormy crossing to Marseilles, head winds delaying us many hours, we thought it well to stay at Marseilles for two nights' rest, and make another halt at Cannes.

He might have seen Cannes as it was in its natural state of beauty, for in 1846 he was on the point of paying a visit to Lord Brougham (who was the possessor of the first villa built there) for the purpose of painting his portrait. But as that arrangement fell through, it so happened that the short glimpse at this time was his first and last. Brief as it was, it was never forgotten. For, before any one else seemed to be astir, we were on the seashore, enchanted by the beauty and the calm of a morning that might be called perfect.

Behind us were the pleasant winter homes in

delightful gardens; in front, the Mediterranean, like an opal, glistened under a sunlight more silver than golden. There was no movement but that slow mighty roll that seems to follow after rough weather, and comes from the heart of the sea like the last sobs of a child after a storm of tears. We had made acquaintance with the rough weather so lately that perhaps the sense of that great calm movement was heightened by contrast. Anyhow the charm was strongly upon us as we sat there silently watching, when, suddenly, as if it might have been purposely for our particular pleasure, into the arena rode a troop of porpoises (some six or seven of them), at first slowly—grandly enough—tossing their helmeted heads and following in line one behind another. Then they began to gambol and tumble, and tumble again and again, splashing and sporting as if gone wild with joy at being alive on such a morning and in such a sea. And glad we were to have been there to see their joy.

But the haven where hotel life would cease for us was what he longed for, so we moved on to Mentone that day, and lost no time in finding a villa to suit and of which to possess ourselves, there being ample choice, as the fear of earthquake had swept the whole place bare of winter visitors.

A record of great happiness was made during the weeks spent at Mentone, for it summed up the return of health, and the joy of being once more at work, the sense, already in March, of summer being about us — the Mediterranean, with its ever-new glories of colour, the neighbourhood of the hills, and the quiet of our simple life, alone with books and with nature.

The Villa Baron was small, but he was not daunted by want of space or the loss of his easels, which his dislike of travelling heavily laden had caused to be sent home direct from Malta. The canvases were stretched upon the wall of the most suitable room, and he made the best of the distance to be got through a door opening from another room. It was his way to make a good distinction between such discomforts as had to be borne and those which need not be borne. Against these he was quickly and hotly rebellious, a great boon in everyday life, as they could at once be made right, and all heart-burning over grievances brought forward too late for remedy was saved for those about him.

Some five or six pictures were, in spite of disadvantages, begun and carried well forward: three from sketches made in gouache at Naples, the picture called "The Open Door," a study of a head in pastel,[1] sent to the Royal Academy exhibition in the following summer, and the landscape known as "The Alps behind Mentone," painted from studies made from nature. While he was painting this picture we made many pilgrimages to the spot. It had been a great joy to find that after a time his

[1] The only experiment he ever carried to completion with pastels.

walking powers had come back to him, and he was able to follow a delightful track leading from our little bit of garden into the heart of the woods. The sight of hotels and villas left behind, in time we reached a point where the Alps rose grandly from a deep valley of pines and olive-trees to the crowning of the summit by the convent of Sant Agnese.

"I feel very certain," he said, "that to render nature truly—that is, to give her inward beauty—one must make careful studies first, either in pencil or monochrome, looking much and well at nature, and then coming away and trying to paint the impression left on the mind. For this reason I consider that the backgrounds in some of Millais' pictures have far excelled the landscapes he painted directly from nature."

The state of mind which Signor knew was produced in himself by the presence of nature—more especially amongst mountains—was the state into which above all things he wished, through his art, to bring the mind of the beholder.

In the earnest desire to produce this state of feeling—or rather to awaken the perceptions to that which is instinctively acclaimed to be the highest—he never lost sight of the true value of the means to that end. He worked as earnestly at the studies in pencil he was making from nature of the rocky structure of this spur of the Alps he was about to paint, as if he was still the student who, for the sake of the discipline, was carefully drawing in the skeleton before clothing it with muscle, flesh, or the folds of any outer garment. But having, so to speak, built up the structure, he felt he was at liberty to subordinate all the material facts as much as appeared to him to be necessary for the production of that particular state of feeling he desired to create. A presentment, however dexterous, of the external aspect only, was what he could never allow himself to be content with ; nor could he ever consent to call such painting a work of art.

He returned often and sat long at the spot where he could best study the subject of this picture, sometimes silently absorbing the beauty of the varying moods of the mountains, sometimes making fresh notes of characteristic features.

" I wonder if any work is as disheartening as painting !" he would exclaim. He often wished that he could find a winter home in such a place as this. "It would be worth anything," he said, "to live amongst such hills and have them to look at at all times. In their nature, partaking of earth and sky — something of the strength and reality of earth with the blue-celestial of eternity." And that evening, his thoughts turning again gratefully to the pleasure of our morning walk, he said simply, " How kind nature is to us ! She takes us aside quietly and says, ' Here is a book for you to see—I don't show it to every one,' and so every day we have a fresh delight."

On looking back there seems to have been a delightful mystery for us about the little pathway. We never knew how far it went, or to what place it led, or why it had been given to us only, so that all the time it was ours no one ventured to trespass upon it.

Only once, on such a tempting morning that we felt obliged to be walking there soon after sunrise, did we see three delightful trespassers. We were standing a little way from the path to watch the—to us unfamiliar—shadows cast on the hills from the sun low in the east, and to notice the delicate cistus blossoms at our feet opening wide their sensitive petals wherever a ray of sunshine fell, when from below came a family of peasants toiling up the steepness. A donkey led the way, laden with baskets filled with household goods, in the midst of which sat a darling child holding on with small hands to the basket's rim, while close behind followed a young father and mother, upright and strongly knit—so probably from the hills.

They passed without a word or look, only the child smiled back at us as we smiled with pleasure at the little figure sitting so serenely amongst the pots and pans, the little face rounded by the becoming coif of a blue handkerchief faded into great beauty; and, when I kissed my hand to her, she enchanted us by instantly returning the salutation with a grace that was royal.

The family must have been up before dawn, most likely taking country produce to the town;

and the child, as part and parcel of themselves, was already sharing something of their happy life of labour.

The weeks passed only too quickly, and we began to be aware with keen regret that the days of our little " Baron " were becoming few. The quiet suited him so well that Signor began to think he might do better work if he could be shut away, see no newspaper, forget the world, and be forgotten ; but again the remembrance of the work yet to be accomplished at home, and the friends he could not spare from his life, came to mind, and conquered his longing for a hermit's cell. And even here friends came to him. Sir John and Lady Dalrymple (the "*Sorella*" of old days) were at Monte Carlo, and we went to them and they came to us. Andrew and May Hichens and Blanche and Herbert Somers Cocks were also in the South of France, and made journeys to find him. They were all rejoiced to see that he had so wonderfully recovered from his severe illness, and thought him looking well ; and so he was ; this we could with very thankful hearts acknowledge. But even to the little Baron, now a paradise where, through open windows, came a scent of orange and lemon blossom, of roses and of heliotrope, news would come to bring the sound of the " tides for ever flowing, the measureless waters of human tears." One morning the news of Matthew Arnold's sudden death shocked and grieved Signor. Six years before they had been brought together through the intercourse held during quiet hours, whilst Signor painted and Matthew Arnold sat for his portrait; and he valued him as a friend and as a great Englishman, and believed the place the future would give him would be a very high one. At San Remo the Emperor Frederick was dying, and people were full of foreboding as to what would happen when his reign ended; this was a real sorrow to Signor, who believed the Emperor's life to be of great value to Europe. With his mind full of questionings why valuable lives were taken away before half their work was done, he exclaimed impatiently, "And people who are like chips in porridge go on living!" and then continued, "Well, perhaps the incompleteness argues for that other existence. Life here, with its intimations of perfection, could never be all that man is intended to know; he must develop elsewhere. I feel sometimes as if the human being was an atom in a great Whole—that we are all but as people moving in a dream, and that the dream is from One Brain."

After the first week in May the weather at Mentone became too hot, and we thought it well to begin our journey northwards to Aix-les-Bains, where he was to try to get rid of gout; we halted at San Remo, and so went on by the glorious valley of the Po to Turin. We seemed to rush through tunnels from one loveliness to another; the magic of spring was on the land—on the landscape of Italy—and nightingales sang

GEORGE FREDERIC WATTS

in choirs, and made themselves heard above the sound of steaming engines and the bustle of stations. He had never before visited Turin, and we spent many hours in the picture galleries. It was worth much to him to find there Paul Veronese's "Queen of Sheba before Solomon"; he thought it a supreme work and in a finer condition than any other picture known to him by this great master. To this and to the Botticelli "The Virgins with Saints and Tobias"; to Gaudenzio Ferrari's "St. Peter," with the beautiful figure of the donor, an old man on his knees; to Bernardino Lanini's "Descent from the Cross"; and to Pollaiuolo's "Tobias," he went back over and over again. On Sunday afternoon the galleries were filled with peasants, men and women alike appearing to be awake to the beautiful in these works of art. Signor was reminded of a story told him by George Mason of a shepherd in the Roman Campagna who stood behind him while he painted. Mason was about to retouch some part of his picture, when this peasant, with a deprecating gesture, cried out, "*Ah, lascia stare!*" and he took the advice of the shepherd dilettante.

Signor was glad to find here the statue, by his old friend Marochetti, of Emmanuel Philibert of Savoy—a mailed figure of the sixteenth century on horseback, sending back his sword to its scabbard. He thought it Marochetti's best work; the one adverse criticism that he had to make was that the Duke's thighs might have been longer. When Marochetti first showed him his statue of Richard Cœur de Lion, he pointed out this fault, which in this work is even more apparent. Marochetti exclaimed, "You are right! if it had not been cast I should have made the change, but it is too late"; and he struck his thigh, saying, "The fault is here; my own thighs are short."

At our destination, the Hotel Thermal at Aix-les-Bains, we secured the *dépendance* of the hotel, which fortunately consisted of our own suite of rooms and no more; this Signor much preferred. In the end the treatment did little to diminish the trouble of suppressed gout which was said to be the cause of all his maladies; but while at Aix he gave himself up patiently to the cure under Doctor Blanc's orders. The place itself, however, was full of charm for him, the weather was glorious, and when other visitors were shut up in hot dining-rooms we took delightful walks, saw something of the poetry of the people and the glory of the evening light upon the hills. We usually climbed by uphill paths to reach wider views and unspoilt country. We crossed little mountain streams that turned numberless busy mill-wheels on their way to the valley; passed peaceful-looking peasant homes, and found little wayside shrines. The Virgin of the Waters had hers, and we stood aside one evening, for we had suddenly come across a circle of white-capped peasant women, their faithful eyes turned earnestly up towards the Blessed Mother and her Child, as they sang their vesper hymn. And Signor said, "Oh, the pity that such a faith should ever be lost."

There was much that was beautiful to look back upon in these walks. The light of the hour the Venetians loved to paint was on the hills, and above our favourite ridge one evening we saw a full moon rise in the crimson of an afterglow.

Amongst the French books we had been reading at Mentone, Zola had been giving us his terrible pictures of French peasantry, and by contrast the Savoyard seemed to us to stand for all that was opposed to this. Their manners were always courteous, while at the same time a distinct sense of independence of character was conveyed. Of the sturdy up-bringing of these children of the hills we had a glimpse, when on one of our evening walks we met and were fascinated by two little girls in the costume of the country—the short-waisted homespun frocks and tightly-fitting caps of white cotton, with thick wooden soles to their little shoes. They had in their arms a number of implements, heavy enough as we knew later. We watched them on their way, believing that with these burdens they could not be far from their own home; but instead of this, on they tramped in front of us, with the wisdom of older years changing their burdens from arm to arm, though indeed the eldest could not have been more than six years old and her sister probably not five. They stopped to ask their way from a woman standing at her door, and we overtook them and found this kindly woman full of compassion for the children, giving them cakes. She told us that they had been up to what, till now, had been their home in the hills, to fetch these things which had been left behind when the family moved to Aix the day before. The children had been walking for seven hours, she said, and their home was still to seek. "*Là-bas*," was the only direction they could give. Signor at once took possession of the haft of a scythe which was of stout oak and bound with iron, and of a child's chair made heavily enough to last out several generations of little Savoyards. I took some indescribable things made of iron which seemed to belong to a mill wheel. Then a small hand from each was so thankfully put into his and mine. We had noticed that each step was becoming more unsteady, and the grateful expression of trust in the blue eyes that looked up at us could never be forgotten. "*Là-bas*" proved to be still some distance off, and I was getting anxious about Signor with his load as we went on and on; but at last the children hailed their mother, who was watching for their coming, though, as it seemed, not racked with anxiety! We explained why we had helped them, and suggested that the walk and the weight they had carried was too much for such small people. This she admitted, but shrugged her shoulders and asked what else she could have done—she must needs send them, as their father wanted these things for his work next day. The children's dogged patience gave us the impression that they would have walked on without complaint—to death itself—had there been need. The following morning we went to see how they were; they were skipping about briskly and well, the mother having allowed them, so she told us, to lie in bed till half-past seven, as a great concession.

While we were at Aix-les-Bains the first exhibition at the New Gallery had opened, and Signor had many kind letters from friends writing to him of his picture, " Death crowning Innocence," shown there for the first time. Of it Andrew Hichens wrote : " The sober sweetness of the colour and solemn beauty of the composition, and not its sadness, for there is little of that, are what bring tears to one's eyes and make one thank God for another beautiful gift to the world." And his words express what was said by many friends. Signor had intended to sell that picture, but when he found that it was liked, and buyers began to present themselves, he settled at once that it was to be of the number offered to the nation. He only required the assurance that he had expressed an abstract truth to which the human heart could answer. " As for thanks," he said, " one would do nothing if one thought of these, one does it for the principle." With letters and books and the visits from the friends we found at Aix, in the interludes between massage and baths, the day became well filled. Lady Somers was in her charming house at Grésy and often came to see us, seldom empty-handed. She brought flowers and books, or it might be a loaf of home-made bread. And we drove to see her at home in her garden of a thousand roses. But the day could not pass without some time being given by Signor to his work. A picture had been maturing in his mind for a day or two, to be called " Peace and Goodwill."[1] While he drew, I, answering letters, had tried to describe him. "Signor is sitting now before a little wax figure we have twisted up together and draped in wet handkerchiefs. The wax lady is poised on the edge of the table, and he, a few feet off, is leaning back in his chair, one knee thrown across the other. All the lines are long and come so well, his figure reminds me of nothing so much as one of his own silver-point drawings. His drawing-book, held at arm's length with one hand, is just supported by his raised knee, the other hand is working away busily. Then clear-cut against the window I see the small head moving up and down, as he sends that earnest direct glance of his from his model to his sketch."

It was surprising to see the beauty that was suggested to his eye by that rough little figure,

[1] The finished picture has, since his death, been given to St. Paul's Cathedral.

and to watch the regal robes that came into existence later when, using gouache, he made sketches from this figure in colour. "Peace," he had told me, "was to be a queen, though she is a wanderer and out-cast from her kingdom. She will turn wearily towards a streak of light which may mean the dawn of better things. The son, her heir, is still only a young child upon her knee."

"Before Signor begins a new picture," I continue, "he does not see the design very distinctly. He has first a very strong mental impression of the ideas he wishes to convey, then he is conscious of a certain nobility of outline in keeping with the idea, but nothing more than that. The rest comes as he works it out on paper or on canvas. He told me that when Mr. Thoby Prinsep was watching his brother (a good amateur artist) at work on a drawing, he said to him, 'What are you copying, James?' 'The picture I see in my mind,' he answered. He was working as fast as if he was copying every line."

We were nearing the end of the ordinary course at Aix, and intended to go straight home, but during the last days there Signor was so unwell that our plans were changed, and Doctor Blanc decided that he must have rest in more bracing air before the long journey. We went on, therefore, to Monnetier (Haute-Savoie), more than two thousand feet above the sea-level, and a week later went home by Geneva and Paris. On the journey to Monnetier we saw Switzerland together for the first time. He had seen nothing of the Swiss Alps, excepting only when passing quickly through the country on his return from Italy in 1853; and he questioned whether Swiss mountains would appeal to him or not. But "Nature, who never did betray the heart that loved her," prepared to reveal herself throned upon the everlasting hills. For as the train drew up at a little station called La Roche-sur-Foron, steeped in the crimson of the setting sun, suddenly a line of snowy peaks blazed out upon a background of giant cumulus clouds. Before there was time for the least change to dim these glories, we were whirled away, still speechless with astonishment.[1]

During the week at Monnetier and two days spent at Geneva, he saw the Alps under various effects of sunlight and shadow. One day, looking towards Mont Blanc, whose summit was lost in cloud, range upon range all glittering as silver with sapphire shadows, he called it "a celestial city." But the sight of those giant peaks and towering clouds at La Roche-sur-Foron remained in his mind as the *Gloria in excelsis* of earth and sky. On a gilded canvas he afterwards painted from the impression the picture named "Sunset on the Alps." There was an early stage when the picture—as it appeared to me—gave the diamond glitter and the height and weight of those mighty peaks; later, something of this

[1] By a kind of luck, which followed him, surprises in Nature seemed to be prepared for his first view of certain beautiful spots. It happened quite five times during the years that he and I were together.

GEORGE FREDERIC WATTS

was lost, as he knew himself. The grey of an English winter seemed to have dimmed his impression of radiancy.

After two days at Geneva, and two in Paris to see something of the Salon and revisit the Louvre, we were once more in England. At Charing Cross a beloved friend was waiting to greet us, and on our door-step Val Prinsep and his wife—she holding in her arms one of a fourth generation ready to embrace Signor. It was good to be in " Paradise Row " again, the more so that anxiety was behind us, and we knew how different the home-coming might have been.

CHAPTER XV

Art in its highest form has always been symbolic, used as a means to suggest ideas. Like poetry, it must in its best expressions deal with what is noblest and best.

G. F. WATTS.

CHAPTER XV

ONE of Signor's first visitors was his old friend Sir William Gregory, who was anxious to discuss a new rule the Trustees of the National Gallery were contemplating, the purport of which was to defer the acceptance by the Trustees of any picture until twenty-five years after the painter's death. The Trustees, so Sir William told him, desired to make an exception in his case. This was not at all pleasing to Signor, who earnestly begged that no exception should be made. He entirely agreed that the only verdict that could be final was that which was given after some length of time—the only one by which he wished his work to be placed. For his own part, he was content to know that his pictures could be housed at South Kensington, or in any other gallery where they could be seen by the public.

Whilst the working hours until late in the afternoon were carefully respected, his friends came as usual to see him during the month we were in London. Miss Janotha came to play to him; she was brought by Miss Mary Anderson, whose portrait he was painting, and still delayed to finish—I believe—so that the last sitting might never come! Another delightful visitor came with Mrs. Leslie Stephen, Mr. Lowell, the diplomat and poet. Mr. and Miss Browning came, he several times; Mr. Auberon Herbert to talk of education, and Mr. Lecky was a very constant visitor on Sunday afternoons. Professor Jowett came for several sittings, and at the last—the hundredth perhaps—declared that he would have been sorry to miss one. The studio was a little republic where any one at work and in earnest about life was made welcome by Signor. That is to say, he preferred these people to idlers, but I often wondered at his beautiful courtesy towards every one. There was one striking example when some strangers, who, it must be confessed, were pretentious, and therefore vulgar, were shown in (by the discriminating servant, not to the drawing-room, but to the gallery); and, while I found it difficult to be civil, he was as polite and as charming as he had been a few days before to a clever and delightful Royal Highness. If the studio could be called a republic, of Signor himself may be used Carmen Sylva's description of the growth and expansion of a heart with the increasing years, from youth, which she symbolised as a castle with its keep, dungeons, and secret chambers, and so onwards, to become at last "a market-place—a cathedral!"

There was no summer this year, and he seemed to miss the sun; anyhow he was constantly so unwell that the waters of Harrogate were once more recommended. He went there only to puzzle the clever doctor who attended him, who at last exclaimed, " You are a unique man, Mr. Watts, and it would take a wiser man that I am to say just what would set you right." The continual drip from grey clouds did not help matters. I believe there was one fine day, for we drove to Studley Royal and had tea with Lord and Lady Ripon. On our way we saw beautiful Fountains Abbey in sunshine. We returned to Little Holland House with the unsatisfactory knowledge that none of the ills he was troubled with had been left behind. Indeed, what Dr. Myrtle told me in private only added to my daily anxiety; the more so that it confirmed the opinion of other medical men, that his condition was serious.

In August of this year a great wish of mine was granted, and Alfred Gilbert came to make a portrait bust of Signor. I had written from Aix-les-Bains to ask him to undertake this commission, and he had promised to do so. Accordingly, one day a cab arrived with all the implements of a sculptor, and I heard the sound of feet carrying heavy weights through the house to the garden studio, quick steps following, which I knew must be those of Mr. Gilbert. I found in the hall a man who looked so young he might still have been called a boy. Almost his first words were, " I cannot tell you how great an endeavour I shall make " ; but though so glad that he was allowed to make this bust, he confessed that it was an undertaking that he dreaded. While his materials were being arranged in the iron house, Signor and he went down to the gallery, and came back talking together earnestly of things deeply interesting to both. They were finding themselves in mutual sympathy. Mr. Gilbert told me he usually required about five sittings for a portrait; in this case he had eighteen. "I want," he said, "to make it my best work—the portrait of a man who might have been great in any profession, and by accident was an artist." In the early stages he tried to give the more transient expression of keen interest and endeavour. "That keen look of his that is like a war-horse," were his words; but as he grew to know Signor better the graver look appeared to him to be the most characteristic. Mr. Gilbert told us he had long wished to make this portrait, and added what Signor was touched to hear, that his friend and neighbour, Mr. Hamo Thornycroft, had once asked him to undertake this as a commission from him. He generally stayed for luncheon, and went round the gallery afterwards. One day, shaking his fist at some design, he exclaimed, "He steals all the best subjects away from the sculptors"; and he went on to say, "Mr. Watts tells me things that are of such infinite value, and they are so simple!"

Towards the end of the eighteen sittings he longed to begin all over again. "How I wish

I had known Mr. Watts when I first began as I do now," he said; "these hours have been priceless, they take me out of myself, I gain so much in every way." He took the bust away, intending to have one more sitting after it had been cast in plaster; but as we had then left London for the winter, it was finally cast in bronze without this sitting and given to us. Mr. Gilbert stoutly refused to make it a commission, and said that had it been so all the pleasure would have gone out of it. Sir Frederic Leighton, when he saw it, gave it high praise. I remember his passing his hand over the planes of the cheek-bone and then to the planes of the coat, saying, "It could not be better," and Signor agreed with him, remarking how far finer a coat became in sculpture when treated in such a manner than any artificial drapery; and they congratulated each other on the disappearance of the bathing-towel from the shoulders of a modern bust.

This year, of Mr. Gilbert's statue of the Queen, Rodin had declared that in his opinion it was one of the finest things of modern sculpture, and Signor in enthusiasm exclaimed, "It is the finest thing since the Colleone."

After much consideration we settled the question where to spend the winter by taking a house at Brighton. There was the advantage of a well-lighted studio, built for a picture-gallery, large enough to take in his big painting of the "Court of Death," and as many others as he wished to have there. His doctor knew and recommended this house, and to 31 Sussex Square we went on November 1. A big platform was built up in this studio to make it possible for him to work upon the "Court of Death." When he went into that room to find that these preparations had been made, his feeling seemed to be a sort of despair at the amount of work that still remained undone. But before an hour had passed he had pulled himself together, saying, "Come, this won't do"; and the frail little figure stood drawn up erect and full of unconquerable spirit. He had worked hard the last day before leaving Little Holland House, upon the "Physical Energy." There were some roughened bits and deep scores he was anxious to fill up. "The idea of its being left in that state was dreadful to me," he said, adding, "in case anything should happen to me." He lived always as a good pilgrim, girt and ready for the long journey whenever the summons should come. The tick of the clock had in it for him the sound of Time's footstep. "I know it," he said, "and remember that each line that I draw is one less, one nearer the last."

Brighton suited him fairly well at first, and as we had spare rooms, friends came occasionally for a night or two. One of the first of these was Mr. Henry Holiday, who happened to be arranging a series of *tableaux vivants* to raise funds for a crèche, which had been closed because of a debt of £300, this after thirteen years of useful work. Signor was interested by hearing him speak of the lady, Mrs. Hughes, who had instituted and carried on the work, and a week later we asked her to come to tea. A delicate little lady appeared, looking most unlike the foundress, manager, and supporter of a big institution. They talked of the work, so much needed in Brighton, where many women are employed either in laundries or in private houses by the day. She told him of the effect the care bestowed on the babies at the crèche had on these poor mothers, who were often influenced by this to keep their homes more clean and wholesome. Presently Signor said quietly that he would like to help her to reopen her crèche, and handed her a cheque, at which she glanced, and, seeing the full sum of the debt, just buried her face in her hands and wept. " I can open it next week," she sobbed through her tears of joy, and his pleasure was as great.

During December an extraordinary thing happened, for he did allow that there *was* a small present he would like to have given to him on Christmas Day! This was a seal, and one of Dutch design was found. On the evening of Christmas Day we began to talk of what might be engraved upon it, and I asked him to invent a motto for it. He was silent for a second or two, and then said, " I think I should like to say, 'The Utmost for the Highest.'" As we were just then reading that delightful translation by John Addington Symonds of the life of Benvenuto Cellini, my thoughts were running on decoration, and I began at once to plan an emblem for this motto. " Shall it be a pool reflecting a star ? " I asked ; and Signor was pleased and answered, " Oh, yes ! a little puddle, that will do beautifully for me."

The picture he was now working at—if one of the many may be especially singled out—was the newly created Eve to which he afterwards gave the title " She shall be called Woman." A shaft of light set up between heaven and earth— the columnar figure — is surely a nineteenth-century reincarnation of the ancient Tree of Life in Chaldean symbolism, which in its earliest form was represented by an upright line supporting the crescent—the symbol of the heavens. It has been suggested that the pillar over the " Lion Gate of Mycenæ " had in archaic Greek art this same signification. It is not likely that when Signor designed the trilogy of Eve, some time in the 'sixties, he had in his mind either the Chaldean Tree of Life or the Greek pillar set up between earth and heaven. He was a symbolist, unconsciously as well as consciously ; but certainly his intention was that in the newly created Eve he should represent the central figure of the universe, and in this respect the Greek vision of " A line of light, straight, as a column extending through the whole heaven and through the earth in colour resembling the rainbow, only brighter and purer,"[1] very

[1] *The Republic of Plato* (Professor Jowett's translation).

much describes his conception. He told me he wanted the figure not so much to stand in light as to emit light. The upturned face is dark in the midst of light, for the human intuitions may take the human mind into a region where reason stops, " dark with excessive light." [1] He explained that it was not an apotheosis of womanhood, but rather of the qualities with which it is natural to associate the term feminine.

For this reason, over the region of the heart and breast the light is concentrated because, so to speak, there is the seat of tenderness, goodness, love. Many years afterwards he seemed to epitomise this idea (though not speaking at the time of this special design) when he said " the evolution of the idea of goodness in the mind of man leading up to the knowledge that Love is all."

I venture to think the picture carries this legend, and is one of the most imaginative of his paintings belonging to the class he described as " ethical reflections."

The Brighton studio showed this picture to an advantage it has never had since. Very often we breakfasted in that room, and the morning light poured down upon the breast of the Great-Mother till it seemed to breathe and scintillate.

One day I saw him add some touches of ultramarine blue, and the effect was to intensify the sense of teeming life, and make more vivid the

---

[1] A quotation from Milton he used to explain his own aim and intention in this picture.

impression of the freshness of this first morning of the world.

Lady Somers happened to be in Brighton; she came and sat before it for some length of time, and exclaimed, " It is the greatest thing he has ever done ! "

I suppose every one whose lot it is to be often present in the workshop, where the true artist's shuttle is working to and fro—a lot that may be called blessed if any is so on earth—all of these must know the impulse that made the Roman shepherd cry out to George Mason, " *Ah ! lascia stare !* " The miracle moment seems to come when the work should be left as it is—so the onlooker thinks. But as Haydon says reverently, when speaking of some change he would have liked to make in a picture by the great Venetian, " Titian thought otherwise." The painter knows what he knows, and must go forward to lose or gain. And if he saw fit to go further, not twenty shepherds nor a whole Academy of artists would deter him.

Perhaps this picture had at this time some qualities that were lost in the final paintings; completion sometimes requires this. I know that to concentrate attention upon the torso he deliberately sacrificed what he told me he had been labouring to achieve — the " Pheidian form " of the lower limbs—by wreathing them more and more with cloud and the fluttering bird-life that garlands her.

In the trilogy of Eve, everything had to be

subordinate to the representation of the three stages through which human life has to pass. In the first, the newly created soul is more conscious of heaven than of earth, the hands are spread out, they grasp nothing of earth's treasures; the foot alone is firmly planted.

In the second stage the sway of the senses has descended upon the soul, the figure is bowed, enmeshed, enthralled; the head thrown back in a sort of abandonment to the overpowering scent of flowers and luscious fruit: the paradise of sense has developed a lower ecstasy. In the third—the Eve Repentant—all is changed, the earthly paradise is wrecked, and the agony of remorse is expressed by the attitude of the tragic figure.

It is perhaps interesting to observe the elemental lines of the three compositions, which are these: | upright, ➤ bent, and ⌊ leaning lines which any country labourer capable of building a wall, or even putting in a post, would understand — the first representing perfect strength, the second entire weakness, the third a return towards the first but requiring support.

It was at Brighton that he completed the little Cupid under the monk's cowl, and named it "The Habit does not make the Monk." I remember a pretty young girl in that studio asking Signor vaguely as she gazed at the picture, "At whose door is he knocking?" and his quick retort, "Oh, at yours, perhaps."

There were many weeks of almost uninterrupted work this winter, and time to enjoy books when lamp-light hours were long; and I read to him either old favourites or from new books that he cared to choose. Amongst them the life of Charles Darwin, by his son, gave him such great pleasure that he wrote to tell the author this, and had a charming acknowledgment and thanks, received with a simple surprise by Signor, as if his letter of praise would carry no more weight than a schoolboy's. Mr. Francis Darwin sent him also a copy of the *Memoirs*.

As has been already said, he deeply regretted that he had not been able to paint the great scientist, who was not well enough to move to London, and Signor was not sure if he went to Down to paint him, as he was invited to do, that he might not himself be laid up with illness.

In February came a sad interruption to this happier time; he caught a bad cold, developed bronchitis, and finally pneumonia, and so, with complications which followed on convalesence, he was hardly at all at work till the middle of April. Considering what this loss of time meant to him, his patience was great; his distress being only that he gave cause for anxiety and required so much care. It was useless to explain what it meant to those about him. Whoever loves and serves knows how the humblest duties of the sick-room give consolation, even a sort of pleasure. Then his thoughts, sleeping or waking, were always travelling far and climbing high; and one morning, soon after the turn towards an improvement had been reached, he told me of a dream from which he had just awakened. As he told it to me in the half-darkened room, the voice enfeebled by illness, I, afraid of forgetting it, tried to write it down word for word, and it was this : " I thought," he said, " that I was climbing up the side of a steep mountain, and I knew that it was the mountain of Fame — Fame in the greatest sense of the word, all that is worthy of the best endeavour. It was so steep that I had to cut each step that I took, and I knew as I went on that the path I made closed up behind me, so that no one could follow where I went ; and I could not find the track of any one who had gone before me. From the foot of the hill I had seen quite clearly the paths made by other men —some rough, some smooth ; but when I began myself to climb, I could not see them at all ; they were all hidden under tangles of thorns and briars.

" While I was still labouring on, making my path, I was suddenly lifted up and allowed for a few minutes to be on the very top of the mountain, so that I could see the whole distance laid out before me. It was more ethereal than I can describe, of a beauty that can only be imagined in a dream. I was looking over a sort of parapet, and there were pillars of some building beside me ; and, though I heard voices, I could not lose one moment of the beauty by turning to see who spoke ; but I was aware somehow that those people had reached the summit, and were to remain there for ever, themselves a part of that great beauty, giving out to it from their own being. And I said to myself, this is the sort of fame for which I have given my life.

"I hope," he added, "I shall be able to keep that vision before me; I think I shall, now I have told you. It as far surpassed in beauty that wonderful first day at Athens when we looked out from the Parthenon, as that surpasses in beauty the little streaks of colour we sometimes see here."

The first welcome sign of convalescence was shown when he asked for paper and pencil, and began to make sketches of the folds he saw in the sheets or blankets. Another, when a little quiet humour began to reappear. And now a voice said from the pillows: "Tolstoi has the milk of human kindness in the brain, it ought only to be in the heart." He had overheard a mention of his name.

When by degrees the strength returned, and after the long interruption he got back to the studio, he decided to stay on at Brighton till the end of May, to have the advantage of another month of work in that fine room. He had great hesitation in proposing what seemed selfish on his part towards our servants, as in the basement of this house they had to live almost continuously in gas-light. But when his wish became known not a shadow of reluctance was shown by any one, and it pleased and touched him that his interests were made the first consideration.

The newspaper critics were very flattering this year, when the New Gallery opened with six of his pictures on the walls. Mr. Hallé had been allowed to glean as he chose from the studio at Little Holland House, Mr. Burne-Jones having sent special requests by his son that Signor would supplement where he himself could not contribute his share, he being hard at work on the Briar Rose series of pictures. They specially praised the "Fata Morgana," to which last year he had added texture and the solidity of Venetian colour. "That sort of thing only makes me feel depressed," he said; "I know it is not a real thing. The 'Heron,' for instance, they are now all praising, had no notice taken of it when it was first painted." Still the assurance that he was not losing ground in public estimation was pleasant to him. No one of his temperament could be anything but encouraged by honest appreciation; and once, after listening to a piece of good writing by a sincere admirer of his work, he said, as if with some pleasure, "It is still quite new to me to find my work spoken of in that way."

Before we left Brighton Sir Frederic Leighton wrote to ask me to add my name to an appeal against the extension of the suffrage to women which was to appear in the *Nineteenth Century* magazine. In talking the matter over with Signor—I think seriously for the first time—I found that we were agreed, and that he believed that feminine influence in politics would have a good effect, especially upon social questions. He recognised the justice of the demand, and regarded it as a natural development consequent on the progress of education. I rather suspected later that Sir Frederic himself was but a lukewarm opponent.

Of Signor's own bias in political matters he wrote in 1875 to Mr. Rickards: "I rather pride myself on being a real Liberal, that is to say, being liberal enough to see and understand that there must be many conditions and many opinions. We may all see a little bit according to our several points of view, and we ought all to acknowledge that while each one may see the light reflected from a different face, each one may see clearly." Towards the end of life he told me that he found in himself no tendency to become less liberal, a tendency he noticed in some of his contemporaries. He said: "I think one thing I have is not common—I do not grow less liberal, I grow more so with years. Men as they grow old have a tendency to fear every change; it is foolish, as change is inevitable, it is necessary for a condition of life and health." His own political views had become merged in the interest he took in the position of the nation as a people of great deeds. Party overruling principle to him was a wrong he could not condone. "I am no Radical or

GEORGE FREDERIC WATTS

Socialist," he said; "I find Conservatives and Liberals are equally to blame for not holding the standard higher, they are much alike in doing just what is expedient. In the newspapers I find nothing but party rancour. In all they have to say there is no reference made to principles, none to religion, and none to patriotism." He saw with dismay that few recognised the responsibility of being a part of the State. The ancient obligation of the nobles to bring men and arms into the field in any emergency, when they gave even to their last groat, was now forgotten. Money that should be laid out for the benefit of the country was too often squandered at Monte Carlo or elsewhere abroad, or in absolutely unprofitable ways at home.

"They don't live, those people," he exclaimed once when speaking of a society more than of persons, "they only vegetate"; and he added, "they are not good vegetables either." "Be sure of this," he said, "that both on the deeds of individuals and of nations Nemesis follows. This is certain, more certain for a nation perhaps, as the individual life is not so long, it may escape here; a nation's life is long enough to be sure of retribution. Of this I am sure that unless we do refer to principles, the principles laid down by the Founder of Christianity, the truest Socialist that ever lived" (altruistic socialism being understood), "our national life is doomed."

"The unequal balance of wealth and poverty

cannot be permanent, a change must come in spite of opposing interests in the security of which men have forgotten that the advantages they possess carry with them duties." He wanted those people in whose pockets lay the money that gives England the reputation of being one of the richest nations in the world, to bind themselves together, as the crusaders did of old, for some one cause; and thus to make a determined effort to change the conditions of misery and degradation which exist in our slums, and which are brought to light when some special case flashes into prominence, and a thrill of horror goes through every humane heart, only too generally to be forgotten. " Some real and strenuous appeal to the heart of the nation might avail," he wrote, "if the ledger has not asphyxiated its pulsations. I feel very strongly that the time has come when party must be merged in patriotism. I know nothing about details or possibilities, but this I know by all that history teaches of human conditions, that, unless all work together, disintegration and decay and death are inevitable. Giving money is right and generous, but the giving of ourselves is the one great and necessary gift."

He thought that a great change might be brought about if mankind could but realise that the present ideal is wrong—all for self and self-advancement, chiefly by gathering money for self—and would instead try for the grand universal impulse towards helping all to reach a happier and better state of things. "A heaven might really dawn upon earth," he added, and continued: "You may lay it down as an axiom that whatever possessions we have remain with us to do harm. Our health even depends upon our mental capacities being drawn outwards and well expended, the constant supply of power goes on."

And these beliefs he endeavoured to put into practice in his daily life, even in the latest years; aware that the chief thought of the home naturally centred upon him, he told me he constantly reminded himself that he was in danger of becoming selfish.

He found it difficult not to feel gloomy when considering the trend of affairs; and Jonah-like he would often preach against Mammon worship, and the hypocritical veiling of the daily sacrifice made to this deity. "Holy Mammon — Divine Respectability — Sacred Dividend," he said once in this Jonah-mood. He told Mr. Riviere,[1] who came to see him directly on his return to Little Holland House, that he was going to propose to one of our sculptors to make a statue of Mammon, that it might be set up in Hyde Park, where he hoped his worshippers would be at least honest enough to bow the knee publicly to him. Mr. Riviere replied gracefully, and for the moment routed Jonah, by saying: "You make the statue, and I am sure you will find worshippers."

[1] Briton Riviere, a brother Academician.

GEORGE FREDERIC WATTS

Signor looked forward much on his return to Little Holland House to Mr. Riviere's frequent visits. Mr. Riviere's hours of work being unfortunately limited by his oculist's orders, during his afternoon walk or drive he was frequently able to give my husband this pleasure. Every design that was made, and every line in the "Physical Energy," was discussed between these two brother-artists. For the purpose of biography Mr. Riviere kindly put into my hands some sixty letters and notes, each one of which makes evident the pleasure and profit he found in talking over matters that concerned his work with this sympathetic friend. For instance, when Mr. Riviere called one day in 1885, Signor had been ill, and this little note was sent down to him : "I am restrained by my doctor from changing atmosphere and temperature, so perhaps you will not mind coming up to see me ; but first I want you to go into my gallery and look critically at my new picture ; pull it to pieces, and let me have the benefit of your judgment and fresh eye. Also please look well at the two pictures of 'Love and Life,' and tell me which you think best. The new picture is 'Hope' ; all the strings of her instrument are broken but one, and she is trying to get all possible music out of the poor tinkle."

Mr. Riviere, who more often came to give either sympathy, suggestion, or practical aid by recommending a model, lending a cast, or a sketch, this year came to beg. He wanted a paper to be written by Signor for the second

Art Congress to be held that year in Edinburgh, where he had undertaken to give the Presidential Lecture in the section of painting. Signor could not refuse, though writing was an effort to him; and he took for his theme, "The Position that Art is worthy to hold amongst us," and how those who desire to see her placed as of national importance can best help toward bringing this about.[1]

As has been said, his picture, the "Fata Morgana," attracted much attention, and Mr. Beck, the Secretary of the New Gallery, received more than one offer from purchasers. One of these would-be purchasers was very insistent, and offered what amounted to the persuasion of a blank cheque, but Signor had put all the recent work into this picture with the intention of giving it to the Leicester Art Gallery, and the offers of purchase were refused. At the close of the exhibition the picture was presented, and a deputation from the Corporation of Leicester came to thank him.

In the reply made by my husband to the speech from the President, Mr. Hodgson, he told them that he had chosen what he believed to be one of the best of his paintings, not only to encourage the efforts made recently at Leicester on behalf of Art, but because he wished specially to connect with his gift the name of a citizen of Leicester, Mr. John Cook. He had first heard

[1] This paper was afterwards printed in the *Transactions of the National Association for the Advancement of Art*, and also in *The Hobby Horse*.

GEORGE FREDERIC WATTS

of the new Art Gallery at Leicester from Mr. Cook, who had suggested that he might possibly spare a small sketch to it. He had seen for himself, while travelling in Egypt, that the name of John Cook was respected and trusted by all there, down to the poorest of the fellaheen; and he therefore esteemed him as one who had upheld the honour of his country and the word of an Englishman.

This summer he painted the portrait of Mrs. Ronald Leslie-Melville for her husband,[1] who had, he thought, been generous in some transaction, as a trustee, in the matter of one of his pictures; and Signor wished to make this acknowledgment.

When the latest gift had been made he sometimes said, with a look of merriment in his eyes, " Now, I am not going to give away anything else," and we laughed, well knowing what would happen.

It was this summer that Signor and Mr. Browning met for the last time; the poet and Miss Browning came to luncheon, and stayed for some time afterwards, going round the many studios. In the iron-house studio he looked earnestly at the painter, and turning to me, said, " I am looking at the little head that has done all this work "—and Signor told him that the smallness of his head had been a matter of distress to him until one day, when painting Sir John Lubbock, the sitter's hat was mislaid, and Lady

[1] Afterwards the Earl of Leven and Melville.

GEORGE FREDERIC WATTS

Lubbock said, "Well, it is not likely to be carried off, as no one can put John's hat on"; but when it was found, Signor was consoled to find it just the size of his own head. Mr. Browning said that he believed poets as a rule had small heads, and quoted as an example Byron, whose brain weighed only seven pounds.

Our poet left with a tribute on his lips, not to the Muse of either poetry or painting, but to a curry Signor's housekeeper knew how to make better than most. "When I want another such curry I shall invite myself," he said. Alas, he never crossed the threshold again; we had left London when he returned there before going abroad, and in December of this year England lost her philosopher-poet.

The only visits Signor was ever induced to pay during these years were to Mr. and Mrs. Andrew Hichens; and when with them for a day or two this autumn it occurred to them to propose that we should try how the climate in Surrey would suit him for the winter, earnestly begging us to make use of their beautiful home during their absence in London. Any reluctance on our part was met with every affectionate assurance, our hesitation being a fear that Signor's unusual hours, or even the necessary canvases and easels, might be inconvenient when they wanted to be there themselves. The house, standing high, yet sheltered from the north and east, was a most tempting solution of the question of winter quarters, so anxiously considered by me and his doctor, who rather inclined to Brighton, while Sir Frederic Leighton had urged Italy. In the end it was decided that we should spend the winter at Monkshatch, and in November we were there established.

"I always told you I built that studio for you," Andrew said, delighting in seeing the canvases about in the favourite sitting-room of the house, oak-panelled and lofty, with a fine organ and piano, thus devoted to both arts, and generally called the studio. As time went on, they told us that they found themselves coming down from London just three times as often as they usually did. Andrew knew just the sort of news Signor liked to hear, and brought it, social, artistic, or political. Sometimes there was music, or they beguiled Signor to play billiards, for which he had a keen eye and steady hand.

If he wished to be quiet, the library was entirely ours, and our evenings when alone were always spent there. As I write, memories of evenings in that room come back to me vividly— the glow of lamp-light and fire-light thrown upon walls lined with well-chosen books, and where the silvery head shone in contrast with the deep colour of the sofa-pillows, while he rested and listened, profoundly interested in the book we had chosen, his expression changing with every theme, alert and ready for comment, or sometimes keenly delighted by some finely balanced argument, for, as it happened this winter, he was being charmed by the mind of Lecky, tracing cause and effect with delicate skill, as we were reading his *History of England in the Eighteenth Century*.

Sometimes—our slight evening meal being over before seven—Andrew and May, when they happened to be at Monkshatch, dined together, while we, with the dividing panels between the rooms rolled back, looked on from the library; and it was as if a charming little bit of real-life drama was being acted to please us, though with perfect unconsciousness. Signor, watching this one evening, said, "I wonder if any other roof in England covers four happier people."

The winter was mild, and if a north-east wind blew we knew nothing of it, for the chalk cliff sheltered us, and its white wall gave back every ray of sunshine at compound interest.

The picture to which he was devoting time was the study of an old horse, begun many years before at the Briary. Andrew took pains to find one sufficiently aged, from which Signor made the notes he required; and on our walks he searched the hedgerows and copses, bare as they were, that he might study structure and growth. "I have been nearly all the morning painting in three bramble leaves," he said one day. He held that "as a supreme end, the thing to be discountenanced is the effort after obvious dexterity, the one quality nature never exhibits." "Force is a great quality," he said, "perhaps it may be called the most effective;

it certainly is in an exhibition where the object is to attract suddenly, but of all the great qualities it is the least delightful, and the one that soonest palls upon acquaintance." I remember that when standing before Holbein's portrait of the Duchess of Milan, Signor said to Sir Frederick Burton, "Conscience seems to have gone away from modern art: consciousness has taken its place." When "The Life of Unrequited Toil," as he named this picture for the Academy catalogue, was mentioned by a critic as "the work of a barbarian, but a very learned barbarian," he was pleased. He steeped his mind in the beauty of the winter woods, and told me he understood the beauty of tree and leaf better than he understood the beauty of flowers.

One evening, not long after we had settled at Monkshatch, the news of Mr. Browning's death was brought by Andrew. Signor had envied that robust and vivid life when last he came to Little Holland House, and we had looked upon

> a great Tree of Life that never sere
> Dropped leaf for aught that age or storms might wreck.[1]

The next day we read his Epilogue, that splendid farewell. Signor added his name to the list of Browning's friends who petitioned that his body might be laid in the Abbey; and he would have been glad to know that there

[1] The memorial sonnet written by Mr. George Meredith.

Mrs. Browning also lay—England's greatest poetess at the side of her poet husband.

Alas, the time of year made it impossible for him to be present when the great solemn act took place, and the nation's great son was laid to sleep under the Abbey stones.

Meanwhile Christmas intervened, and on that feast of the children young people came to Monkshatch, and made it bright—even merry. Their mother, Lady Lilian Yorke, brought as her offering to Signor the first copy he had seen of Professor Drummond's address, "The Greatest Thing in the World." The first evening that we were alone I read it to him, and to every line he gave his adhesion, in the end saying, "That contains the whole of religion. Do not let us read anything else to-night."

The winter months as they passed found him so well that the idea of a winter home in the neighbourhood—a cottage, perhaps, to which a studio could be added—was constantly in our minds. One lovely sunny morning Andrew came in from a walk, enthusiastic about a site for a house he had found, and a quarter of an hour later we were standing on a little sandy knoll, well wooded and possessed of some very fine trees, and as it then seemed, building our cottage in Spain. "Too delightful for accomplishment," Signor thought; but Andrew saw no difficulty, if the land could be secured. I find this note in my diary, some weeks later, when the cottage in Spain had become a very probable cottage in Surrey: "After Signor went upstairs Andrew and I talked over the house plan. He refused to allow Signor to make any outlay himself, refused to listen to my representation of the risks he ran in spending time and money on a house which might after all not be found to be permanently suitable, and one which must have expenditure on details which would probably be of no value to future tenants or purchasers. He allowed he would not do it for any one else, but for 'the beloved little man'" (as he and May liked to call him). "As a matter of investment he assured me that he was making a good one, as a matter of pleasure he knew he was only doing exceedingly well for himself." And so it came about that, with all the trouble lifted off our shoulders, Andrew bought the coveted bit of land from the squire of Loseley, and asked Mr. Ernest George to make the building plans, over which we had many consultations; and in April the house was begun.

It was now that Hallam Tennyson wrote to tell Signor of a desire expressed by the Master of Trinity, as representative of a committee formed for the purpose of arranging for a subscription portrait to be painted of Lord Tennyson for the hall of his old college. His father, the son wrote, was of course much disinclined to sit, and had made objections to every suggestion. He was at last reconciled by Hallam's proposing to try to induce Signor to come down to

GEORGE FREDERIC WATTS

Farringford for this purpose. To hear this pleased Signor, and made him willing also to make the effort.

Always dreading that on a visit illness might overtake him, and so give trouble to others, Signor decided to refuse the invitation to stay at Farringford, and the Herbert Somers-Cocks, absent themselves on the Riviera, wrote begging us to make use of the Briary. This matter being arranged, and that other essential stipulation, that the portrait should not be undertaken professionally, we went to the Isle of Wight towards the middle of May. The Hallam Tennysons came to welcome us at Yarmouth and drove us to the Briary, where we were told by Mr. and Mrs. Andrews (who were then in charge, and friends from old Little Holland House days) that the poet himself had come over many times to remind them that as the weather had been wet the house must be well warmed !

Early next morning a light wind stirred the curtains, and a grey dawn showed fair and clear to prelude twelve days of almost unbroken weather—May at her best in the Isle of Wight. We pushed the French windows wide open after breakfast, and went out upon the lawn. A cuckoo flew past, so close to us that his caressing note was quite distinct to Signor, as we went to look at the clematis montana he remembered being planted, which now was rampant to the roof, and for the Christmas-tree he and the little people at the Briary had stuck into the ground seventeen years ago, now well grown and flourishing.

We were at Farringford by eleven. Lady Tennyson greeted us as of old — even more tenderly—with eyes brimming with gratitude, and after a few minutes the poet joined us. There was talk of everything but painting, and later we all, save the dear lady on her sofa, walked back to the Briary through the sweet old-fashioned garden, gay with spring flowers. Signor and Lord Tennyson walked in front, falling naturally into their old habits, recalling old days and stories that made them laugh. But the poet had had a letter from a stranger which had touched him where he was made vulnerable because made poet; and he complained bitterly of the intrusive writer, working himself up so much that in the end he exclaimed in answer to Signor's remark that "such intrusions were but the cost of fame "—" I wish I had never written a line in my life." Whereupon Signor took up his parable and remonstrated, " Ah, now you would not have made your Arthur speak like that ! " And the great man instantly turned penitent, and putting out his hand, said, " Well, there, look at my hand ; it is the gout ! "

For these two days they were much together, Signor still delaying to arrange for the sittings, and Lord Tennyson being under a promise to his son to let the suggestion come from the painter. However, as he was saying good-night that second evening, obedient no longer, he said, "When are you going to paint me?" and an arrangement was made for the next day. Early next morning Signor woke with all the symptoms that the undertaking of such a portrait inevitably brought, and hours of depression followed when comfort seemed far. Indeed, as the time for starting grew near, I began to fear the day was to be wrecked in this nerve-storm. I had hastily to scribble a note to Hallam begging him to come himself with the carriage they were sending, and I also arranged that canvas and paints were to be hidden away in the carriage before Signor appeared; and thus interested in other things while Hallam talked to him, without a thought of his work he was driven off. A quarter of an hour after our arrival a message came to me, in Mrs. Hallam Tennyson's sitting-room, to say that "Signor was at work, and that they were both quite happy." After a beginning had been made, the dread of the undertaking seemed to pass like a cloud, and from this morning all went well.

The ten days that followed were very precious days. The Isle of Wight was dear to us both from old associations, and every kind of arrangement was made at Farringford to make it, to the utmost, delightful. Then for the last week Geraldine Liddell came to us bringing (as her friends well know) her gift for taking up all their interests and pleasures in her two hands, and giving them back to them doubled. With

GEORGE FREDERIC WATTS

this fresh contribution the days became such as to make one grateful to memory.

While the portrait was being painted in Lord Tennyson's room his son sat beside them and read aloud. If the sitter was given a little respite, he liked to take a turn in the sun; and would take one of us with him, to admire his shrubs then in full blossom, perhaps to enjoy his Judas tree, of which this year he was particularly proud. Once under a laburnum he asked me if I thought "dropping wells of fire" was not a true description. Some critic had written that it was not fire at all; "not coal fire certainly," he said, "but little golden flames of fire, or so at least it seems to me"; and he looked up into the branches with the eyes that saw and could reveal the most secret movements of nature, and that yet by the irony of fate were extraordinarily shortsighted.

He spoke of his friend Lear that morning, and of the music to which he had set some of the poems. "He put a sort of diaphanous veil over them, that was all"—so he expressed it, and seemed to prefer his setting of his words to any other. Sir Arthur Sullivan mistook the poet's intention when in the song—a lullaby from "Sea Dreams"—he turned the line

> Baby too will fly away,

intended to be sportive, into a sort of wail. He told Signor that, as a rule, he did not take long to write a poem. "When I come to a hitch," he said, " it takes me a long time to get over it," and added that he used to have the whole construction and almost all the words in his mind before he wrote a line, but that now he wrote more as it came to him. Of the poem " Tears, idle tears, I know not what they mean," which Signor thought consummate, Lord Tennyson told him that it had seemed to flow from his mind without difficulty.

When I was young I had heard Mrs. Cameron quote a remark made by Lord Tennyson after reading this poem to her, which seemed like an acknowledgment from him that it was something of a creation evolved by an unconscious effort of his brain. Perhaps the best things are done in this way, and so with apparent ease. The picture of " Hope " by Signor is of all his work the one most generally popular, and he often said that it had given him no trouble whatever. Once when talking to Sir Clifford Allbutt[1] of conscious effort in work, he mentioned that at times he was quite unable to summon up a single creative idea; at another time the ideas seemed to crowd on him so quickly he had difficulty in restraining them. " That is when the tide of life is at its fullest," Sir Clifford replied. " All nature is rhythmical; there is the ebb and the flow in our bodies and in our minds. The greatest work can only be created at high tide."

Signor was now working upon a second

[1] Now Regius Professor of Medicine at Cambridge, but for some years our neighbour in Melbury Road, when holding an appointment under Government.

GEORGE FREDERIC WATTS

portrait, not being quite content with the texture of his canvas, though later he overcame the difficulty, and in fact this was the portrait completed for Trinity College. On the second canvas, in place of the college gown, he used the ermine of the Peer's robes, and when the present Lord Tennyson was Governor of New South Wales he presented it through him to the Art Gallery of Adelaide.

As the portraits grew, the grandeur of the poet's head in life seemed to be more and more revealed. I noticed this to Signor, and he replied, "That is what a portrait painter should do, not by accentuating or emphasising, but rather keeping in mind those lines which are the noblest. What I try for is the half-unconscious insistence upon the nobilities of the subject." Certainly the poet's whole aspect was full of these nobilities.

What a reminiscence a modern Dutch water-colour artist (Maris or Mauve) would have made of these characteristics as we saw them in the beautiful setting of the woods in May. Signor had been at work at Farringford, while Miss Liddell and I had spent the morning together under a big elm on the Briary lawn, and when one o'clock came we went to meet the party, as Lord Tennyson and his son had arranged to walk back with Signor. We had just climbed the little rise that led to a broad green glade when the three came in sight, and we both exclaimed! For down the great aisle of elms they came, a

GEORGE FREDERIC WATTS

white Russian deer-hound flashing like silver through the sun or shade, and the central figure the poet, a note of black in the midst of the vivid green, grand in the folds of his ample cloak and his face looming grandly from the shadow of the giant hat. "Monumental" Signor would have called him. The slight stoop and the heavier step of age made the youthful figure of the son look all the more what he was, his father's vigorous staff and prop. And then our eyes fell upon the delicate grey figure of our beloved painter on the other side, the grey hat crowning silver hair, a grey cloak taking pleasant folds while he stepped like a boy, light and neat in every movement. Lord Tennyson was playful, gave us a smiling greeting, and put out the crook of his walking-stick for us to shake hands with.

As we went on towards the Briary the teeming life of nature seemed to turn their thoughts to a life beyond this life. Lord Tennyson quoted with regret the saddest epitaph he knew, written by a friend who had no belief in a future; and then with moistening eyes he gave us the triumphant words placed over a woman's grave: "I have loved, I love, I shall love," but given in the terse Latin—"Amavi, Amo, Amabo."

At different times Signor and Lord Tennyson had confided to each their conclusions upon religious beliefs, and Signor told me he had found that their ideas were identical. "The poetic mind," he added, "must find its religion either in the human type father, son, and mother—this was the tendency of Rossetti's mind,—or in the cosmic unity, though this is more rare, as it does not touch the sensibilities. The world cannot get on without a personal God. One whose law is stronger than himself, is conceivable—He may know that this is best. The Greeks perceived this truth and called the law 'the Fates.' The Hebrew conception of a god who can break his own laws to exhibit his power is not so convincing of greatness as is the Power that works within a self-imposed order for higher purposes than the human mind can comprehend.

"The Divine Essence is the law Himself; He can no more break a law than He can do away with Himself. This has been perceived in part, for in the earliest miracles, such as the feeding of Elijah in the desert, God does not enable him to do without food, as Omnipotence certainly could have done, but uses means to give him that food." There is but one symbol that to Signor's mind represented a truly religious conception of the Creator and His creation : " A breath issuing forth becomes matter ; controlling this matter are the laws—force which propels and gravitation which controls ; and there in its immensity you have the whole universe. The conflict produced by these laws explains all phenomena." And he continued : " I think my idea of the law of conflict is best illustrated by the shuttle, which has to go backwards and forwards to create the web. That idea of the shuttle quite falls in with my thought that all creation is the garment of God. I can conceive of a state of happiness when human beings become one without loss of individual consciousness, just as a woven piece of linen is one, though composed of an infinite number of strands.

"I can easily conceive that humanity may have passed through stages of progression, from the infant to the child, until at last it is the full-grown man, and in his manhood struggles for centuries with unformed ideas; destined at last to see all clearly."

But the end of May had arrived, and one portrait [1] at least was complete. Signor felt that he must get back to work in London; so our last day came round, and the last hours were spent in the Farringford study, listening for the last time to the poet reading his own poems. They were wonderful hours, and when the good-byes were said, Lord Tennyson stood under the portico waving farewells until the carriage had passed out of his sight; and he from ours, for this life.

While we were at the Briary, a place much associated with his friends the Tennants, Signor had a letter from Dorothy Tennant, which said

[1] The portraits of Tennyson by Signor are these, namely: the first, a profile (1857) now in the Melbourne Gallery; the second, known as the Eastnor portrait (1859); the third, painted at the time when he painted Lady Tennyson and the two boys; fourth, Sir William Bowman's, and at the same time one in the National Portrait Gallery; the sixth, in his doctor's robes, now at Trinity College, Cambridge; the seventh, in his Peer's robes, now at Adelaide. Both these last were painted in 1890.

not much more than this, " I am to be Stanley's wife"; and to her wedding this summer he consented to go, not to the Abbey, but to the gathering afterwards at Richmond Terrace. A great act of friendship, but he was very happy —made welcome by a hundred of his friends who little expected to meet him there.

CHAPTER XVI

Nothing, to my mind, is such real religion as to live joyously; the purest of joys to make others happy.

G. F. WATTS.

CHAPTER XVI

THE summer of 1890 was on the whole a good one for the work in the garden, and the sculptor seemed full of vigour; I remember that he drew up the blind one morning in my dressing-room, where he thought the best view of his statue was to be got, and said:

"You don't think I've lost anything, do you?" and he went on to tell me the difficulty he had in getting it forward towards completion. While he was working merely to give the impression of power and strength he was able to satisfy himself more easily, but now, when he was trying to perfect each part, the difficulty of keeping that original expression of power became greater and greater.

"I wonder if I shall ever get what I want," he went on, "not a man but a type. Five thousand years of activity, and the grace of as many achievements; I should like to write the roll of great names on the pedestal: Genghis Khan, Timon the Tartar, Attila, and Mahomet."

This spring a few friends were anxious to

subscribe for the casting of this statue, and he was consulted. He said, " I should not approve of any such scheme, even if the work was done, but it may be a failure now for all I know, or never finished." And yet in 1886 Mr. Millais had been to see it and declared that it wanted "not a touch more." He begged Signor to have it cast, and added with his usual generous enthusiasm, " I'll subscribe to the casting."

The fact that the sculpture had to be done out of doors no doubt enabled him to work as continuously as he did through all the hours of daylight; and when he used the expression, " I must live in the light," he was prompted to say this by a physical need of which he was partly conscious, as well as by those needs of the mind for which the word light was used figuratively. He told me that it was astonishing how much better he felt for these early hours, and continued: " I feel as if my mind was clearer, and as if I knew something more. Very often in the morning the perception seems to come to me that all this that I am doing is too small for me,—and then it goes!" And speaking with regret of the shortening of the days so soon to come, he added, " Whether I have much time or little left there is much I want to do, and I must not lose a moment of it. I must have no nonsense," he said, taking himself to task for frittering away time, and at eight o'clock at night he wondered why he felt so tired.

GEORGE FREDERIC WATTS

"Dear me, it's always harvest-time with Mr. Watts," a white-smocked labourer remarked to me some years later in our country home.

There was not much "nonsense" either in the studio, where the "All-pervading" was being especially worked at; and it was now that he painted the portrait of Lady Katherine Thynne. He had been much struck by her beauty a few years before, when she was brought by her mother, Lady Bath, to see him, and this year he asked to be allowed to paint her. As he showed it to Andrew and May Hichens he tried to extract the compliment he liked best, that it was not like his work. But Andrew for answer threw his arm round Signor's two shoulders and fairly hugged him with joy, protesting, of course, that nobody else could ever have painted it.

After one of the last visits paid him by Mr. P. G. Hamerton, the distinguished etcher and author, he wrote to Signor: "I shall always remember our conversation, which certainly touched upon some of those profoundly important ideas as to theory and practice on which great art must be built, whether the artist consciously formulates them for himself or not. It seems to me that you are living in a region of thought which is not only far above art as a trade, but even above art as a profession. For you it is what it ought to be, a vocation, a mental expression. May you long live to follow it in that way!"

And Signor did not separate the art of living from the art of painting, or either from the religion of life. "How happy we are to have work at which we can worship all the time," he said; and once when he spoke to me of the poet's mind, I perceived that he unconsciously described his own.

"You don't suppose that the insight with which a poet's mind is endowed is just his ordinary reasoning powers? It is something different—it is contact with a spirit greater than his own. If the aspiration is theirs, amounting to nothing more than a sensation, it is sufficient to produce that aim at assimilation that is called prayer. It is the same sort of thing that makes a plant force its way through a crevice to get the sun's rays.

"Now it seems to me that the great poet always turns the spectator into a poet, makes him the poet for the time, by a kind of hypnotism. The greater the poet the more he makes you feel this; he lifts you into his own region.

"The great artist and poet (one and the same) is not only a prophet himself, but one who is able to make prophets of others, to play upon the human instrument till he makes it generally send forth a prophetic sound.

"And the highest expression in art is that which would be the highest expression in poetry. They are not different although their limits are. The highest sentiment," he continued, "can never be presented to one without a large measure of reality; it is the artist's means, as words are the poet's, yet neither reality to the painter nor words for the poet can be said to contain the whole of their means. There are two sets of realities—the mental and the material.

"Drawing from the model, for instance, is like looking in the dictionary for a word; you will not write poetry till the words come to you without having to turn them up in the dictionary every time.

"The greatness of an art depends upon the power of the artist for selecting those facts which are necessary to produce the impression of a great idea upon the spectator."

I recollect that one day when talking to Lord Rosebery, Signor had said that there were things that could only be done in art at the sacrifice of some other things. For instance, fire might be painted to look absolutely natural, but to obtain this effect higher qualities had to be sacrificed. He added that an artist had to learn exactly what the limits of his art were—what was essential and what was superficial; and Lord Rosebery answered, "Is not that true of everything else in life?"

"The artist," Signor told me, "should try to render the essential facts of nature rather than the reality; were this not so, a cast from nature would be more valuable than a bit of good sculpture. If a picture which is unquestionably well painted and well designed should fail only in that quality which makes another work of art seize and hold the spectator—though technically a less accomplished work of art,—I should say that this is due to the method of the painter. He has given you the whole intellectual idea at once and too completely. A suggestion of something much larger and better can be given by a far less good thing." This to some extent explains Signor's attitude to amateur work, but apart from the pleasure he himself found in any natural expression of mind, he believed in a further value, and wrote : " We should make a stand against the notion that Art, as an expression of ideas, emotions, or pleasures, should be left to professors alone. It was formerly used as naturally for expression of these as limbs are still used for progression, or attainment of material objects we desire to seize. Now it is as though these natural means were never to be employed excepting by paid agents. It is as if it came to be thought no one should ride, or skate, or play lawn tennis or cricket but the professor. Those who give their lives to the practice of any of these things, will, of course, become more proficient than those who use them for recreation or personal improvement, but the latter objects are the most important. It should be much the object of those who have influence, to retain and develop the natural sources of interest, and outlets for individual expression, often little comprehended. What is wanted is to encourage the sense of art, not to make artists. The modern mind revolts against the dogma that life is to be accepted as a state of inevitable unhappiness, and that labour is a curse. More healthy instincts make us feel that the more delightful we can make life the more we can rejoice in the beautiful, and the more we can find pleasure in labour and occupation the better, even for our most moral and religious instincts."

When looking at an amateur drawing, I can remember Signor saying, "I think I like strange things that are of course no-how, but that go anywhere, up through the ceiling!"

I have heard Sir Clifford Allbutt and Signor agree that the necessity or, perhaps better, the love of the mysterious, was an essential and valuable part of the human mind; far from being all disadvantageous or an impediment to progress, it had been in the main a stimulus towards something transcending man's best efforts. Signor said: "It is in fact the poetic element; and what in the superstitious mind is mere dread, in Browning and Tennyson is aspiration. You cannot take away the mysterious from man, he cannot do without it."

During these years, Doctor Allbutt often came to see Signor after six o'clock, and had long talks with him. One evening as he left he said, "How I wish we had a secret phonograph to take down all Mr. Watts has been saying." And I add in my journal: "Oh, if we but had!

GEORGE FREDERIC WATTS

There is a simplicity in the words he uses—in the way he says them, that makes both range of thought and its meaning all the more impressive, but it is impossible to catch that peculiar grace and charm."

When trying to outline my husband's life of thought and of work, I wrote to ask Sir Clifford Allbutt if he could still recall some of their conversations, and received in reply a letter which appeared to me to be so valuable a contribution that I begged to be allowed to include it in the memoirs. The permission was kindly given, and the letter falls into place in these years.

"St. Radegund's, Cambridge,
"*Jan. 3rd,* '11.

" Dear Mrs. Watts—I never felt the frailty of the human mind, or at any rate of my own, more than when you asked me if I could call to mind any part of my conversations with Watts—I venture to call him now by the name which he has made immortal. I hope they were inscribed on the inner recesses of my brain, but I can now recall only such fragments as by their inadequacy and by their want of setting would defeat our purposes. But what remains with me like a revelation, is that quality of his conversations which in unique degree impressed me, and I am sure all who knew him, with a sense of wonder and admiration ; namely, that they were not exactly, as I seem to have said, 'sustained' at so high a level, but that no

GEORGE FREDERIC WATTS

'sustaining' was apparent; he moved in the loftiest sphere of thought and imagination without an effort, as in a home. As I write now it comes into my head to compare his conversations with those of others of his contemporaries whom I had the good fortune also to know. Among those who are gone I may name, for instance, our common friend, Fred Myers, and Jowett, George Eliot, George Meredith—to whose tea-table Leslie Stephen carried me occasionally—Sidgwick, Maitland, and so on—all these great and masterly minds; but in each and all there were differences—whether for better or worse I know not—but something other than perfect ease in Zion. In two or three of these there was a certain defensive irony, brilliant in itself but not Watts's childlike seriousness. In others there was a note of effort or of anxiety, or of yearning, or a dread of preaching, profoundly sympathetic, but not the serenity, the crystal peace of one who lived habitually in 'one vision, future, present, past.' I suppose it cannot have been with him, as it is with the rest of us, who have to climb for our best moments, who often lose them, and have to recapture them again; so that for us some hours are weary, some dissipated, many simply dull. Watts seemed to be always calmly in possession, as a child born in the palace who took all its ways unconsciously, and finding that we were not familiar with them, naturally and without the least assumption showed us the way. I fancy that Wordsworth's conversation must have been of this kind. Watts seemed not to have climbed up, or fought up, or gyrated up, or been educated up to these heights, but to have been always there. The truth must have been, of course, that with him the phases of development were early and rapidly traversed, as indeed we may see in his art, which also was there all the time, from the 'Dead Heron' to the 'Innermost.'

"Among those with whom I might have compared him were those strong and lucid spirits who gain their compact certainties by condensing all subjects to fit into relatively lower categories, thus ignoring those inconvenient qualities of some of them which vaguely whisper of other and less tameable philosophies. But it was the glory of Watts that not only was he a mystic but that he walked hand in hand with the ineffable, ineffable as to words, but not inexpressible — expressible in a language of which he had the secret. This, it is true, is to wander from his words to his painting. Still his familiar walk with the transcendental in his own language gave him a kinship or growth with it such that he could suggest much of it even in plain English. If now and then he found the need of rhetoric in his pictures it never appeared in his conversation, which I repeat had the spontaneity of childhood. Perhaps the friend I have known nearest to him from this point of view was Stokes; but Stokes needed momentum; one who did not know

GEORGE FREDERIC WATTS

how to make the openings would be baffled by an angelic and perennial but wholly silent smile. And Stokes was not shrewd, he was innocent. But Watts had (how from his tower he had it I do not know, nor how 'George Eliot' had hers) that harvest of the quiet eye, and I hasten to add of the humorous eye, which revealed to him all the little wiles of us lesser mortals. I remember his astonishing me by a rapid excursion on some trivial account into finance, betraying amid his blameless and high-minded devotions to nobler ends as shrewd a grip of the world as the worst of us. And no doubt you remember many an occasion—I remember one well—when his sense of humour and his gentle acceptance of rudimentary persons were moved by the proposal of some chance acquaintance to suggest to him a 'subject' for his 'art.'

"I have spoken of him as a mystic; had he not been a mystic he would not have had that message for us; the flute-players we have always with us.

"It was to see for us what for ourselves we could see but in part, or in the mists, that he invented that splendid language of his brush; and, to return again to his conversation, how naturally he would talk of his pictures, becoming as it were the 'Interpreter' in the *Pilgrim's Progress* and regarding himself as but an instrument.

"It was a part of his serenity that he did not

talk in flashes, but with calm summer radiances. I remember one of these conversations about 'The Man who had Great Possessions';[1] I had ventured to say that the irresolute right hand, half closed, and with the jewel on it, told a story words could hardly tell, when he answered with pleasure that such was his meaning, his deliberate representation on the canvas; and when I went on to speak of the many traits in pictures and poems which seemed not to have been deliberate, but to have emerged out of the creative instinct, to be recognised by others—while he would not deny this notion, it was not very acceptable to him; so that in this conversation one learned more clearly how in him, of all artists perhaps, though here we shall remember Goethe, the analytic and the creative reason went hand in hand. One might think of him with Spenser, but without Spenser's archaism, for of affectation Watts was incapable, even in thought. And in Watts the analytic reason seemed not to dissect and disintegrate his ideas, but to add a finer and more subtle chiselling to the form. One might see this also (I speak as a physician) in the exquisite poise of his physical organisation, a perfect servant of his will, but soon put out of tune by errors or lapses in its management. It was probably in part for this reason that he had to live so retired a life, and not from unsociableness, for none was more uniformly gentle and

---

[1] The picture entitled "For He had Great Possessions," painted in 1893-94.

courteous to his friends, or more glad to receive them in the intervals of his work. A little conversation I remember on this subject, quite in the last months; taking up a long slender cedar stem with a slim pointed brush at the end of it, he held it away from him at arm's length, watching the steady point and saying, 'When I see that point tremble my work will be done.' Like his creative and analytic temper those sensitive hands were as nervous as they were steady and strong. For such a finely strung instrument pain was intolerable; under pain only might his will or self-command be shaken; he felt pain, and so apparently did the rugged Michael Angelo himself, in proportion to the depths of his nervous organisation.

"It is, perhaps, not fanciful to attribute to this almost unique blend in him of the analytic and the creative reason, in which by the way Leonardo also is not to be forgotten, the blend of the classical and the romantic, of his unique colour invention with his love of abstract line. We know how he loved the Elgin Marbles, and continually drew inspiration from casts of Greek marbles in his studio, these and his enormous memory for form and colour enabling him, to the wonder of his friends, to work in the absence of the living model; and how magnificently independent, he who runs may read in the 'Repentant Eve' and many another of his female figures. I recollect an occasion when, as he was passing his hand over one of these casts from the Greek, he was reminded of a remark of Ruskin, 'I suppose you find much charm in this figure; to me it says nothing, for it is without life or colour.' Ruskin, Watts added, had no apprehension of 'abstract form.' And as we went on to speak of line, Watts made a remark I had heard him make before—that 'the beautiful line is one which does not return quickly into itself, being part of a giant curve'; but on this occasion he proceeded to illustrate it with many an example. Thus, taking up a piece of chalk and a deal board, he drew such a line, but was not satisfied with it. 'I often practise this,' he said, 'but rarely get it right; when I feel it flowing right,' he added, with a laugh, 'it almost makes me feel sick.'

"On another day he bid me look at a cast of a wrestler, pointing out on the thigh not only the bulk and form and tone of the muscles, but also their swing to gravitation, their swag—a feature, he said, too often forgotten. Such was the classical poise of this gloriously romantic spirit. Once for a few weeks Watts had on his chimney-piece a small neat water-colour drawing of a farmstead with a ploughman in the foreground driving a team of grey horses. The picture contained no hints, gleams, or mysteries, but was just precisely happy in its midday atmosphere. I wondered what it could hold for him, beyond the fact that it was painted by some kinsman or friend. He guessed what I was thinking, and his answer was this: 'Well, it says exactly just what there was to be said about that —and no more.' The golden mean. And here, down deep in his temperament, lay the secret of his mastery over himself, and over his stupendous visions, visions which must have dazzled or blinded one born without this choice sense of measure. It would be false to suggest that Blake was without it, he had much of it; but it is true, I think, that it was not always strong enough in him to give him the universal measure of his ideas which made Watts at home in Zion.

"And this was as true of his conversation, of which I am trying to write, as of his painting, in which I am but a dilettante. Still, as one to whom his painting speaks as on the whole none other has done, I may say in this respect that his classical temper was sufficient to give him an easy mastery over the expression of his passionate ideas, but not so scientific as to carry him outside life to allegorise abstractions. Watts was the greatest, the most poignant of realists; *quicquid agunt homines*. His classical habit sufficed to purge his passion, never to damp or attenuate it. And it ministered to that trial of all men, one of which we often spoke—the elusiveness of our standards. Profoundly as he had studied the works of his great predecessors, his visits to their works (at any rate in later life) were comparatively few; just as likewise he could dispense with the model, and was indeed above any particular model. Poetry we have always at our elbow, and in this our standard should not fall; but pictures and statues, great violinists or orators, are not of everyday life; and Watts thought that we lost these standards not only, as I took it, by our bad memories, but also in part by our worldly lives, by our dissipations. As he had to protect his sensitive physical organisation so he protected his standards, by continual communion with the highest. It seemed to him that it is for this reason that mankind needs forms and ceremonies—they must be; but because of the hardness of our hearts; and yet there is the certainty that we shall put the letter before the spirit. They must be; because in the midst of the world they keep us up to the mark; they fasten to ideas which without them would slip down or out of sight. These reflections I give very imperfectly and diffidently, but he would speak after this kind, explaining how by a cloistered life he avoided the tyranny of letter and custom, dispensing in his own case (which he was always careful to distinguish from the duties of others) with the congregations and adventures of men. All life had to be a compromise, and this was his compromise. And it was this habitual living in him of high standards which made it easy for him (without, as I put it, having in each time to get up 'momentum') to take up his old canvases, even his oldest, again and again, and to work upon them without loss of energy or of continuity of idea; and in the same steadfastness to create his horseman 'Physical Energy' as he used to interpret it, with that slow deliberate growth which, biologists tell us, makes for endurance.

"In conclusion, I would emphasise in my impressions of the converse I was privileged to hold with Watts, that if he lived somewhat apart, if he habitually dwelt with the Muses, for certain sacred hours of the day alone with them, yet this did not consist in, nor engender in him, anything alien from mankind. His sweet courtesy was the mirror of his heart in this respect; and his works spoke eloquently of his mission for the purification and ennoblement of human passions, sorrow and pain, and of his profound pity and healing. Again and again I have heard in his conversation how generously he felt towards his brother-artists—glowingly of those who lived devotedly for their art and for the best in them; of such he would often name Burne-Jones. If then he seemed to live apart, or to speak with the coolness, or rather the calmness, of detachment from common life, it was but a detachment from its discords and confusion. For in all his conversations one feature was eminent, one which was unforgettable, something more than breadth, more than all dimensions—the wholeness of his ideas; not in art only, nor religion or politics only, but in the unity of each in all. In his conversation as well as in his pictures he never seemed to have to convey one into the other, nor were they merely associate in his mind, nor did they only interpenetrate each other—they were fused into one being. In talk or in painting one could never with him think of, nor could he speak of, any one of these as departments of life, or to be contemplated apart, or of each as not belonging to the whole. And herein lay his essential difference from allegorisers, moralists, and philosophers, excellent and indispensable persons with whom undiscerning folk would sometimes confuse him.

"This is the poor all I have to say; shadow indeed beside his light. And I regret that I have been able to give no specimens — no *logoi* — of Watts's conversation. I ought to have made notes of some of them, for the ripeness and fulness and sincerity of his conversation lent itself to such reminiscences. I sometimes reflected that he had in common with Jowett the faculty of dropping precisely upon a truth with the quick certainty with which a bird hops to a twig. But such sayings of the great seer you may have from others, and with them your own mind is stored.—Believe me, dear Mrs. Watts, always yours most sincerely,

"Clifford Allbutt."

Signor had often said that he believed that his best chance of going down to posterity at all worthily lay with his design "The Hemicycle of Lawgivers," and for some time the condition of this fresco at Lincoln's Inn had distressed him very much. A veil of London blacks (especially where the draught from the door struck from

GEORGE FREDERIC WATTS

below it, drove the impurities in a straight line over the centre) seemed likely to obliterate the whole work.

The Benchers were anxious to have it looked to, and Professor Church undertook to see what could be done. He found the dirt was removable, though not with bread. It was finally gone over inch by inch, sometimes delicately rubbed with cotton-wool, sometimes only breathed upon with a fine spray of methylated spirit. Professor Church was present every day directing the one man he employed there. He had said that it was doubly a labour of love—for the painter and for the fresco. Not a particle of colour came off, but in one or two instances the colour came through, where an alteration had been made.

When all was finished two or more coats of a preparation of paraffin wax were given to the whole fresco, and its safety for the future is believed to be assured.

This autumn (1890) the Queen of Roumania was paying a visit to England, and while passing through London signified her desire that Signor should dine or have luncheon with her. As he was not able to do so, the Queen graciously offered to come to see him. The writings of Carmen Sylva had charmed him, and when the beautiful lady came he was not disappointed. Indeed he would have liked to have painted her. He was charmed with her mind, with her voice and gesture, and found something in her beauty of the type of Lady Mount-Temple. He thought her one of the queens that Ruskin dreamt of, who were royal in giving. He told her he was about to paint a picture, taking as his subject the words, " What I spent I had, what I saved I lost, what I gave I have." She made him repeat the words, and said, " Thank you, you have given a weapon into my hands," and they discussed the symbols he should use. He made a little study in gesso for the figure, and the picture was painted the following summer. The Queen left us full of hope that she would return to England next year, but illness prevented this, and Signor never saw her again, but he did not forget her charm or her graciousness.

As she said good-bye and I made my curtsey, I kissed her hand; she instantly took me by both hands and kissed my cheek. She had brought a large party with her, amongst whom were Professor and Mrs. Max Müller and Miss Alma Strettell, the gifted translator into English of the Songs of the Dimbovitza, collected by Carmen Sylva.

Our winter was again spent at Monkshatch, where there was now the new pleasure of watching the progress of Limnerslease, as we decided to call the new house—" Limner," to keep the remembrance that it was built for an artist, and the word " lease," as having a double meaning, for we played a little with the old English word " to leasen," which meant to glean, our hope being that there were *golden years* to be gleaned in this new home.

GEORGE FREDERIC WATTS

" I cannot say how much I look forward to it," Signor said. He had made a great experiment, and was following the system of the American Doctor Salisbury. Hitherto he had lived much more on farinaceous foods, always very carefully prepared by his devoted and clever cook. Now she put out all her skill to make minced beef as perfectly palatable as might be, and it became the staple of his food, working in time quite wonders for him. After a few weeks he lost all sense of stiffness and pain in the joints, and, what was of the utmost importance, the circulation became good once more, as Doctor Bond declared when after an absence of some weeks he held his pulse and found it free of that tension which hitherto had given so much anxiety.

We saw a rare sight during this December. There was much white mist, which hung like a pall for some three or four days. The temperature was low with many degrees of frost, and we grumbled a little, not knowing what was preparing for us. But at last the sun shone out, the mists cleared off, and a new world spread out before us. Every blade or twig, every pine-needle was strung with a mass of glittering crystals! The bare trees seen against the sky seemed to have some strange new foliage; their very character was changed, for the weight of ice was so great that every branch swept downwards in a way that made it impossible to say whether the trees were oak or elm or sycamore. They looked like none of these.

GEORGE FREDERIC WATTS

The herbaceous garden was in blossom again, as all the dead stalks of Michaelmas daisies and other late plants became clusters of crystal flowers! Andrew brought in a spray of larch which actually bore four measured inches of ice upon its slender stems. This strange scene lasted for quite three days.

The winter was on the whole dark, and instead of painting, Signor took to using red chalk and made a series of twelve drawings.

In May these were exhibited in the Old Bond Street Galleries, a sale being arranged by Sir William Agnew that enabled Signor to purchase the new house from Andrew, which as a matter of business was now convenient to both. For some years Andrew was still the ground landlord, but he permitted Signor to make it freehold by a further purchase in 1899. In March the finer days allowed of painting, and he had but a few last touches to add to complete his large picture of Naples, which we hoped he would have sent for exhibition to the New Gallery. But he was curiously indifferent to comments made by the critics when his well-known work was re-exhibited, and instead of sending "Naples," he chose to send "The Deluge," a picture that had during the last five or six years become well known; and Mr. Hallé could not persuade him to send his portrait of Lord Tennyson. A few of us, who took, no doubt, a smaller view, would have liked the world to know what good work he was still doing. However, he did allow his portrait of Lady Katherine Thynne to go to the Academy, and on varnishing-day his brother-artists pleased him by their congratulations.

The epidemic of influenza raged this spring in London, and on our return to Little Holland House Signor was one of its victims—an attack at first so little serious that he seemed to be throwing it off, but there gradually developed a very different condition, and days of great anxiety followed. Doctor Bond thought it well to ask Sir Andrew Clark to come to see him. After the usual terrible silence while the consulting physician makes his examination, Sir Andrew said heartily, "You are mending, Mr. Watts; you will have to do a great deal more work yet." "I want to," Signor answered simply, " and better "—with an earnestness that made Sir Andrew echo the words, " And better ; that's the true spirit of him ! quite undiminished." And his cheerful visit helped towards improvement, though downstairs he allowed that Signor was far from being out of danger. There were many days of anxiety when our kind Doctor Bond would appear soon after seven o'clock each morning for his first visit, in riding-boots and spurs, bespattered with mud from his gallop in the park, bringing to the sick-room the very breath of health and vigour to help us. Sympathy too !— for one day after a bad night when my heart was failing me, I remember his looking at me brightly and saying, "Now, look in my face, Mrs. Watts; *I'll be in tears* when there's any need of it."[1] And so he would—keen sportsman and hard rider though he was. When recovery set in Signor spoke of this illness and the possibility there was of a very different termination.

"I fancy it was near, but I have never had any fear of death; it has no horrors for me beyond the pain of leaving those who will grieve for me. I think I have shown in my work what I think of death."

During this illness Dr. Clifford Allbutt, our friend and opposite neighbour in Melbury Road, was often at Signor's bedside. Doctor Bond asked this favour of him as his own house was distant in Westminster, and it was, I know, a service rendered from the heart. He came across one morning when Mr. Thomas Hardy had had breakfast with him, and he told Signor that Mr. Hardy had been to see the collection of chalk drawings and had come to think that after seeing them he must himself begin art all over again.

"I must certainly begin Watts again," he added, for the Allbutts had reminded him that this was Melbury Road where "every one was more or less a Watts fanatic."

During the convalescence Doctor Allbutt had a half-way of meeting depression with sympathy, and yet with the assurance that there

[1] The sorrow was for us. He lost his kind doctor in 1902.

was nothing seriously the matter, and he always left Signor very much the better for his visit.

A visit from Sir William Bowman remains a vivid memory. He had heard that Signor was ill and came without any thought for himself, though I did not think him looking well. He told me at the time that he was doctoring his coachman, who had a very severe attack of influenza; alas, a few days after this Sir William was also a victim. Doubtless this illness was a severe strain upon his constitution, and the following spring, after pneumonia, he had "passed over to the other side." He stood by Signor's bedside holding his hand and talking earnestly; these two so much akin in spirit, and each with the light of it visibly shining through the frail shell of its dwelling-house. Signor spoke of what he hoped still to do in the short time that was left, and Sir William answered, "We have neither of us much time left now."

The purpose of his visit was to ask to whose charge the pictures had been confided which Signor had bequeathed to the nation, for he wished to put into practical form an old intention that the portrait he possessed should eventually be placed with the collection. Signor told him that he had bequeathed them to the Trustees of the National Gallery—that he had in fact presented them—but as there was no building to receive them, he had meanwhile put this matter into the form of a bequest. He explained that his wish was to leave the Trustees free to dispose of them as they might think best. His object, he explained, in painting the class of subjects he had chosen to leave as a series, was not intended to represent the art of the time, but rather that side of art which touches upon subjective and abstract thought—what is called symbolical, and is so much ignored and even decried.

Sir William answered by telling him that he had perceived from the first that Signor's view had been that the spiritual and the imaginative was the highest possession of the human mind, and that he had therefore made it his object to dwell upon that side.

It was a solemn and beautiful half-hour, and though that same autumn Sir William drove over from his Surrey home, Joldwynds, to find Signor well and settled at Limnerslease, it was at the side of the sick-bed that the true last meeting of minds took place, and there that the real farewell was said.

The result of this talk was that the portrait of the artist painted by himself in 1864 was presented by the widow, Lady Bowman, to be placed with his work in what is known as the "Watts Room," with this inscription on the frame:—

> Bequeathed by Sir WILLIAM BOWMAN, Bart.,
> In testimony of the love he bore the painter.

After this illness a week spent at Monkshatch helped him to complete recovery, and he went back to work with returned power. Almost the first canvas he began to work upon was the picture we then called the "Epitaph picture," subsequently named "*Sic Transit*." The weather was fine, and for the first few days he worked in the garden studio with the door wide open. It was one of the pictures that cost him little trouble. The quality of the canvas, which had been prepared with plaster of Paris soaked in water for many weeks to remove all lime, had a texture that suited him. It was begun on the 11th July and was taken to Limnerslease, to be carried on further when he went there in November for the winter. Baron de Cosson invited him to choose a helmet from his collection, then at South Kensington Museum, and one was found belonging to the very best period.

He made more than one study of this; the beauty of the patina and the curved lines of this bit of armour were a source of wonder and delight to him. Besides the studies, the helmet was twice painted in the picture; first in the foreground, where it was very carefully completed. But the composition was unsatisfactory to him, and one morning it was painted out. When he called me to look at the change the improvement was evident. He told me he knew it would be, but had hesitated about making it, because, he said, it was really well painted; adding, "Donders would not have doubted for a second—that is the difference between us." We had just been reading the memorial account of this remarkable Dutchman whom he had twice painted.

The Surrey home was an unqualified success. Such a home, he said, was what he never thought to possess, and his enjoyment of it was like the enjoyment of a child, as my sister said when he called to us to come and hear how delightful the sound of the wind was among the trees. Though built for the winter months, it soon became the home where the greater part of the year was spent by us. He allowed himself more holiday, especially this first year when the garden below the wooded hill was but a bit of stubble-field, and everything had to be planted. But the little bits of gardening he did himself in the wood were his chief interests, and he was very happy when, wearing a strong pair of gardening gloves, he pruned back tangles of bramble and thorn with a reaping-hook, no one else being trusted to do this for fear too much of the beauty of wild nature should be lost; and quietly from a full heart he said, "How I do enjoy this life."

A fallen fir-tree was given a chance by being propped up, and honeysuckle, wild roses, and dogwood were planted about the root and over the bare stem, a work to which he gave nearly a whole day! I regret to say the tree refused to live, and he suffered it, after a year or two, to be cut up and carried away. For the dark hours he soon had his "niche" made in our little sitting-room, and there he went to rest, to enjoy our books, or to talk, according to his humour.

GEORGE FREDERIC WATTS

If in the mood, he would tell stories from the Greek mythology, or from Homer; and his listeners sometimes enticed him to this by pretending to believe in the invulnerability of Achilles, which always stirred him to indignation; but in the end he would be led to tell all the story of Troy—of Achilles and Briseïs, of Helen and Priam, and so on, with delicate definement of each character—of Agamemnon's praise of Teucer and his reply, begging the king not to urge by praise one who was already too keen. These simple touches out of the knowledge of human nature, he thought, placed the book above any other but Shakespeare. "He too was gigantic," he said; "they run and skip where other men toil with difficulty; surely they were children of some giant race."

He was indignant that Achilles, the creation of Homer, who makes him refuse to fight without armour, and indeed to receive a hurt from Patroclus,[1] should by later writers have had given to him physical characteristics which robbed him of all his heroic qualities.

During the winter the picture "*Sic Transit*" was completed, and he gave it that title, preferring to use these two words only, without the addition of "*Gloria Mundi.*" His intention in the picture was not so much the passing of the glory of the world but rather the end of all human existence.

[1] I have not been able to verify this; if it requires correction the error is mine. After a long talk with Signor in 1899, the Master of Magdalen (Oxford) wrote to me that he had not been prepared to find him so minutely acquainted with Homer and the Homeric study.

When I read a letter to him from a preacher who had used this picture as the text for a sermon, Signor remarked, " He makes the mistake of imagining a person, and not taking the shrouded figure as the symbol of human life ended, and with all its possibilities laid away."

The portrait of Mr. Walter Crane brought him praise from his brother Academicians that astonished him when he met them at Burlington House on the members' "varnishing day." " Millais," he said, " used the word 'sublime.'" The critics also praised, and continued to announce that it could not be recent work till Mr. Crane published a letter giving the facts. Signor was much surprised, and said, " I assure you it is cared for because of the absence of texture, that which to me is its great defect."

To the Academy Exhibition he sent " She shall be called Woman " ; and about this picture he had some correspondence with Mr. Calderon, and with Sir Frederic Leighton, who wrote :—

"8/4/'92,
"2 HOLLAND PARK ROAD,
"KENSINGTON, W.

" DEAR SIGNOR—You have perhaps been wondering at not hearing from me, but the fact is that immediately after the business of the Council was over on Monday, I rushed out of town for a short rest, and only returned last night. I was much done up, and wanted to sulk alone away from London ; to-day, I have deferred writing till I should have been to Burlington

House and seen the members of the hanging committee, and especially Calderon, with whom I knew you had been in correspondence, and with whom I had talked over the subject of your letter before leaving. I need not tell you that whilst I cannot admit that his feelings towards you are the same as mine, or that you are to him the same very dear and honoured friend that you are to me, he entertains for you a truly affectionate and appreciative friendship; we took, therefore, your letters warmly to heart. He tells me that he has written to you, and I find that he has said exactly what I myself feel. You know how keenly I appreciate and how deeply I acknowledge the high tone and the dignity, to say nothing of other qualities, which are ever present in whatever comes from your mind, attributes too rare, alas, in the art of our day. I feel that this nobility of thought and imaginative force are fully present in your 'Eve.' Calderon tells me you fear its fresco-like look; to me, however, this quality seems thoroughly suited to the work. On the other hand, under the strong light of an exhibition room one feels that there are, perhaps, inequalities in the execution, and a lack in places of completeness that you would be the first to acknowledge and see in the new surroundings; these are, however, much lessened by a removal from the immediate level of the eye—now the question, I gather, is what you, as a matter of feeling, think about its place; it is now in the long room in one of those transverse angles (like your 'Cain' a few years ago and Holl's fine 'Duke of Cambridge'), but there is a moderate-sized picture under it. That the picture gains in finish where it is there can be no doubt. It would look less well on the level of the eye; nevertheless we are anxious to know what you feel about its not being 'on the line'—just as a full-length portrait is not put on the line as a rule. Nothing would grieve me more, few things as much, as that you should be pained in this matter; but this you know. Write me a line and believe me—Ever your affect. FRED. LEIGHTON."

This picture was considered a lamentable failure, and even Sir Frederic Leighton regretted that it had been exhibited. Signor must have been aware of this, but he made no comment. He knew that I was disappointed by the silence, but explained to me that no final verdict could be given now, and that he hoped the picture had not been painted for a season's exhibition. I find I wrote of it in answer to a question Signor had received as to the intention of the design, and before sending the reply I asked him if he approved; he did so, and told me to put down these words:—

"It is not so much, or rather not at all, the Eve of Genesis, nor of Milton either. It is an incarnation of the spirit of our own time, and a hope for the future. It is intended to suggest the very essence of life—strong, fresh, vital, electric — an embodiment of the ideal inheritance of humanity from its mother, of the spiritual, the loving, the beautiful."

One very great pleasure Signor found this summer in the collection of Lady Waterford's paintings at 8 Carlton House Terrace. He went many times, and at each visit his admiration increased. "She never makes a mistake in movement, in proportion, or in expression," was his answer to one of the many who cavilled at what they considered a want of correct drawing.

Another satisfaction for him was the rumour that possibly Mr. Tate would set apart a room specially for Signor's work in the picture gallery he had then offered to build for the nation. Lady Pembroke and Lady Brownlow drove down to Streatham to see this generous donor of what is now the National Gallery of British Art, to tell him of the series Signor had long wished to paint, and of the pictures already completed, and they found that he was anxious to have these pictures. Lady Pembroke had entered into the idea of the "House of Life" very earnestly when she was with us in Surrey, and it seemed to her like the launching of that ship of his dreams. It was but salvage of some wreckage; but nevertheless that he lived to see his pictures placed in a noble gallery was certainly an accomplishment of his hopes he had not looked for.

"I do not want any recognition now or in

the future," he wrote at this time, "excepting that which is due to a desire to throw my mite into the scale with those who endeavour to aid the cause of real progress. I have long been accustomed to look probabilities in the face. Perhaps a day may come when it may be thought there was more presumption and vanity in leaving these pictures to the nation than anything else."

As a representative of the medical profession, Signor had asked Sir Andrew Clark to sit to him; and in June of this year, 1893, the portrait was begun. As the painting progressed he liked to have the sitter so far removed from him that it became impossible, on account of deafness, to hold any conversation. He was, therefore, glad of a third person, and sent for me as a listener. Sir Andrew talked well, and when telling a story out of his wide experience of mankind, he carried one along, for his descriptions were powerfully dramatic.

He was a strong man and held strong opinions, which he expressed in very forcible language. "I tell my patients never to speak of over-work to me; there is no such thing. I have people coming to me every day telling me they are suffering from over-work. I tell them, 'No! you are suffering from mismanagement, or you are suffering from rest!' Affectionate women are often at the bottom of it; they bring odd foods at irregular hours. Three meals a day of wholesome food, and a man should work for sixteen hours. The Latin proverb says, 'Work is life'; I say more, it is the very life of life. Those who produce nervous work must, in the nature of things, have infinitely more sensitive nerves than the ordinary human being. When they leave off work they become aware of these nerves, they begin to think about them, and that sets them going. Authors have these nerves—all brain-workers have them! Painters have them, Mrs. Watts."

This I knew very well, and yet I can affirm that in my home my wonder was ever at its serenity. Speaking to Signor's old and intimate friend, Mrs. Leslie Stephen, I once said, "As you know, he is supposed to suffer from nervous excitability; I find him calmer than most people." Before our marriage he had constantly warned me that I had made myself an ideal that was not himself. Some eighteen months afterwards he asked me if I had not found out that he was very different from what I expected. I answered, "Only in being much less irritable than I thought you would be."

Nervous he naturally was—how could it be otherwise with such an organisation? The spirit in him might well be compared to the flame of a candle consuming the material (a symbol an Eastern visitor once gave to him, and which he liked). The condition so well known to brain-workers induced at times an anxiety which was without reason. He made himself positively ill, and for many days—once when my train, shunted to allow numberless excursion trains to pass, delayed my return by some hours, and there was no possibility of telegraphing to explain what had happened. I remember that Sir Edward Burne-Jones told me that he himself never saw his dearest ones go out of the house without mentally seeing them carried back on a stretcher!

A phase of this anxiety in Signor's mind was one from which no one could save him. It was, I believe, a ghost of the difficulties he had to encounter in early life, and one I should not touch on here, but that it showed itself more often when he was writing letters, and hereafter these may come to light and so be misleading. His letters were often written before dawn, waiting for sufficient light to begin painting, an hour when the proportion of things is too commonly distorted; or they were written after work was over, and he was thoroughly tired, which had the same effect. Sometimes these letters were replies to requests for aid. He never got inured to the pain of refusing even printed appeals!

Only twice in our life together was there the slightest ground for disquieting thoughts about money matters. Even then his solicitor told me that in his opinion there was no cause for anxiety whatever. It was then, however, that he wrote (in 1891) to one friend of " our having to exercise parsimonious prudence," and adds, "of this I am not ashamed since it is not the result either of extravagance or speculation."

He wrote in this mood to Mr. Gladstone, and I believe to Lady Pembroke, Sir Frederic Leighton, and others. That he was usually calmly free of any anxiety on this head is proved by the way he, with a perfectly free mind, deliberately over and over again refused opportunities for making money. If I knew of the depression the cure was easy, for his "pass-book" never failed to bring reassurance.

These "invisible riders," as Emerson named this physical—or should it be called psychical?—infirmity, drew him also to a self-depreciation that would have made one smile, but that it so greatly partook of the nature of "that divine disease humility." The habit of his mind was calm and serene. "There is nothing so religious as to live joyously," he said, "to make others happy," and he certainly lived to do this. Once when a number of young people about him were set to think what their wish would be supposing a fairy offered to grant it to them, Signor's answer was quickly given, "To be fortunate to every one whom I may happen to come across," and to me it seemed he often had his wish.

The children who came occasionally to Limnerslease were a great joy to him. "I like to have these little lives about," he said; and the children of his Blanche, Verena and Arthur Somers-Cocks, came sometimes, and my sister's three girls, or my brother's little daughter and son, this little boy being with us when he was only three years old, when Signor became his devoted playfellow. He liked to have a young child's opinion on his work, and was delighted when, to a humble inquiry as to whether this critic liked a portrait he had just begun, the answer came promptly, "No! it is too smudgy."

With these little people Signor, when enticed to play wolf or crocodile, became very agile, and ran very fast and lightly. In the evening he often spent half an hour by the little boy's bed, pretending to be a stork that pounced at the white-robed figure dancing about on the bed. If Signor's stork became too vivid for the child's imagination, he would call a truce by saying, "No storts in dis country!" "Dou are to come up the nights I *are* tired," he exhorted with forefinger up, after this excuse had been made for missing the visit the night before, when Signor's conscience had suffered acutely because the promise to go to him had not been kept.

When the Somers-Cocks children were with us we played more sedate games in the evening, and if this happened to be a game of cards—"Old Maid," for instance—they were both entirely occupied in trying to shield Signor from the disaster of being "old maid." And sometimes the daughter of Signor's old friend Sir Henry Taylor brought little people to see him—her brother's children and others; and amongst these a little girl, who had lost both

George Andrews photo.   *Emery Walker Ph.sc.*

The garden doorway, Limnerslease

GEORGE FREDERIC WATTS

father and mother, was brought to us first by her, and as she lived near us at Little Holland House she often came to play in the garden there, and not being very strong, sometimes came to stay with us in the country.

And this Lily by name and by nature grew deep into our love and, circumstances being favourable, she came to make her home with us. Signor was certainly well loved by all these little people as well as by his older friends. However much he might bewail his other disadvantages, he would always allow that he had been singularly fortunate in having many dear and real friends. A few of these contrived to give him a great pleasure, and a still greater amount of astonishment, as, for instance, when four of Messrs. Broadwood's big men arrived and placed a grand pianoforte in the studio. At first it seemed to be a mistake, but a letter came from Mr. Hipkins, Broadwood's manager, to say he was instructed to send it, and later we came to know that Mrs. Henry Holiday was the arch conspirator.

As great musicians came to play to him sometimes, and his little cottage piano was most unworthy, this gift was a real boon.[1]

It was well that he kept the open door of his love for the young who were growing up to reach his heart, for like the rest of mankind a long life brought him many a sorrowful loss.

[1] The givers were Lady Brownlow, Lady de Vesci, Mr. and Mrs. Henry Holiday, Mr. Hipkins, Lady Lothian, Miss Geraldine Liddell, Lady Pembroke, Mr. Ruskin, and Lord Wemyss.

In October of this year, after not much more than a few hours of anxiety for him—as the serious nature of the illness was not made known to him till the day before the end—he lost his friend the Poet Laureate. "The news of the day fell heavily upon him," I write on October 6; and on the next day I say further, "Signor laid up—ill and depressed; he took up a scrap of paper and began to write. When he showed it to me I knew that he had had that longing divined by Browning, to—

> . . . forgo his proper dowry,—
> Does he paint? he fain would write a poem,—
> So to be the man and leave the artist,"

and coincident with this sorrow he became ill, and was laid up for several weeks. So strangely sensitive was his organisation to mental impressions that more than once I saw such an effect from sorrow; probably his physical condition at the time being low, and contributing to it. He was thus prevented from being one of the number of pall-bearers, as Lady Tennyson and her son wished; and that he could not have this last privilege was an additional sorrow to him. The last message he had had from this friend had been brought by his son some months before: "Give them my love ten times over." The last from his lips; but how often through the years that followed, even to the last hour of consciousness, the voice continued to speak to him! After reading from the poems one day, as the book closed, he said, "How they take me into the blue! There is such an all-pervading sense of the spiritual, and yet the mind is so sane, so well balanced."

But never again after this time of loss could he bear to hear those lines in Ulysses unmoved :—

> It may be that the gulfs will wash us down :
> It may be we shall touch the Happy Isles,
> And see the great Achilles whom we knew.

To Signor's mind, the three arts being so distinctly one and the same, he was at times almost rebellious that he himself was limited in expression to one only. In his dreams alone could he create music, and this not infrequently; but one such dream I remember more clearly than any other, his description of a magnificent anthem that he had just awakened from hearing, of which he told me had it been possible for him to write the score down, it would have stood for ever as one of the great things of the world. "'Hallelujah, God is great,' were the words," he said; "it was quite superb in its grandeur."

When Signor thanked my sister (Mrs. Edward Liddell) for a letter he had received from her, in which a description of village life had much pleased him, he says : "But the poet turns everything to poetry. Why do you never write? you to whom the gift of words has been given; a gift I envy more than I can say. Words won't come to me! If I try to come at them, they seem to fly over the waste and I only see a whisking tail! Or I may come upon a throng of wild horses; if I ever entrap a few of these they usually assume an extravagant high-falutin shape! I think it is too bad of you who have these obedient to your command,[1] to keep them eating their heads off doing nothing; if I had these at all tractable, I would make them do something, if only in a carrier's cart."

Once when the longing for poetic gift was strongly upon him he would fain have put into the form of a sonnet the idea that the light of the sun hides the light of the stars from us; just as the light of reason hides the higher and further off—the spiritual. "A child looking at the moon thinks it a far greater light than Sirius," he said, "though Sirius is a million times bigger than the sun."

He was laid up through October and November, but these illnesses, if not too crippling to mind as well as body, were not without compensation. A detachment from the routine, even of the artistic life, with its leisure for thought, free from interruption, was certainly a gain. New subjects for designs presented themselves to his mind in greater numbers than could have been painted in a whole lifetime. Once it was the procession of Life, beginning with her birth in a primæval dawn, and led on through all vicissitudes, till at last in some new sphere, surrounded by all beautiful and delightful things,

---

[1] A life "of great love and much serving" had by force of fate replaced the life of dreams.

she is robed by Faith and Hope and crowned with an olive wreath by Love.

"How exquisite it might be," he said, turning to me a look bright from the vision. "Art," he continued, "should be a great cosmopolitan language, and for that purpose should dwell upon subjects that unite all mankind. It might even be a medium for giving vitality to such interchange of ideas as are common to all nations, and in this way might possibly become a binding together of nation to nation.

"The mission of art is threefold—to delight the senses, touch the sympathies, and rouse intellectual, and therefore spiritual, activity. To delight the senses only is where art stops, at the level of that for which G——'s well-invented word is 'the mawkeries.' Perhaps painting may be said to represent ideas, poetry and prose to suggest ideas, and music to create ideas. These are generally the characteristics of each, but they do not belong exclusively to any."

To his mind the order of the qualities of the fine arts were these: firstly, imagination; secondly, the intellectual idea expressed; thirdly, dignity of form and noble line; fourthly, harmony of the composing lines; fifthly, fine colour; sixthly—the last and quite the lowest —realism. He held that dignity of form included reticence, the absence of any exaggeration, or the violation of any of the essential truths of nature.

His own aim, he said, was not so much to

teach as to present a range of ideas, to be suggestive of much more to the spectator; and added: "These subjects of mine are not new, I don't attempt to be new; there is nothing new to be done in that way; they are annotations which, appealing to a different sense, may call people's attention to a broader and higher level of thought than is common. Fairy-tales keep their place very much because all the extravagant and impossible feats are woven about and upon some really great truth of human nature; their teaching is generally good."

He regretted that the aim of the modern artist was not more in the direction of, and on a level with, the best thought of the time. The art of the Middle Ages he found distinctly characteristic of the age. It represented its mystery, its superstition, its piety, and its simplicity. Venetian art represented the splendour of its commercial prosperity, with the burst of fresh life from the renaissance of the Greek. When reflecting on a collection of modern pictures he had lately seen, he said: " In the whole place there seemed to be nothing that one could call great, none of the righteousness of beauty which belongs to the bird's song and the movement of the clouds; all distinct from mere charm. Splendour of colour in itself lifts you away from the mere material. Art has come to be looked upon more as a part of house furniture than as a means to make men better. The art of Michael Angelo, even if it were destroyed to-morrow, would live for ever in the work of other men whose minds have been moved by it." The re-birth of thought from age to age was often present to his mind as a sort of living stream, which represented to him the eternity of imaginative work.

"I would like to have done for modern thought what Michael Angelo did for theological thought." Such was his aim. And later from the next room through the open door I heard him say to himself, "If only I could do better work!" and I was reminded that this is what Carlyle had called "the only reasonable and justifiable complaint."

His unshaken belief that a serious expression in art was of value to a nation, made him venture to offer paintings both to Canada and to the United States of America. To Canada he sent, in 1886, his picture "Time, Death, and Judgment," and to the United States, in 1893, a version of "Love and Life," at the same time expressing a hope that it might become the nucleus of a national collection. He said, "Of course I do not present the picture as an accomplished work, but simply as an example of effort in a direction."

CHAPTER XVII

I WOULD lead to that church with many doors which is illuminated by the great light shining through many windows — the eternal truths preached in the Sermon on the Mount especially.

G. F. WATTS.

Limnerslease on the south side

CHAPTER XVII

WHEN Signor was once more well we returned to Limnerslease, and during the winter he took to riding again. The wooden pavements over the long distance from park or fields round Kensington had made him give up this pleasure when old Little Holland House ceased to exist. Now all his love of it returned. Lord Aberdare took much trouble to find for him a delightful Welsh pony, who to this day keeps her shape and good looks, though a pensioner aged twenty-eight. She was a handful with almost any one but her master. Doctor Bond rode her one day, and on his return seriously questioned whether Signor ought to ride her; she had been too much for him, he said. But under her master's light hand she never pulled, and he trained her to stop at a word from him, even in the midst of a gallop. Close to Limnerslease there runs a delightful ride, part of the Pilgrim's Way, known by the name of the Sandy Lane, delightful in being in all weathers soft to the hoof of a horse. Cantering along neck and neck through the aisle of trees in winter beauty—under archways of bearded "traveller's joy"—Signor's spirits always rose. For many years we enjoyed rides along this lane, or wandering over the heaths and the commons with which West Surrey is enriched. There were days in March especially, when the blues and purples of this English landscape were divine, and on these rides he filled his eyes with colour.

In the studio the new work included a little opalescent goddess descending to earth through rainbow skies—a figure as transparent as if made with rain-drops. He called it "Iris," and the picture was bought almost at once by Sir William Agnew, and is but little known.[1]

Signor was also carrying forward a subject, then still unnamed, that we spoke of as the "*Gemini*," but to which he afterwards gave the title "In the Land of *Weiss-nicht-wo*." Much of the rich colour of the Surrey landscape went into this picture. The two little figures just hint at the natural and the spiritual in human nature. The dark-complexioned, dark-haired twin is stuffing grapes into his mouth, while the other, fair-haired and wide-eyed, holds out his little hand, upon which a butterfly has alighted—the emblem of the soul. My husband was interested in this human characteristic: "the double dwelling-house" of the ancient Egyptians, the two horses of Plato's charioteer,

[1] This picture is not to be confused with the painting of a girl in which the iris flower is introduced, once in the possession of Mr. Rickards, who gave it that name.

the first Adam and the Second—the carnal and the spiritual of the New Testament; and in the modern presentment of this same idea, when R. L. Stevenson's genius gave it a new form, and conceived of the same man as having two separate visible existences. Like other super-sensitive souls whose ideals are unattainably high, in a moment of self-depreciation I have known him just touch upon his own dual self, the Doctor Jekyll and Mr. Hyde! I could only laugh. Could it be otherwise when before my eyes I saw the daily life of quiet endeavour —the obvious consciousness in his mind "that life was an emanation from the divine which returns to the divine"—(his own words)? Much more often when he spoke of the dual nature he was alluding to the transcendental and the practical — the Grail and the quest for the Grail.

This record must fail greatly if it does not convey the truth that he habitually dwelt upon a high spiritual plane, and that from this he did not step down to do the common things of every day, but rather that the everyday duties were lifted up by him to take their place, in perfect harmony, on the higher plane.

"Religion," he said, "is the earnest endeavour of every moment. It is the contemplation of those intuitive ideas which lift man as far as possible above his own pettiness, and from the materialism that necessarily occupies him so greatly. Religion is the constant desire to do right; not saying merely, 'I want to do right,' but the strong desire itself, like some powerful spring in machinery keeping up the motion of the whole by its pressure."

He held that waste of time was irreligious, waste of daylight, waste of any material possession. Order was religious, so was industry, cleanliness, punctuality, so that even the smallest duty well done became to him part of the religion of life. If the outline of the religious life was not bounded for him by definite theological doctrine, this did not mean for him any emancipation from any precept of conduct; rather the contrary, the voice of conscience was all the more paramount. "The lamp of truth is always here," he said, "in the conscience of man; now and then a son of God comes and turns the light up."

To him the religion of Christ was love to God and to man. He believed in the learning to love God in the wonders of creation; in learning to love man by desiring to do as we would be done by. "Individuals alone," he said, "can excite love in the fullest sense of the word; but the general desire for the general good, and the readiness to give up something for it, is what every one may try for. Without that endeavour," he said hotly, "whatever the religious belief, whatever the profession, it is nothing but hypocrisy; and if this is being tried for, whatever the belief, I trust that neither you nor I would ever say a word against it, let it be as mystic as they like. No religion is worth anything if it does not sound the note of sympathy."

His definition of Faith was this: "Faith is the elevation of the material reason into the region of the spiritual idea." This, to his mind, excluded what is mere superstitious belief, or mere assertion; or that which had been taught in childhood and had become a habit of mind —these, he said, do not deserve the name of Faith.

"Prayer, in so far as it implies that the mind has been uplifted towards an ideal of all goodness, a going out into the infinite, is invaluable to man, and marks the great distinction between him and the lower animals. It is answered so far as it is high and holy aspiration, being an exercise of mind which thereby creates the condition it prays for. After all, we do not know that mind power has not a material existence somewhere, just as much as electricity has. If will-power could be brought together as a concentrated force, it might have very astonishing results. At present it is too broken up."

He was, perhaps, more often aware of his "subliminal" mind than is common; he knew that it took him to a verge where reason ceased to be a crutch, but where dim glimmerings of the unity of all things—the reconciliation of the conflicting elements in human nature, and in human conditions—came almost into sight.

That he usually and without effort attained to the adjustment of the practical and the visionary could very clearly be seen in all that he thought and did; and, as years increased, attainment to this became easier to him. "More and more," he said once, "I see that nothing is so necessary for the religious condition of the mind as absolute simplicity. We know what we have got to do, and the only thing is to ask ourselves whether we are doing it as well as we can." He saw that matter and spirit, being bound together, must work together sanely and equally. Not to use our reason whilst we are making the endeavour to understand in what the religious life consists, was, he maintained, as if we were told that our four fingers were made for service but the thumb was not to be used. Of the importance of reason to man in the use of his more spiritual faculties, he chose one day to make a little parable of the human hand. The first finger he called Reverence, the second Devotion, the third Faith, and the fourth Hope, to the thumb he pointed as being Reason. "With the four fingers," he said, "man can cling like a monkey, but he cannot thread a needle; he cannot, in fact, do any real work without the thumb."

Liberality, in action and in thought, was to him part of the religious life; what was illiberal or narrow was not, and so had no part in true religion. When the Salvation Army were suffering from unjust attacks in the newspapers, he said to me: "I do feel so thankful for Canon

GEORGE FREDERIC WATTS

Farrar's letters, not so much because they coincide with my own views, as that they please me because they uphold that principle that we owe this justice to one another, at all times to look upon actions and intentions, not from our own personal and particular point of view—these may be narrow and are certain to be prejudiced—but from the side opposed to us." At another time he said, "Always be on your guard against strong convictions — well, not perhaps against strong convictions, but against their narrowing the scope of your vision." On looking into a book which he told me belonged to a class of religious thought with which he could not sympathise, being dogmatic, exclusive, and narrow, he was glad, notwithstanding, to find that he was able to read it with less irritation than would have been possible some years before. By this he judged that his sympathies were not narrowing, but widening with age. To one who found real spiritual help in ritual, he said : "Why strip belief of all its grace and ornament? Slight things are often of great value ; beautify your principles as much as you like so long as you remember that religion is action, not fancy. Nature is full of beauties we cannot find a reason for, except that beauty is the reason, as beauty completes. Religion without beauty is poetry made into hard bald prose; the idea may be there just the same, but it does not come to you on wings."

There was nothing strained or unnatural in

his rule for the conduct of life. "Duty cannot be well done unless it is a pleasure; if a duty is always irksome, there is something wrong, and it should be seen to. The religion of our lives ought to be so spontaneous that we are almost as unconscious of it as a strong man is of his good health."

In the precepts given by Christ he found the perfect law of liberty; and when speaking of that party amongst the Jews who so fiercely resisted his teaching, and resented any forward movement as impious, he said: "They were not looking at the hour but trying to stop the hands. This people, in spite of themselves, were giving the world its greatest religious Reformer—greatest, because Christianity is the Open Door. In spite of every narrow difference in creed, one section of Christianity banging the door upon another, Christianity itself is essentially an open door. Creed is nothing in itself, but it is the outline; and that is absolutely necessary. No nation but the Jews have ever formulated such great truths and principles. Their prophets were seers such as the world has only once known. Side by side with these truths, they had the darker characteristics of their barbarian condition. While they formulated the duty to God and to the neighbour for all the Christian world, they left it also a legacy of fanaticism, superstition, and cruelty.

"The repression of thought has often lost to a nation the lessons of highest value to it. The edict of Nantes eliminated from France a valuable element of which our Puritans are the counterpart. There should be no repression but that of crime ; lead, but do not coerce."

Charity, liberality, and serenity were the chief characteristics of his mind. A very true analysis of his nature was given me by Mr. Aubrey de Vere, who said that, to complete the human being, the characteristics of the man, the woman, and the child were required. As a part of his charm—perhaps the most obvious part—the child in him was very evident ; the delicate tenderness of the woman in his nature could only be known to those in the closest companionship. "I should be very sorry if I did not think of things for you," he answered to my grateful thanks for some little act done for me, a trifle, but one of the little flowers so easily trampled on by busy feet. Then there was, of course, the quick response and understanding of the joys and sorrows of others ; the nerve that quivered where some poet had touched the sublime, and equally shrank from words that were unkind or critical of others. The man in him was found in a certain sternness towards himself (I used to tell him that he was "unrelenting" when he urged himself to keep to the early hour for rising, while nature was pleading against this), in the unusually large view he took of everyday matters, and again in the true Englishman's love of manly games. Denied the physical vigour, he could only be a spectator ; but he was always keenly

GEORGE FREDERIC WATTS

interested in fencing, polo, and cricket, and in fact in all games and feats of strength.

During the last months of his life he was walking with my brother in the garden at Limnerslease, depressed, and talking of the weight of years, and of his many hindrances to work. My brother, who had not seen him for many months, noticed that he now stooped and his step was slow. But suddenly a sound reached their ears, and Signor stopped, instantly arrested, and said, "That's a cricket-ball," and he was off, as alert as of old, to watch the game being played in our field close by. "What a born sportsman he is!" exclaimed my brother.

In March of this year, 1893, Signor was asked to lay the foundation-stone of the new Lecture Hall and Library in connection with the South London Fine Art Gallery, and he undertook to perform a public act for the first and the last time in his life. But for this, the little function would not be worth mentioning; but it so happened that it also became part of the history of that Fine Art Gallery, so full of unusual occurrences that the incident took its place quite naturally. With the early growth and progress of this Institution we were closely connected. The Council was composed of busy and successful men and four or more ladies, in all some fifteen in number, with Sir Frederic Leighton as President. The meetings were often held in the President's studio, when nearly every member of the Council attended, including Sir

Edward Burne-Jones and my husband! Perhaps neither of these two was ever seen at a meeting of any other Council. Sometimes these were held at Camberwell, and on two or more occasions at Little Holland House. Sir Frederic told me that the work connected with the Gallery had cost more time and labour than the affairs of the Academy had ever entailed upon him.

I once saw a large-sized portmanteau absolutely filled by letters from Sir Frederic to the original founder, Mr. W. Rossiter. To many of the members it was a singular opportunity for seeing Sir Frederic's power of taking infinite pains with whatever work he might put his hand to; his self-control under trying circumstances, his tact and resource. On the Council Lady Burne-Jones was his right hand; she had the whole business at her finger-ends, and was ready to prompt or suggest in a manner that gave her husband great opportunities for his fun; but he was surprised and proud in all seriousness. In one letter he writes of these labours: "Georgie I haven't seen for days—she is somewhere behind a heap of Rossiter's correspondence for the last seven years. I can see only the top of her head, but believe she is pretty well."

The founder and director of the work, Mr. William Rossiter, had been the first member of Frederick Denison Maurice's "Working Man's College." He desired to bring art to the people of Camberwell, and Sir Frederic Leighton, Sir

Edward Burne-Jones, and my husband gave him their names as supporters.

The first collection of pictures was housed in a small dwelling-house, and the Council speedily met to consider the possibility of building at once a fire-proof room. To this Signor was the first contributor. Having passed through many vicissitudes in its early and romantic history, it is now a very large institute in the Peckham Road, Camberwell, a "Leighton Memorial" Technical Institute having been added by Mr. Passmore Edwards, with other generous gifts from him to the original building. When laying the foundation-stone Signor expressed his hope that the Picture Gallery would always be open to the children of Camberwell. He believed that even very young children might be conscious of the influence of beautiful art. He had heard the lady who specially looked after the child-visitors tell many beautiful and pathetic stories of her experiences amongst them.

During this spring of 1893 our neighbours at Limnerslease, General and Mrs. Palmer—the tenants of Loseley—brought Mr. Meredith to see Signor. Not having met for more than twenty years, this was a great pleasure ; and besides, my husband was most anxious to paint Mr. Meredith, and Mrs. Palmer, to accomplish this, had persuaded him to stay with them. In the years that had passed the finely-cut sensitive features had lost nothing, and Signor became only more

GEORGE FREDERIC WATTS

desirous to make the record. Sittings were arranged for, and the portrait begun. What interesting mornings followed! Those who have had the pleasure of quiet talks alone with Mr. Meredith can understand. His whole conversation during the five mornings that he spent in the studio left an impression of the hopefulness of his outlook, confident that progress was being made in the right direction. "We have the rise and dip of the wave, but mankind goes forward," he said. He believed a better balance was to be brought about, by a return to more natural conditions. "We want to be stripped of conventionalities—women more so than men; circumstances have so moulded women that they are seldom their true selves." He thought that co-education would be one means for such advancement. To Signor he remarked, "I believe that this age will be ranked as the most heroically striving of any time," and he attributed much of this earnestness to the work of Carlyle. Of this he said: "It will last, but how it is impossible to say; whether as classical work or as absorbed by his generation and transmitted, none can say as yet. He has taught all earnest people to-day that they have to take life seriously and do some work for the world—that there is a yea and a nay, and they must make choice of one or other."

"The longer I live the less patience I have with merely worldly people," was Signor's opinion. "I see what great changes are inevitable all over the world: what preparations are they making for this?" They then spoke of Tennyson, Mr. Meredith saying that he was the most natural, the most spontaneously natural, of human beings. "So was Carlyle," he added, "though perhaps less direct. He had the look of Lear encountering the storm on the Cornish coast," Mr. Meredith continued. "You have given him that look in your portrait," at which Signor expressed his regret that the portraits were failures. Carlyle as a sitter was submissive, but Signor was conscious that it was wearisome to him. "I said I would sit, and so I will do so," he said doggedly when Signor apologised.

Talking of Mrs. Leslie Stephen—for whom they had an equally great admiration— Mr. Meredith said, "I want to make a portrait of her when I get her more by heart." Signor mentioned that "George Eliot" had said that she did not draw from life. "Oh, I do!" Mr. Meredith answered emphatically, "but never till I know them by heart."

Mr. Meredith knew this part of Surrey well, and loved it for its associations. He had walked all over our heaths and commons with Mr. John Morley, and called him "the most delightful of companions."

Some months before this visit, Signor had written to Mr. Meredith recommending an artist for some special commissions; and Mr.

Meredith then wrote : " You are he that carries our standard for us, as will be fully known in another age. I wish to see you. The restriction is heavy on me with your letter inviting. Adieu, my dear Watts. Know me ever, while breath is in this body—Yours cordially,
"GEORGE MEREDITH."

When writing to me some three years later he called my husband " Your Titian of Limnerslease." The letter has an accidental countersign, and this the postscript explains. " Signed by the mediation of a casual pin with my blood, but I dare not attempt another letter and I leave it to your mercy."

During the winter and spring of this year the collected works of Sir Edward Burne-Jones were exhibited at the New Gallery. This was a triumph for his friends, and of these Signor was amongst the most enthusiastic. He was amazed at the wealth and glory of the colour when the pictures were collected, and realised more than ever before the greatness of this friend as an artist. " Just a little painter painting pictures," Sir Edward had called himself in a letter some time before, and now he only shivered and said he had certainly not been brought up to believe that there were two Days of Judgment !

Whenever it had been possible for him to do so, Signor had attended the Academy election to record his vote for Sir Edward ; the attitude of the majority in that body upon the subject was a matter of very painful annoyance to him.

The spring and summer passed well for him; he was constantly at work on new pictures. "Faith" was being carried forward. "Faith listening to the persuasion of Nature hearing the great voice of Eternity," he said of this picture.

Monsieur Leon Benedite, Director of the Luxembourg, paid him a visit this year. Monsieur Benedite's mission to England was to purchase some representative works for the great French collection. He chose a version of the "Love and Life," which Signor felt it an honour to present to France. He wrote: "I feel greatly honoured by the invitation to contribute a work of mine to the splendid collection at the Luxembourg. I will send my picture as soon as it is completed, and as it belongs to a class in which I have endeavoured to identify art with thought, and for which I have never intended to take money, I beg to say that the honour of its acceptance is only too great a recompense."

Of this picture he also wrote at various times: "The picture is often cited as a failure, especially with reference to the fragility of the figure of Life. I may have pushed this slightness too far, but I wanted to insist on the weakness of human existence far down among the lower creatures but for the vivifying and uplifting impulse of sympathy." In another note he says: "My female figure is fragile, for what is life in the midst of the immensities? Love I have only suggested as powerful by wings, for material muscular forms seem to me to be out of character in a design which has to do only with the purest abstractions. Also I made the figures perfectly nude, for they are only symbols, and have nothing to do with aught but the simplest conditions; in like manner the surroundings represent nothing but the very simplest ideas. There are the rugged steps of the path which leads from the baser existence to the nobler region of thought and character. This religion of Love has been acknowledged from the earliest times—then with an uncertain utterance, but now beginning to be acknowledged as the foundation of all."

When at work upon the " Physical Energy "[1] this autumn, he said to me : " I am doing the most difficult part of my work, trying to give a sense of deliberate largeness to the lines. No good music is without that deliberateness of precision, the distinctness of enunciation that Coquelin spoke of as characteristic of the good actor." A friend, in speaking of " Physical Energy," called it "impressionist"; Signor replied: " All art is impressionist; the men who use the term do not carry out their own ideal. The aim of their impression is to make evident their own dexterity; the aim should be to give the impression of some great truth of nature, something so far too great for expression that finally

[1] The title "Vital Energy" was never given by my husband to this group, nor used by him in speaking of it at any time. He objected to it because it did not convey his meaning.

it must remain indefinite. The infinite looming large behind the finite. That is the impression which great art alone can convey. I do not wish my man to be like any model you could find anywhere, and I do not wish my horse to be like a natural horse. I want them both merely to represent the characteristics of the human and of the animal." He wished to convey the idea of mastery over the animal, a mastery so complete that the man begins to look beyond. He had at last satisfied himself, by having got the trampling action in the horse arrested for the moment, and impatient of control. But the difficulty of completion seemed to make the work endless. "I never come to it," he said, "but I see something fresh that I must do to it." The limbs were removable, and sometimes without an arm or a leg he seemed to be better satisfied; he thought that a piece of sculpture in fragments was more impressive than anything that had been completed could possibly be. The imagination fills the blank really better than the artist can, yet at the same time one thinks how much finer it would be if it were complete.

It was very wonderful to sit in that garden, the roar of London so far off that the bird's song and the rustle of the breeze among the leaves made a pleasant sound about one. And many hardy flowers did well and were gay, but beyond all was the great white group, the conqueror and the conquered; Signor, the

GEORGE FREDERIC WATTS

creator, working vigorously with hammer and chisel, and the clever fellow-workman ever ready at his side, prompt and helpful in all respects, full of quaint wisdom, full of the deepest devotion to his master. This year for the first time Signor went down to the sculptor's studio before it was light, with a candle in his hand, and told me he found the dim light extraordinarily instructive. The tap of the hammer could be heard there sometimes at four in the morning. In those early hours, like Esdras, "the thoughts went up over his head." I find this note of mine: "He told me that this morning he went out in the twilight, and saw the light grow, and as it did so he felt the earth move in its courses—'Myself more distinctly a part of the great universe than ever before.'"

He had a great wish to see Mr. Ruskin again, and I a great hope that he might be able to paint him. The inappropriateness of this omission from the number of the men of mark represented by Signor's hand was so obvious. He told me that in former years he did not make the attempt, as he knew the very presence of the critic would make failure a certainty. Now in these later days the critical faculty was allowed repose. He had heard from Mrs. Severn and from Sir Henry Acland of the deep quiet of that once active mind—"speaking little and in short sentences," Sir Henry had said. But Signor was not well on the morning when we were to start for Coniston; the journey was put off, and another opportunity did not occur.

A commission from the Benchers of Lincoln's Inn, for a portrait of Lord Selborne, begun the year before, was completed, and that of Sir Andrew Clark for his national collection. The last sitting for this took place only a few days before the illness which ended fatally a fortnight later. Signor was pleased with Sir Andrew's definition of old age: "A mental incapacity to accept a progressive idea." The great physician did not reach old age; neither in this sense did his painter.

One day when Signor had ended a delightful talk with Sir William Richmond, as this sympathetic friend was leaving the studio, he said to me that he found Signor's interests and range of thought wider even than they were. "Well, to grow still at seventy-eight is youth," he added. Sir James Knowles spoke in much the same terms, and gave me his interpretation of the saying, "Whom the Gods love die young"; which was, that in mind they never grew old. Of this Sir James Knowles wrote to me later: "I am so glad you like my interpretation of that old proverb. This is how I put it down:—

> 'Whom the Gods love die young,' the proverb told:
> The meaning is they never can grow old
> However long their list of labours past;
> God-given youth is with them to the last.

You have the proof of this before your eyes

every day, and long may it be so! I send him my best regards."

Once, speaking of his own feeling, Signor told me the only difference he found in himself as he grew older was this—" I am interested in more things, and I feel younger instead of older. I know I am quite as eager, quite as much striving for improvement in my work, as I was at the beginning of life."

In the beginning of 1894 my husband received the following letter from Mr. Gladstone :—

"Biarritz
"(Address to D— Street),
"*Jan. 26th*, 1894.

"Dear Mr. Watts—I indulge to-day in what is to me a very great pleasure. It is the pleasure of writing (with Her Majesty's sanction) to say that the offer of a Baronetcy which you long ago declined, is now renewed through the medium of this note.

"You had then an ample title to the honour; that title has since been amplified, and further elevated by well-known causes.

"I earnestly hope that you may be inclined to accept it, and I hold this hope in the interest of British Art, which must always receive some healthful impulse when public honour is awarded in quarters the best entitled to it.

"Pray make my best compliments to Mrs. Watts, and believe me—Most faithfully yours,
"W. Gladstone."

GEORGE FREDERIC WATTS

When my husband found that I was entirely in agreement with him, he replied as follows :—

"Limnerslease, Guildford,
"*Jan. 30th,* 1894.

"Dear Mr. Gladstone—The renewal of the offer, formerly respectfully declined, is to me a greater distinction than would be ten Baronetcies ! I do not speak of the inconsistency of accepting now what was so declined, because I do not think consistency in itself an especial merit ; in this world of changes we may not stand still, but the reasons which formerly prevented me from accepting the honour have, if anything, increased in weight with my added years. In addition to my natural shrinking from the publicity which must and should accompany all social distinctions honourably carried, I feel strongly that the proposed honour which, fittingly bestowed on the statesman, the lawyer, soldier, and the like, those whose exertions have reference to the immediate and material power of the nation, and whose services can be easily appraised, cannot as fittingly be bestowed on purely intellectual efforts in the domain of literature and art ; here I think some such conventional but well-understood distinction, such as the Universities bestow in their honorary degrees, which do not imply material position, would better meet the requirements of the case. I value social distinctions more I think than most people. They have always been the natural outcome of civilisation, for the influence they have and ought to have; therefore, I think they should be justified if bestowed, and their duties comprehended if inherited. So distinctions, associated with social success which I have no talent for, or political consideration which I do not comprehend, would not fit my shoulders. I will not occupy your time, dear Mr. Gladstone, with all the reasons which I might give for the repugnance which obliges me again to decline the honour your kindness would invest me with.

"They (my reasons) are sticks which would take too long to sort and arrange into a bundle, especially as my fingers are clumsy at that kind of work; but please accept my deeply grateful thanks, and believe that it is, as you seem so amiably to put personal interest into the matter, with real regret that I cannot bring myself to profit by your flattering intentions. I must also ask you generously to interpret the crudities of my letter, and construe my defective utterance; I am pretty bad at saying what I would.

"I do not know whether the expression of Her Majesty's sanction is merely conventional, or it would be becoming in me through you to make known my grateful acknowledgments. Please take charge of the matter for me, and believe me to be, dear Mr. Gladstone—Very sincerely and gratefully yours,

"G. F. WATTS.

"I have not forgotten the drawing.

"The Rt. Honble. W. E. GLADSTONE."

GEORGE FREDERIC WATTS

At his refusal his two friends, Sir Frederic Leighton and Andrew Hichens, were both somewhat vexed. Sir Frederic's reasons were primarily (as he wrote) "a great unwillingness that there should be any honour held by an artist in this country that should not be yours"; and Andrew's regret that the title, representing as it did an acknowledgment from the nation of his services, should not be made evident abroad and at home. Signor was sorry that they differed, but the simple feeling that the addition to his name would be distasteful to him was as strong as ever.

During the last two winters our reading, though always varied according to his inclination, had been mainly upon the history of man's spiritual development through the ages. We read of the search by the different peoples of the ancient world in the Hibbert Lectures, the Gifford Lectures, "The Records of the Past," and some of Professor Max Müller's series— "The Sacred Books of the East." He spoke of it as "that splendid search made by mankind from the earliest times towards that which lifts him into the infinite, drawn towards it as a flower is drawn towards the light." "The longer I live the more the spiritual conditions of humanity become interesting to me; so much so that, though I won't say they extinguish other interests, they do over-lie them. In this present time the scientific seems to war with and overpower the spiritual, but they must ultimately be found to be reconcilable, for man cannot get on without them."

He sometimes said that he could accept any conception of the Creator that he knew to be too vast for his understanding, but he would not accept anything that was too small. "I can't bear the little peddling way religion is represented, as if it were part of a very bad piece of ornamentation—nothing grand about it, —no reach."

He believed that in the next century the Christian creed would have to be purified from encrustations. "It will have a great sifting, probably a great saviour"; he held that the fiercest future conflict would yet be creed against creed. "Christianity needs to be restated and put upon a different basis."

I was interested in, and was now trying to learn, something of ancient symbolism. He liked the little concrete signs I found, especially when connected with the religious aspirations of the race to which they belonged. He called it a language which expressed the highest ideas of man, and thought it a fine study, much beyond the acquirement of antiquarian knowledge; as much so as the art that has something to reveal is beyond the art which is a mere fringe of ornament. He was impressed by the description in a Zoroastrian writing of the visible form of a beautiful maiden who arrived to greet the dead after they have crossed over from the here to the hereafter;

and who in answer to the Soul's question, "Who art thou?" replied, "I am thyself, thine own deeds have made me." He referred to this at times when he had taken himself to task, and said, "I don't want that figure to be ugly."

Rossetti painted the two lovers meeting their own souls; and Signor had long ago painted " The Happy Warrior," over whom leans the embodiment of the ideal for which he has fought and died.

At this time I wrote, on a lovely morning in April: "'The Breath of Life' seems to be in the air. On our ride Signor begins to search for the unfound word which Professor Max Müller calls 'The Self,' but from which it is difficult to divest the 'Myself' that has so long been associated with it. 'The Word,' 'The Life,' 'The Fire of Life,' the 'I Am,' Matthew Arnold's 'Tendency that maketh for Righteousness,' even our own word God, seemed to him to contain but a fraction of what the word should convey. He tells me that he is conscious of this Presence—seeks after it and knows that in every great effort of the human mind, from Egypt to Greece, from Greece to Wordsworth, in the poetic philosophy of India and in all sacred books of the East, there is to be found a consciousness of that Presence. 'In those Parthenon fragments, in all great art, I hear the organ tone; in my own work I am always trying for it. Yes,' he added, answering something I had said, 'religion is nothing unless it is the music that runs through all life, from the least thing that we can do to the greatest. After all there is very little to be said; we know we have to desire to live well, to love goodness and to aspire after it, that is for God: to live in love towards all, and to do rightly towards all, that is for man.

"There is only one great mystery—the Creator. We can never return to the early ideas of Him as a kind white-bearded old man. If I were ever to make a symbol of the Deity, it would be as a great vesture into which everything that exists is woven."

CHAPTER XVIII

Unless *Art can be identified with the active springs of life and the broadest and most progressive issues of the thought of the day, it cannot be great.*

That cannot be great which does not appeal to what is great in us; greatness speaks the language of greatness; that only is great which appeals to what is noblest in us.

G. F. WATTS.

CHAPTER XVIII

THE building of the National Portrait Gallery had now reached a stage of completion, which made Mr. Lionel Cust, the Director, anxious to know Signor's intention with regard to the portraits he had bequeathed to it.

Of the number of the men of mark portrayed many were fortunately still with us, but there were also many who were not, and whose portraits therefore were available. Upon hearing from Mr. Cust, Signor consulted Sir Frederic Leighton, and from Dublin he wrote in reply :—

"I am delighted to find that you are willing to let the National Portrait Gallery have your splendid series of portraits at once. Depend upon it that you have this time fulfilled — and admirably—your aspiration to serve your country. We at the Gallery shall indeed be proud of our acquisition, which will artistically and historically be a treasure to those who follow us as well as to ourselves."

"It is identifying myself with a great national object," Signor said when he had finally decided.

GEORGE FREDERIC WATTS

The Gallery opened with fifteen portraits in oil-colours and two drawings presented by Signor. More than double that number are now placed there, while some still remain in the Watts Collection at Compton, until such time as they shall be required. In the summer of 1896 Mr. Arthur Balfour wrote to ask Signor to become a Trustee of the Portrait Gallery, explaining that for him it was to be but an honorary position entailing no obligations. He accepted this offer, and upon one or two occasions, when the Trustees met, was able to be present; and he always took much interest in the new acquisitions. There were four women of mark whom Signor would have liked to include in his series—Mrs. Barrett Browning, whom he never had the good fortune to meet; Mrs. George Lewes (George Eliot), whose portrait he was afraid to attempt, perceiving the difficulty that it would have presented; Miss Florence Nightingale, whose portrait he found he was unable to complete; and Mrs. (Josephine) Butler, for whose heroism he had a deep veneration. Her portrait was painted, and at Limnerslease, where she came to stay with us. Very lovely in her youth, in age her delicate sensitive nature still gave true beauty to a face that bore but too plainly the marks of an heroic crusade. When she saw the portrait for the first time she said but a few words. She left the room and went to take the rest which at intervals was now necessary for her. Before she came downstairs to dinner she had written what she had not been able to say to Signor.

"When I looked at that portrait which you have just done, I felt inclined to burst into tears. I will tell you why. I felt so sorry for her. Your power has brought up out of the depths of the past, the record of a conflict which no one but God knows of. It is written in the eyes, and whole face. Your picture has brought back to me all that I suffered, and the sorrows through which the Angel of God's presence brought me out alive. I thank you that you have not made that poor woman look severe or bitter, but only sad, and yet purposeful. For with full purpose of heart she has borne and laboured, and she is ready to go down to Hades again, if it were necessary, for the deliverance of her fellow-creatures. But God does not require that descent more than once. I could not say all this aloud. But if the portrait speaks with such truth and power to me, I think it will in some way speak to others also."[1]

In 1895, being anxious to raise a reserve fund for the working expenses of the Home Arts and Industries Association, Signor wrote a letter urging its claims on those who could afford to subscribe; and furnished with this I undertook the distasteful work of begging. The strength of the letter lay, as I told him, in the fact that he who now pleaded for gifts of money had himself always lived like a pilgrim and given

[1] This portrait (so far) remains in the Compton Gallery.

like a prince. The fund was eventually augmented by many generous gifts from strangers and friends. But the donor of the largest subscription was one day announced to me by Signor, who told me that he intended to paint two portraits for this purpose. I was strongly opposed to this, dreading for him the risk of a nervous strain, and said all that I could to dissuade him; so much so that he gave way, and I thought the matter had ended. But I was obliged to be away from home for two days, and on my return I found that he had arranged, with the connivance of Miss Liddell, who was taking care of him in my absence, that a sitter should be accepted, and accordingly he painted two portraits. Both his subjects were sympathetic to him, and he fortunately suffered no nervous anxiety whilst he was painting them. The first of the two sitters was the Rev. Alfred Gurney, the second Mrs. Charles Coltham Rogers. This year he painted Professor Max Müller for the national collection, and Alfred Gilbert as a gift. He also began to paint the portrait of the beautiful Duchess of Leinster; but fate destined it should never be finished, and one day, early in June, he saw her for the last time. As she stood in his studio dressed in the deep mourning of recent widowhood, listening to her sister's singing, exactly behind her was the figure of the Messenger of Death. Signor looked at her and then towards me, to draw my attention to the grandeur of the living form,

GEORGE FREDERIC WATTS

even when in competition with the ideal. He had not so fully realised the dignity of her beauty till that day. Strange to say, the Great Messenger was in very truth drawing near her.

The beauty of Mrs. Rogers was of a type he found very great pleasure in painting, until after the sittings were over and the picture finished, when he began to be critical of his work; and in fact, later, so much so that when he had been laid up for a day or two he asked to have it put out of sight before he came downstairs, saying, "It is such a grievous disappointment! I hoped it was better." A few days later Lord Wemyss came in. Critical as he ever was, he exclaimed, "He has never done anything better," and returned to the portrait over and over again; then as he disappeared through the hall door into the street he turned to me and called out, "Long live Mrs. Rogers!" Signor certainly followed Titian's advice, and looked at his pictures as if they were the work of an enemy.

A new young friend, Lina Duff Gordon, the great-granddaughter of the Lady Duff Gordon of Careggi days, now came to find him, to take as it were an inherited place in his affections; and this she soon did, and few ever held a higher. She often came to us at Limnerslease, and my eyes were pleased by the sight of her gold by his silver when she sat beside him as he rested in the niche.

Among the old friends of this year came one who had not seen him for some forty years, Mr.

John Jenkinson. He told me he found Signor " as full of life and fire as ever." As it sometimes happens, the younger and stronger fell beside him one after another, while he himself, who had always been so frail, was still indefatigably at work, and still with undiminished love of it youthfully striving to do better.

This summer he heard that Sir Henry Layard was laid up, and went to see him. I remember his pathetic words of greeting, " Most of our old friends are gone, Watts " ; and a few weeks later he had followed them.

As I turn over my notes for the years 1894 and 1895, it seems to me that they were more full of loss than any. Lord Aberdare—much missed, for he was to the end one of the most faithful in coming to Little Holland House; Sir Henry Rawlinson; and then our dear and beautiful Mrs. Leslie Stephen, of whom Signor said, " It was a life that gave strength to one's own by merely knowing that it was there " ; his dear Blanche, so young though already a widow — all these he lost within one year. Then in November 1895 he took leave of Sir Frederic Leighton, and saw him no more. On the afternoon of January 25 came the last of the many telegrams he had been receiving ; and it told of the end. " Half my life is gone with Leighton," he said, in his grief, and his last words that night were, " I shall wake happy thinking it is a bad dream " ; but the night brought but too little sleep and forgetfulness.

GEORGE FREDERIC WATTS

The very diversity of their way in life made the friendship what it was. Each honour to Lord Leighton had been an honour to Signor. He coveted laurels for him while he cared for none for himself.

"It is the unaccomplished career," he said, "it is *that*, I think, that makes his loss so terrible to me. I have seen it always rising, always going further, always successful. I felt this seat in the House of Lords might mean anything! He was a fit man for any difficult position. He would have been greater as a statesman than as an artist." "It was a life lived with the highest purpose and aim," he said, and *he knew*—" A highly honourable and precise mind." These were some of the tributes he gave to the friend whom he had known for some forty-five years. As he talked of him with those who knew Lord Leighton best, it seemed to me that nothing was so remarkable as the infinite variety of that nature. A new facet would to the last shine out to surprise even his oldest friends. The little flowers of courtesy were never forgotten by him ; neither contact with the world nor a life that was filled to the utmost with work and business had power to make him neglect an opportunity for kindness — and he recognised simple goodness and loved it.

For some time Signor thought that he would never care to go back to Little Holland House, but the work was there that could not be accomplished elsewhere, and work was paramount with him ; it was indeed " the life of his life."

He was now thinking out his picture of " Love Triumphant." Possibly the sorrows of the previous year had had some influence upon his thought, and he turned to it as a consolation. The small canvas was the first upon which he began to work. He wrote of this picture : " Time-constructor and destroyer — sinks and falls ; Death sleeps who once put all to sleep ; Love alone Triumphant spreads his wings, rising to seek his native home, his abiding place." Before this picture he once said : " You see I want to plant the feet of Love distinctly on the ground. In this life all that is spiritual must get its impetus from the ground beneath our feet. That must be recognised, though there are minds to whom the truth appears to be irreligious. It seems to me that too often in the so-called 'religious picture' of modern times, I miss the great organ tone : there is an entire absence of spirituality." To strike that " organ tone " was what he strove for so earnestly.

It so happened that during this summer the Directors of the New Gallery expressed themselves as desirous to have a collection of Signor's work for their winter exhibition (1896–1897). He was averse to the idea ; but as it was urged he consented, and accordingly one hundred and fifty-five pictures were arranged in these galleries. In the fifteen years that had passed since his work was exhibited at the Grosvenor Gallery there was naturally new work to add, and many of the earliest paintings were obtainable as they had been traced. For years I had taken some pains to do this, so that he might leave, as far as possible, a complete list for use in the future. As a preface to the New Gallery catalogue Signor had been writing a few words upon the pictures, and he said at the time to me: " I want it to be understood that I do not attempt to teach in any narrow or particular way. I want the suggestion made to be as far removed from what might be called dogmatic as the symbols I use are removed from the realistic. I feel myself that I have a rough sense of something that is larger than the ordinary range of thought, though I cannot explain this in words, for the use of them is denied me. Later on what I have aimed at will be better understood." And when he talked of his pictures, and the naming of them, he said: "You cannot adequately label them, because they represent ideas much too far off, taking one outside experience. I want them to take you as music might, and lead you further even than I myself intended. If I write a few words of explanation with them they will have to be very few. One can say perhaps that I mean not Death himself but his Messenger, coming under various aspects."

And being sad because of his consciousness of the possible he knew that he never achieved in the actual, he envied first one man's powers of attainment and then another's, saying that if nature had but done as much for him, the result would have been different. This I had to deny, saying, "You try for something elusive. You want to go down into 'the crystal roots of the Tree of Life' before you send up your branches into the heavens." "Well, I suppose that is it. I don't want to be anecdotal, or fanciful, or realistic, not even poetic; what I want to paint is the spiritual."

And in the same mood, with the sense of failure in his mind, he said, "I wish I had done more with the long span of years, but I have had a good deal to contend with, wind and tide have been against me." It was a pleasure to him that this exhibition brought him many letters of gratitude from strangers, often written "out of the deep." It was the kind of testimony he liked best to receive; and once when a writer spoke of courage and consolation gained through some picture, he said, "The whole reward of my life lies just in those few sentences."

On February 23 of this year (1897) he attained to the 80th anniversary of his birthday, and as I had heard that the Directors of the New Gallery wished to present him with an address, we went to stay at Little Holland House for a day or two. Mr. Comyns Carr, Mr. Charles Hallé, and Mr. Leonard Lindsay brought him an address of congratulation inscribed on vellum, signed by men distinguished in Politics, Arts, and Letters. To a sonnet by Mr. Algernon Swinburne the first page was dedicated, and Mr. Comyns Carr read this in such a manner that no one present could listen unmoved. The little ceremony was all the more touching because of its being informal, and indeed all that Signor could have wished. We were alone but for Miss Liddell, my sister, and Mr. Marion Spielmann, who came in to offer congratulations. The Directors, Secretaries, and Staff also presented him with a bronze portrait-medal—" Our Titian of Limnerslease" it may well be called, as the resemblance is accentuated. It was the work of Miss Elinor Hallé. The words of the sonnet by Mr. Swinburne were these:—

> High thought and hallowed love, by faith made one,
> Begat and bare the sweet strong-hearted child,
> Art, nursed of Nature'; earth and sea and sun
> Saw Nature then more god-like as she smiled.
> Life smiled on Death, and Death on Life: the Soul
> Between them shone, and soared above their strife,
> And left on Time's unclosed and starry scroll
> A sign that quickened death to deathless life.
> Peace rose like Hope, a patient queen, and bade
> Hell's firstborn, Faith, abjure her creed and die;
> And love, by life and death made sad and glad,
> Gave Conscience ease, and watched Good Will pass by.
> All these make music now of one man's name,
> Whose life and age are one with love and fame.

The President and Committee of the Arts and Crafts Society also presented him with an address " as a tribute from a body of artists, to an artist, who, during the course of a long and laborious life, devoted to the arts of painting and modelling, has ever pursued them with a sincere and constant enthusiasm of their highest forms and the expression of the noblest ideals."

In the afternoon we had a merry party of some eighteen children; some of these great-grandchildren of friends of long ago.

A fortnight later Miss Elinor Hallé and Miss Geraldine Liddell planned with great courage to give an evening party to meet the painter under his pictures. There were to be two Hamlets, possibly for fear one should fail, and the party was understood to be in honour of Dr. Joseph Joachim as well. Signor promised he would go, and remained firm; though from time to time he let us know that he hoped it would give as much pleasure to others as it was misery to him. Once there he was perfectly happy, surrounded by old and young friends. Sir Edward Burne-Jones and Doctor Joachim were in the vestibule when we arrived, and the three stood talking together for some time. Then came the many, the rooms filled, and all was sight and sound. When the music began, Signor sat by Professor Joachim, a galaxy of beauty around them. Many of the beautiful faces on the walls had come that evening, some with just a little history added, but no beauty lost. Mrs. Percy Wyndham was there, Lady Lytton was there, May Prinsep (Mrs. Andrew Hichens), Lady Airlie, Lady de Vesci, Lady Wenlock, Miss Violet Lindsay (Lady Granby),

Lady Somers, and others. There was colour and light and music. The concert suite of Bach for small string orchestra, which was given by a group of artists, "who played to the two Masters with Love as the rosin to their bows," (as a friend wrote), Mrs. Frederick Liddell, one of Dr. Joachim's favourite pupils, being the leader. He had previously said, "I will play as much and whatever you like"; and the choice made was the sonata in E of Bach for harpsichord and violin: this was the contribution of the "master of the violin"; and Mr. Fuller Maitland accompanied on his own harpsichord. The next choice was the "Frühling" sonata of Beethoven, and this Dr. Joachim gave with his old friend and colleague Miss Agnes Zimmermann at the piano; and the pictures glowed, and from their harmony of colour and rhythm of line gave out an answering echo to the great masters of tone. It was a wonderful evening, well thought out and carried to perfect success by the two hostesses. We went back to the quiet of Surrey woods next day; Signor was well, and for him, in looking back, the pleasure of the evening quite outweighed the prelude of disquietude.

Perhaps no portrait from Signor's hand ever gave more unmixed and lasting pleasure than did a drawing of Lord de Vesci made at Limnerslease this spring. The silver wedding to be kept at Abbey Leix in June, made him wish to offer something to give pleasure, where he had long given affection and admiration to an unusual degree. Lady de Vesci was not in the secret of the sittings for this portrait, and Signor had the pleasure of a child when he led her into the studio to discover what he had done for her. Her first words repaid him to the full for all his anxious fears when he had assured himself that the portrait would not satisfy her.

The enthusiasm of Mr. H. E. Luxmoore for his picture of "Sir Galahad" resulted in Signor's finding the original sketch for that picture, and painting and presenting it to Eton College, where it is now placed in the Chapel. During the first collective exhibition of his works at the Grosvenor Gallery, Mr. Luxmoore had written to enquire if the small version was available, and Signor had replied:—

"Little Holland House,
"Kensington,
"*Jan.* 23*rd,* 1882.

"Dear Sir—The little 'Sir Galahad' does not belong to me. I feel greatly flattered by the opinion you express of my works exhibited in the Grosvenor Gallery.

"I have always regarded art as belonging to the region of thought and taking the stand of literature, as in the same way reflecting honour upon an epoch and a nation. I am not so vain as to suppose anything I can do can be placed in such a category; but I hope through failure of achievement the earnestness of the intention may be evident when the works are taken as a whole. Something more than a hope of this is en-

couraged by the sympathy I have found—since the opening of the exhibition—among the best intellects of the day. Thanking you for your encouragement.—Yours very truly,
"G. F. WATTS.

"I feel that art should be able to throw a side light and stimulate reflection upon subjects whose more direct enforcements might be (especially in youth) met with impatience and even resentment. I should like my picture to be illustrated by Chaucer's description of the young squire. In generous and perhaps unthinking youth, seeds of good and evil may be sowed by very unexpected and apparently small means."

Mr. Luxmoore's ardour had not lessened during the fifteen years which had run their course between the two exhibitions. He therefore wrote again, and received the following reply:—

"I recognise that from several points of view art would be a most valuable auxiliary in teaching, and nowhere can lessons that may help to form the character of the youth of England be more important than in the great schools where statesmen, and soldiers, and leaders of thought receive their first impressions. Reminded by your letter, I have looked out a study of 'Sir Galahad' the size of the picture now in the New Gallery, and will endeavour to finish it with the object of presenting it to Eton; pleased to identify myself with an institution so famous, and to be

(I hope) famous in the long (I trust) story to be told."

The picture was placed in the Chapel by June 4, 1897. Some two years later, when we were in Scotland, and at a time when Signor was seriously ill, the Rev. S. A. Donaldson, who was about to preach at Eton on the subject of this picture, wrote to ask some question. The sermon had been preached before the letter reached us, and this delay I wrote to explain, and added : " I have been able to tell Mr. Watts in a few words the subject of your letter, and he was much pleased, and said, ' I want my picture to have a voice—we need it.' "

One evening towards the last days before the exhibition closed, I went somewhat late to look round once more. I was standing near, not before Signor's portrait[1] but looking, I think, at " Time and Oblivion," when a little old lady, a stranger, moved towards me, and pointing to that portrait, said, " Isn't that a beautiful face for a painter ? " to which I answered, " Yes, I do think so, and I must tell you that you have said this to his wife," whereupon she covered her face with both hands. " Oh," she said, with a sort of sob in her voice, " then a blessing be upon you." We talked a little together, and I asked to be allowed to send her one of Mr. Hollyer's reproductions from that portrait. I knew later that, though rich in every other way, she was in purse poor ; but that in her little

[1] Lent to the exhibition by Lady Bowman and now in the Tate Gallery.

room she had portraits of Beethoven and of Mozart, and between these two Signor was placed. She became a very dear friend.

On June 29 of this year Signor was asked by Mr. and Mrs. Tate to meet Lord Carlisle and Sir Edward Poynter at the newly completed gallery at Millbank. Mr. Tate took Signor round the galleries and spoke tentatively of his bequest, but did not ask him directly if he would give his pictures. However, Sir Edward Poynter asked me if he should write to Signor and propose it, and when I told him this, he replied, " Oh, I am glad they want my pictures"; and a few days later they were carried away, and he saw what he called the accomplishment of all he had worked for. The " Love Triumphant " and the " Court of Death " were added later. This summer was given to work upon the " Physical Energy." " I never go to it but I see something fresh to be done to make it better," he explained, adding that he never lost sight of the ideal he had before him, " to create a figure that should suggest man as he ought to be—a part of creation, of cosmos in fact, his great limbs to be akin to the rocks and to the roots, and his head to be as the sun." When he first thought of making this group he had a dim idea that he would set a sort of Theseus on horseback, but he soon found out that such a type was unsuited to action. While the idealist worked, his fellow-workman, who, from his aspect might have been a Diogenes, worked at his side, round-eyed with wonder, full of quaint humour, a man who had never lost a chance of acquiring any knowledge that had come in his way, and who did not forget to make use of it at the right moment. "Learn, madam! when there's nothing more for me to learn I won't want to live a minute," he once remarked. "It's all right, madam," he answered, when I hurried to tell him Signor was calling for him, "I'm often lost for a minute or two." When preparing to put Signor into his smock he turned to me a look somewhere between pathos and pride, and said, "The best of the whole lot of slops this, though made by a very unprofessional hand," which meant his own wife's. I loved to tell him praise of his master, and one day I thought that with a little exaggeration I might satisfy him when I said, "Thompson! the other day a gentleman in the Gallery said that Mr. Watts was the greatest man alive!" But he accepted it whole, merely remarking, "That's nothing at all, madam! I've heard that scores of times and a great deal more, I can tell you. Nobody will know the half, not even the half, of what Mr. Watts is, nor what the work is that he's done." He also gauged a characteristic of his master's, of which not all his friends were aware. It was the one Signor showed when he considered the matter of the symbol of death suggested by Verestchagin, and answered, "No, I will not." Thompson's arts of persuasion once in some matter had failed signally. When it was borne in upon him that the "No" was final, the affair was concluded by this summing up : "Oh, he's remarkably hard to handle is Mr. Watts ! nobody's going to *coax* him against his will."

A chance visitor to the Gallery in the spring of 1899 happened to say to Thompson, " I should like your master to paint me, but I am afraid he won't." Thompson, looking up at the stranger, and being pretty certain that he was Mr. Cecil Rhodes, said cautiously, "I'm not so sure of that "—and he was told to write. "I dropped on the whole thing by accident," Mr. Rhodes wrote later, when his wish had also been made known to Signor both by Lady Granby and by Lady Stanley. "I saw the notice outside your house that the public might look at your pictures, and your man was very kindly, and thought you might like to paint me."

Signor explained that he would like to undertake a portrait of Mr. Rhodes for his national collection though not as a commission, and Mr. Rhodes promised to sit, though he was leaving England almost immediately. He came for his first sitting on May 18 ; with him was Lord Grey, and they were soon joined by Lady Granby, who arrived to make a pencil drawing of the Colossus. On the next day he came again and, being alone for the first half-hour, Signor explained to him that the series of portraits he had painted, and to which he liked to add from time to time, were of the men who make England—the prominent men who may hereafter be found to have made or marred their

GEORGE FREDERIC WATTS

country; and he added with candour, "I am not sure myself which you are doing." Signor told me this afterwards, and that the words " extension of Empire" conveyed to his mind but a qualified gain. He admitted that progress must entail the supremacy of civilised man—it was a law of nature—a force that could not be restrained; but he regretted the means! Too often civilised man, to attain his ends, had used means that the primitive savage could not have surpassed in cruelty.

One morning Mr. Rhodes arrived alone, and when I went for a moment to the studio to see that everything was there that was needed, I found him standing at a little distance from Signor, and therefore not well able to make him hear. As I was leaving the room Mr. Rhodes said, " Don't go away, Mrs. Watts, I should like to talk to you." I had gone into the studio with a very faint interest in my husband's sitter, knowing very little about the real man, and I expected to find a man of the world with a brain full of great enterprises, but these chiefly matters of investment and speculation. In a very short time this was swept from my mind as if a portrait, drawn on a slate, had had a wet sponge passed over it. I was under the spell of a great imaginative mind. " England extinct!" he exclaimed. " She is only just beginning to live." As he talked that morning he outlined his gigantic scheme for British ascendancy from Cape Town to Cairo, and I could not help saying, " No wonder all the world hates us "; and he answered quietly, "You are perfectly right." The ideal he looked to was: "For the Empire of the race that I believe to be the best, and which will be the best, if we educate the youth to their responsibilities, and teach them that their work is paramount." When speaking in terms of high praise of the fitness of the British race for colonisation, I asked him to what he attributed this quality. "Well," he answered, "I think it is the village life, and if I may say so the village church," and added that it was with the men who came from towns that difficulties usually arose. He talked of books, the poets he cared for, and of Art. He looked at Signor's rendering of the Sphinx which I brought to show him, and he was moved by it —looking at it long and silently. He told me the story of the dusky king who desired to be buried seated upright on the summits of his kingdom, so that even in death he might look over the limitless expanse below him, and of his own anger when the skull of that king was offered to him as a trophy, and he discovered that the tomb had been desecrated. He set to work at once to make reparation to the people, to whom he gave a hundred head of cattle, that there might be sacrifice and reburial. "What a poet that man was," he said, and so I thought is Cecil Rhodes. Yet he spoke with unusual simplicity and directness, and reminded one of the English boy fresh from school. Signor had some little time before received a letter which had moved him profoundly. It was written by a stranger to tell him in the simplest language that in a dark hour of life in a grimy northern town a photograph of his picture of "Hope" had arrested attention at a moment of extreme crisis. The photograph had been bought with a few remaining shillings, and the message pondered, and so for one life the whole course of events had been changed. The letter concluded with these words: "I do not know you, nor have I ever seen the face of him who gave me my 'Hope,' but I thank God for the chance of that day when it came to me in my sore need." I read some of these simple words to Mr. Rhodes, and when I next looked up I saw in his moistened eyes how deeply they had touched him. Signor went with him afterwards to see the Memorial that was being made to commemorate that little heroic band—Wilson's force. Whilst we were there the father of one of the brave fellows came also to see the Memorial, and Mr. Rhodes went to speak to him. "Your boy died for his country," he said, "and now I want him to teach others to be ready to do the same." There was but little time for these sittings, as Mr. Rhodes was on the point of leaving for South Africa, but he managed to come three or four times. Once at half-past six he and Lord Grey arrived and stayed for breakfast. That morning, after the sitting was over, Signor took Mr. Rhodes into the garden to show him the "Physical Energy." He was visibly im-

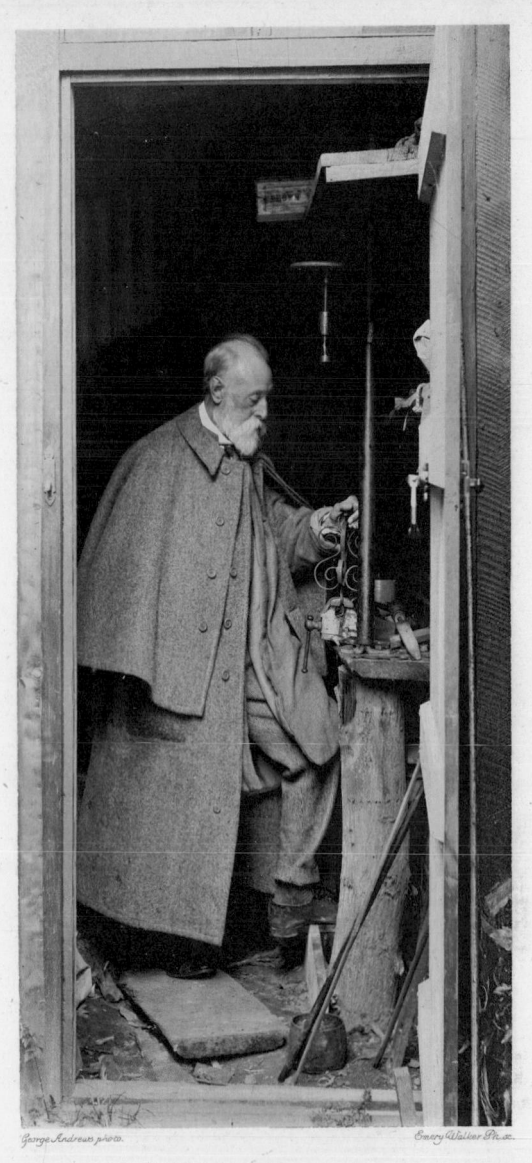

A Limnerslease workshop

pressed, and said : "That's what I should like to have to commemorate the completion of the Cape to Cairo railway. I would write on the base the names of the first subscribers, and the words, 'These people believed that this scheme was possible.'"

I possess a letter written by Mr. Rhodes a few days later—I believe these letters are not plentiful—and in this he writes : " I could not help just writing a line and thanking you and your husband. It was such a pleasure to come to you. Your home was quite different from anything I had come across in my rough life."

Alas, the portrait was left very incomplete, and my husband never allowed any one to see it. Nevertheless Mr. Lionel Cust prevailed against my hesitation later, when Signor was no longer here to refuse ; and it is now in the National Portrait Gallery. I have had letters from people who had known Mr. Rhodes and who said that, incomplete though it is, the true spirit is alive in the portrait. The enthusiasm Mr. Rhodes had shown for the "Physical Energy" induced Lord Grey after his death to ask Signor to allow a cast in bronze to be taken from the group, that it might be set up in the Matoppo Hills,[1] as the Rhodes Memorial ; and to this Signor replied :—

---

[1] This scheme had to be given up because of the difficulty of transit. It now forms part of the memorial to Mr. Rhodes near Cape Town.

GEORGE FREDERIC WATTS

"Limnerslease, Guildford,
"*April 5th*, 1902.

"Dear Lord Grey — The death of Mr. Rhodes has caused me, I will not say profound regret, but profound sorrow. I regard him at this present time as the last of great Englishmen of his type. My statue, intended as an emblem of the energy and outlook so peculiarly characteristic of him, shall be dedicated as you propose, if the model can be left, as I believe it may be, in a state which will not prevent me from completing it later, if I should have time and health. I feel somehow that its incompleteness has a pathetic appropriateness. It is only in this way that I can offer it, for I much feel the completed work belongs to the Government, as the Government offered to cast it and find a site. I did not feel I ought to accept the generous offer in the unfinished state of the work, but if I can ever finish it I shall look upon it as belonging to those gentlemen whether in or out of office. So if you will undertake to see your idea carried out, you shall have the model to be used for that purpose, the model still being mine. But not for money! the gift so far shall be my contribution, and up to that point my identification with a great personality; more so as I remember he expressed a wish to put the statue up at Bulawayo.

"I am sure you are deeply grieved by the death of your great friend and great man, for he was a great man even though making mistakes,

and perhaps to make mistakes. I believe Alfred himself would make mistakes in an age so full of complications as ours.—Very sincerely yours,
"G. F. WATTS."

The offer from the Government to cast and erect the statue, referred to by my husband in his letter to Lord Grey, was made (I think unofficially) this year, 1898. He was not able to accept the offer, for, as he wrote soon afterwards to a correspondent: "The unfinished and likely to be unfinished state of the work made me unwilling to profit by the generous offer of Lord Salisbury's government to cast it at the expense of the Treasury. It is still my hope and intention to complete the design."

It was due to Mr. Rhodes that in these later years Lord Grey became to Signor a valued friend, and this when older friends were being each year withdrawn from life.

The country was now mourning the loss of Mr. Gladstone. In our Gallery the quiet steadfast eyes looked out at us as they looked upon his painter half a century ago in the studio where no conflict was discussed more recent than that around Troy. To honour the dead that day, a little sheet of paper lay under the portrait, and in Signor's handwriting the words:

> Whatever record leap to light
> He never shall be shamed.

They were almost the first words he had used on hearing of Mr. Gladstone's death. The portrait went almost immediately to its destination in the National Portrait Gallery.

Quickly following on this loss, the world of art and his numberless devoted friends suffered yet again in the sudden death of Sir Edward Burne-Jones. We had been at Brighton for a few days, and were returning to London, when at the station the fatal news was flaunted on every placard.

What a wealth of sympathy, tender or wise or humorous, went with those words from Signor's life, only those who knew them both in their inner life could know. Sir Edward wrote to him in 1881 : " How deep I am in your debt for loving friendship now this many a year —but I do give you real love back too." And a few weeks after her great loss Lady Burne-Jones wrote to Signor : " You never failed him from the first."

These years were on the whole too uneventful in their peace to leave much to record except of the thoughts Signor gave me, the books we read, and the work he accomplished ; or of the friends who came to see him, bringing to him pleasant variety.

"Our life is a calm one, not humdrum," he said ; "that it can never be with us"; and his wish, " to live—well !—perhaps twenty years more," as he expressed it, was the sign of a new vigour acquired through his life in the country. He was surrounded by beautiful nature, and nothing in nature could ever be stale to him, as he said when telling me that the night before he had looked out at the moon and stars with a feeling that he was being shown them for the first time. With his mind full of thoughts of "the great whole in which we like molecules of the blood rush round one little hour, and return to the great Heart to be renewed again and again," he had a spring of new life for ever rising in his own heart and mind. He was always so glad when the day of work began, and the duty of a night's rest had been got over. I often wondered at the quiet joy that seemed then to come to him; but as the old Egyptian poet said, "That transporteth man to God even the love of the work that he accomplisheth." "A new day," Signor said one early morning, "let us begin our chant of praise for it and see how well we can praise." On one cold December morning at five o'clock he awoke to say, "Oh, I am so glad the night is passed." "Why?" I asked, seeing that he had slept like a child. "Because I want to get to my work," he answered, and then, if ever, I understood the life and hope there is in all creative work. Nearing eighty, frail and delicate as he was, neither creature comforts nor even necessary rest were grateful to him when compared with this work, that in its nature partook of the creative and of the eternal.

One day when Andrew Hichens sat beside him while he rested in his niche, they talked of *Paradise Lost* and its first small market value; and Signor quoted a contemporary of Milton's who wrote, "The old blind school-master hath writ a book, which, if it hath not the merit of length, it hath none other," and added that now, perhaps, it was the second book of the world. "It shows," he went on, "that the most unreal, the spiritual portion of man, is the most real and lasting." Andrew answered, "Yes, imagination is more abiding than fact." "And why?" Signor continued, "because the spiritual activities of the mind are the heritage of all nations and of all times. The active public life of the moment appears to be the important one. The Wars of the Roses were in their day all-important; what are they now to England, or the rest of the world? only an episode in history, and interesting so far as they helped or hindered the expression of mind in its various ways: this ought never to be lost sight of." And he did not lose sight of it. Whatever doubts he may have had about the ultimate place his work should be given, of the dignity of his calling and of his aims he was absolutely certain. "There seems to be in human effort a part that is progressive and transient, and another that is stationary and eternal,"[1] are words he would have answered to with his whole being.

The true question to ask is this, "Has it helped any human soul?"—Signor's own words —and he continued: "It is said of literature, but is equally applicable to art. I think the great sculptor of the Parthenon must have done so.

[1] *The Rise of the Greek Epic.* By Professor Gilbert Murray. 1907.

GEORGE FREDERIC WATTS

Gothic cathedrals certainly have. Yet these which conferred actual and immortal life were, to the masses of the nation intent upon eating, drinking, fighting, and getting rich, but vague and visionary complements to the more material and important considerations of everyday life.

"Paradox as it may seem to be, it is safe to assert that the most visionary manifestations of human activity have ever proved to be the most solidly based, and are the most permanent."

During this winter, when our specially chosen books took us into the thought of the ancient races of the world, I found that to Signor the idea of the rebirth of the soul—even many times—through the ages was one very acceptable to his mind. He thought it consonant with the highest conception of omnipotence, and a theory into which retribution following upon sin might fall, without imputing to the Almighty qualities which to human wisdom seem incompatible with the title of the All-loving. When speaking of this theory of rebirth he often said that he had a dim intuitive feeling that in some former existence he had been a Greek.

When trying to find any racial characteristic in his temperament and his work, these words of his, though spoken with no great seriousness, may be taken into account. The bias of sentiment and association would have inclined me to find in him the characteristics of the Celt, but I think that he knew himself better. The imagination that produced chaos passing to cosmos is not that of the Celt, which, as I understand it, is a fine fancy that takes it to the borderland where fairy vision and practical fact become confused as in a dream. The insight into nature inclines it more to reveal the weird, where the "little people" become visible.

In art, whilst in Signor's work the absence of ornamentation is a marked feature, in Celtic art—so far as it can be judged from efforts too early merged in Gothic art to be justly placed by the side of any art that has attained to full flower—the most striking feature is the elaboration of intricate patterns, very emotional, and most interesting as telling a story in symbols.

Matthew Arnold, when writing of the Celtic genius, affirms that the Celt is without what he calls "the eternal conditions" necessary for success, which are "balance, measure, and patience." "The Greek," he continues elsewhere, "has the same perceptive emotional temperament, but he adds to this temperament the sense of measure." Lord Holland, to whom Signor had once remarked that probably, if we knew it, each one of us was mad upon some point, told him that he was quite the most sane person of all his acquaintance! The endeavour to see the true proportion of things was the habit of his mind, and characteristic of his view on any subject, excepting always where he had to judge of himself—there perhaps the sense of measure did fail him! In the matter of patience and persistency, however, these qualities he did allow that he possessed. "The only quality," he once said, "I can look back upon and say that I had, to save me from being nothing at all, is persistency: I never faltered." And to Mrs. Henry Ady he said, "The fitful accomplish nothing. All I have attained to is the result of strenuous and persistent effort now for over sixty-eight years."

Professor Gilbert Murray writes of the Greeks that "the idea of service to the community was more deeply rooted in them than in us, and that they asked of their poets first of all this question: 'Does he help to make men better? Does he make life a better thing?'" These were the questions that Signor asked himself daily and hourly. I remember how pleased he was when Verestchagin agreed heartily with his aphorism, "Art should be used to make men better."

"Every day that I live I grow to care less and less for pictorial excellence. In fact, if I could just get rid of technical imperfections, which necessarily are a hindrance to the utterance of my idea, and which make it, so to speak, disagreeable in the utterance, I should be content."

He wondered if his work ought to be called distinctly English, and wrote: "With ten times my ability to express my ideas and manifest my objects, I could not but fail, because I aim at qualities of all least likely to be sympathised with in modern times and northern climates—grandeur of form and dignity of line."

GEORGE FREDERIC WATTS

It has been said that the Celt never forgives; now the injunction to forgive seventy times seven was to Signor the supreme commandment. He told me that it had once happened to him to be very angry with some one person, and to feel so for some time; and then, thinking over it one day, he had come to see that it would be better to put away all the angry feelings, and to try to believe that circumstances had been too strong; and with that he made a great effort to conquer himself, and after doing so he felt a strange influence like something celestial passing over him, as if a higher power had laid his hand upon his head. It was something he had never known before or since—a glimpse of the divine. I believe this happened to him in early life.

His precepts were: " Give people, even when you have much reason to think badly of them, the benefit of the doubt. We find it difficult to know ourselves, how can we judge others?" He had, in fact, never in his life repeated anything that he had been told that could prejudice or injure any one's character. His old friend, Miss Duff Gordon, once bore testimony to that. She was told something discreditable of some one, and Signor was quoted as having mentioned it. "That I won't believe. Watts never repeats anything that is damaging of any one." He made a habit of weighing the variable and apparently contradictory essences of individual character, saying that they were accounted for by remembering temperament, heredity, circumstances, and habit, all of them acting in various ways upon the original basis of character, which is chiefly affected by temperament. Temperament, he thought, affected actions far more than intellect did. "A man may think he believes all sorts of doctrines, and may live as greater than his creed, or *vice versa*." "On temperament depend our opinions and our actions."

"I believe," he said, "that even a good thought does not die as it passes through the mind. I like to think it has existence somewhere, and goes on for ever. How much more important does it become that we should teach ourselves to be generous, large, and charitable."

His sense of order was unusually strong, considering that the artistic gift so often carries with it a great disregard of this. He liked to have a great care in small matters, saying: "It is so bad for our moral nature to have ragged ends." This delicate care apparently belonged to the same order of things as did his silverpoint drawings. He once got a daub of ultramarine upon his coat sleeve, and though the coat was known by the name of "Squalid"—it was so ancient—it had never had such a thing happen to it before. Looking down upon the blue stain, he said dejectedly, "I feel as if I had done something that has degraded me as an artist." His servants were often reminded that he required to have things done very precisely, sometimes adding this little counsel of perfection: "Remember the daisies!"—pointing out that one of the smallest and commonest works of nature was thus exquisitely finished; therefore the smallest things in life should neither be ignored nor slurred over.

To the Greek mind, so I have read, "the good and the beautiful were one and the same thing; and that is the first and the last word of the Greek ideal."[1] This ideal was certainly Signor's. And to him the word "good" conveyed a signification of unusual value. It so happened that once during the last months of his life an appreciation of his work was being read to him which, while placing the artist extraordinarily high, was so free from any hint of adulation that it gave pleasure anyhow to the reader, who paused for a minute and, glancing from these heights of appreciation back to early days when he must have been quite unrecognised, said to him: "Some of your friends of that time would have been surprised if they had read this. I daresay you were to many of them just a good, kind man," using the word "good" rather slightingly, in the sense of a mere easy habit of good nature; and was rebuked for this by the quick answer, with a look and gesture that made the words sound like a fervent prayer, "Oh! I hope I was that." With him to be "good" was supreme, and the first and last aspiration of his daily life. The humblest duty or the highest range of art were as one to him; each a part of a great whole, of which some day it

[1] *The Greek View of Life.* G. Lowes Dickinson, M.A.

might be written, "And God saw that it was good."

During the summer of 1898 Signor had undertaken a work the size of which might indeed have daunted a man bearing fewer years than his, for he was now in his eighty-second year. He had heard from Lord Brownlow, the Lord-Lieutenant of Lincolnshire, that the county intended to put up a statue to Tennyson. As he had known the poet so well, and had visibly before his eyes the grand figure of his friend, with its " monumental aspect," which he thought might possibly be unknown to sculptors of a younger generation, he asked Lord Brownlow if he might be allowed to make this statue, not as a commission, but offering his work, if the county undertook the expense of casting. This was agreed upon, and he made a small model in wax for approval by Lord Brownlow and the committee.

To enable him to carry this out, he arranged with Andrew Hichens for the purchase of a small farm-house close to our gate, where a fine old barn was available for such work. The colossal figure was built upon a trolley, and could therefore be brought out of doors with ease. The central idea was the poet's regard of nature, pondering over the root and stem of a little flower. The dog, awaiting the conclusion of the long pause for thought, sits patiently looking up into his master's face. "It is," Signor said to Canon Rawnsley, "the lesson of the flower in the crannied wall repeated, but it needs repetition." The statue was built up in *gesso*, but unfortunately the fundamental mistake of a shallow base gave a great deal of trouble; the first figure was broken up, and a new beginning had to be made.

The purchase of the barn, with its picturesque roofs, gave an opportunity for turning what had been for centuries a cattle-yard into a garden— a very charming cloistered garden; and there Signor often went in the intervals for rest.

A new interest had grown up for us both in the last two years, the building of a chapel for the new village burial-ground, his gift to Compton. He did not design it, but suggested that, if we proposed to hold a class, the people of Compton might like to come to it and be taught to make simple patterns to decorate the walls; so that by this means a special and personal interest in the new graveyard would be acquired by the workers.

This year, on a most glorious day—the first of July—the Bishop of Winchester (the present Archbishop of Canterbury) consecrated the ground and chapel, Signor walking in the procession in his doctor's robes. The class, begun entirely for pleasure, developed later into a village industry for terra-cotta modelling. The whole was undertaken, and is continued, on account of his great interest in the arts and crafts of the country, and his belief that we must have great craftsmen before we can have a national art. I remember that as we left the

Alexander Fraser Tytler, photo.
Emery Walker Ph. sc.

In the Barn Garden, Limnerslease

door of the New Gallery, after visiting the first exhibition of the new Society of Arts and Crafts, he said, "Well, I come away feeling as I never do from our summer exhibition of pictures, that these men are real artists."

With many interests and many friends, he kept perpetual youth in heart and mind. On one of the latest birthdays, Lady Wenlock wrote to him: "I send a little book that I discovered might be new to you when I had that happy visit to your Paradise of a home. I wonder if you remember that I mentioned the *Livre d'Or*? and I could not help quoting to you one passage: '*Combien de temps reste-t-on jeune?*' '*Tant qu'on est aimé*,' which seems written for Signor the beloved." They had been friends for many years, and any one who has had the privilege of knowing her will understand that she held a special place with him.

CHAPTER XIX

THE World is a workshop in which a wonderful fabric is being carried on, the progress of humanity.

G. F. WATTS.

CHAPTER XIX

SIGNOR had been very hard at work both upon the statue of Tennyson and in his painting-studio working on the "Court of Death" and on "Love Triumphant," and was feeling very tired, when suddenly he turned to me and, to my delighted ears, proposed that we should go to Scotland this summer. "Why should I not be your brother's tenant at Dalcrombie Lodge?" he asked.

The proposition was made by telegram and accepted by telegram. "Great joy here," were the words from the old home. Signor had never crossed the Tweed—I had never had any hope he would, when suddenly this wish of his sprang into existence, and early in July we went. We were all praying for brilliant sunshine to greet his eyes when he awoke in the Highlands on the journey north, and that Scotland would greet him radiantly. But she did not. She rolled herself in a white sheet of mist, and, for the first twelve hours, he saw nothing beyond an arm's length. She reserved her beauty for the next day, when he woke in the home of my childhood on a perfectly radiant morning. By eight o'clock we were standing on the shore of Loch Ness, looking down its full length, on a morning that we called Scotland's reward for wet days. The first impression of those blue hills and drifting veils of moisture he afterwards painted; and he knew then what I had meant when I had told him of the colour of our Scotch hills, different from but quite as beautiful as any in the Greek islands. "You see colour in Scotland that is not to be matched in any other part of the world," Sir Frederic Leighton (who was no Scot) once said, when Signor had laughed at my Scottish prejudices.

Two days later we drove up to the higher ground where, amid moor and lochs, the little lodge we had taken was ready to receive us. A shelter, brought for the purpose of serving as an outdoor room and studio, was soon set up. It could be easily turned against any wind that blew, and there he almost lived, and, from its open doors, painted many landscapes always with the same conscientious care as ever. On the very first canvas to come upon his easel he painted a rendering of Scotland as he first saw her, shimmering in blue and silver, when he looked down the full length of her longest loch.

He had not been at Dalcrombie many days before a new phase of life opened. He tramped across moors, was rowed about on a little loch covered with rocking water-lilies; he had picnics with young people beside brown rivers, and sat out to watch the sun go down without fear of chills.

Mr. Evelyn Heseltine had his yacht on Loch Ness, and more than once Signor was tempted to make expeditions on the *Leda* ; and the kind hosts anchored here and there that we might land and show him other Highland glens and brown rivers with their falls.

It was a remarkably fine summer, and if now and again it rained, " it was just to varnish the picture," our painter declared. Certainly an hour or two of rain steeped the landscape in fresh colour. It was quite a new life for him, and we made many expeditions. One was very memorable. The oldest crofter on the place, in his ninety-second year, had confided to my brother that before he died he would like to go just once more to the top of " dear Dunyardil," and my brother was bent on getting Signor up to this high point also. It is a beacon-hill, one of a chain that traverses Scotland, and upon which the Fiery Cross once blazed from south to north.

We had a glorious day, and after luncheon in a cool green glade, the party, numbering twenty, set forth single-file up the narrow track of the ascent. Signor, the old crofter, and another of the party were mounted. Signor's great black horse, borrowed from a farm near, looked like a war-horse of the Middle Ages, and the riders helped to make the string of pilgrims through the deep fern look all the more picturesque.

GEORGE FREDERIC WATTS

The rock holds its bare glittering head "in the illimitable air," and wild goats live in its caves and hollows; on one side it drops steeply into the brown river at its foot. It is connected with the Cuchulain Saga by the story of "The three Sons of Usnach," Deirdre, the wife of the eldest brother Naoise, having left her name to the rock, "Hill of Dearduil," while Naoise in all probability became Loch Ness.[1] The old crofter, James Gow, told us that day that the rock was once the castle of a princess. When the three sons went back to the false king and to death in Ireland, Deirdre, having foretold their doom, sang her lament, weeping as she looked back on Scotland.

> Beloved is the land—that yonder land
> Albain full of woods, full of lochs,
> Sore is my heart to be leaving thee;
> But I follow Naoise.

Some forty feet from the top the riders dismounted, and the three horses were left in a patch of green mountain grass, which I remember was starred with the largest white flowers of the Grass of Parnassus I had ever found.

There was a scramble to get to the top, but the view there was magnificent. The old crofter felt he was one step nearer heaven. He took off his blue bonnet, and reverently bent his head, and in beautiful-sounding Gaelic answered

[1] "The old reciters spoke irregularly. Some said 'Loch Naois' with an open sound, and some said 'Loch Nĭs, Nĭs' with a close sound."—Notes on *Deirdre*, by Alexander Carmichael.

to nature's call to prayer. Then he asked for my brother's two children, and gave them a Gaelic blessing.

There were many beautiful days to remember, and an afterglow we called the "Twilight of the Gods." Some days after seeing this twilight at half-past ten at night, Signor set himself patiently to paint the rocky sides of the hills when staring out in the sharp light and shade of midday. I said, "But the night you saw that afterglow there was nothing visible, it was that simplicity which made them loom up so grandly, so solemnly." "Yes," he said, "I know that, but it was *there*, and, however much I may mystify it later, the anatomy must be all there. To give the sense of something more that one does not see, is the key of real impressionism. The modern impressionists forget that. They give you an empty effect with no hint of something beyond.

"Depend upon it, nature's system of evolution produces the best work, it is the opposite of the impressionist. You may lose something at times, but so does nature."

In the little shelter, not more than seven feet square, he was happy with his work, and made many studies of hill and moor. He also carried forward a picture of some size he called "In the Highlands"—a young girl with her lap full of flowers, which was more or less a portrait of our child Lily. But he allowed himself more leisure for enjoyment than he had had for years, and was astonished at his own vigour. He liked to see the strong Highlanders about, and watched with pleasure a Highland lassie stride across the moor, notwithstanding that she brought a telegram to remind him of the existence of London with its streets and slums. Then in contrast his thoughts turned upon the bareness of human habitation on these wild hills, which, for numberless reasons, were ceasing to keep alive the best race of men and women—as hillsmen are well known to be in every country of the world—and he was grieved.

We hoped that this time spent among the hills would have added years to his life, but in the end we made one bad mistake; we stayed on longer than was first intended, and the weather changed. We went down to a lower level, to another lodge, for a visit of two nights, and Signor caught cold and developed pneumonia. Not till the beginning of November was he able to be moved to Limnerslease.

Meantime the war in South Africa broke out, and while our Highland soldiers were leaving Inverness-shire in high spirits, promising to be back in a few weeks, Signor, from his sick-bed, seemed to have a sort of prophetic insight. "It is going to be a dreadful war," he said, and, like a seer of old, he added, " I see blood, blood, blood everywhere "—and all through his illness he begged that the subject should not be mentioned.

The dear old crofter, hearing he was seriously ill, made a walk of eight miles to inquire for him, and "The Lord be the doctor wi' you," was his benediction to me. As Signor became convalescent, he began to take much interest in the conflict. The ready sacrifice, and the patriotism called out, naturally appealed to him. Like Mr. Ruskin he felt the horrors of war had a redeeming grandeur that an inglorious peace was without. He wished to trace for himself the larger forces behind the men of the moment who appeared to bear the responsibility of it. On this subject he said, "They might just as well say when they look at the clock, that the hands made the hour." "The poet," he thought, "too often ignores the condition of conflict and its necessity, especially that state of effervescence amongst men which leads to war. Wars can never cease, because men are driven to it periodically by a force they cannot control, and which is inherent in nature. They will recur and recur again, unless co-operation brings about a revolution in the natural character of the human being."

The law of conflict, he perceived, was actively at work in the production and development of conscience. "Conflict for self-preservation in the savage becomes in the process of development conflict against self,—the self-abnegation of the saint."

This war seemed to rouse in him the martial patriotism he had shown in 1859. He wrote to a civilian who had volunteered: "I trust you will come back safe with the splendid experience of the battlefield, compared with which every other experience must be tame. Every man who volunteers is to be envied."

When, some time before the war broke out, he had spoken of the state of affairs in the country to Lord Grey, he had said that England wanted a good squeeze to make her think—and to him at this time he wrote :—

"Limnerslease, Guildford,
"15th Dec. 1899.

"Dear Lord Grey—I didn't want the squeeze to be quite so close ; in what shape do you think it will leave us ? I will not quote the words of Francis the First after the battle of Pavia, but I think a good deal has been lost, although the conduct of the troops has been beyond praise. I want more blue jackets for the future, and have been advocating the establishing of a number of training schools all round the coast, the more the better, in which all the children of the slums we can get hold of may be taught judiciously and pleasantly (this would want good looking after) to be not only sailors but active intelligent citizens, capable on any emergency. It is evident that every man among the Boers is capable at short notice of being turned into an efficient soldier ; so it was with us in the Middle Ages. I would have had these ships so built that they could readily be strengthened into serviceable little war-ships, carrying perhaps one serviceable gun. I think an immense reserve, which could become at any notice soldiers or sailors or both, would be better worth paying for than nearly two millions of paupers and criminals; many so taught would probably go to the Colonies, some into the Merchant Service (which we might subsidise, and which is now mann'd almost entirely by aliens), and nearly all might be relied on to do good service in case of need; but it is not our habit to look into the future, and Germany will soon be mistress, I believe, of all.

"What a grand fellow was Hubert Harvey;[1] and how delightful in the midst of all to think not a few in the rank and file are cut out on the same plan; our soldiers—officers and men—have been magnificent.

"I don't know whether you will be able to read this scribble; I write in bed and under some difficulties.—Very sincerely yours,

"G. F. WATTS."

He saw that England's defences should be on the sea, and every effort and every expenditure should be made and borne for that object. I find in a note made by him, probably in answer to some query in a letter, that he says:—

"I think the character of my designs must prove an opinion adverse to war. It is therefore not necessary for me to attempt expression in words, nevertheless I confess to feeling that nothing will put an end to it—even approximately—but exhaustion. The story of humanity since the beginning has been written with letters of

[1] *Hubert Harvey, Student and Imperialist.* By Earl Grey. 1899.

blood, that of religion the most stained, perhaps, of all.

"Wars are dreadful, but less demoralising than much that seems to be inevitable in the direction taken by natural activity in times of peace. We may deceive ourselves in thinking we are spreading civilisation by war, but the deception is less degrading than the belief in money-grubbing, gambling, and drunkenness, as the best way of spending existence. The Temple of Mammon, the Turf, and the gin-shop will do more to bring about the downfall of a nation than any amount of fighting. It seems to me apparent that man must be in conflict with his fellow-men, but this conflict need not be cruel, his conflict with nature is not so. It should be less a fight, one against another, than a generous emulation as to which should do better than the other, and universal peace must not be supposed to be absence of universal struggle.

"The attainment and dread of the scientific ideas which for thousands of years have haunted the mind of man, may some day take a concrete form, and people may cease to form antagonistic interests, and, instead, combine in co-operation to build the greatest universal empire possible. Probably when war shall have become too disastrous and exterminating to be contemplated by humanity, it may cease. Aggrandisement by the sword and gold cannot be the last word of the human race. It is not success in arms, or commerce, arts or science, or in the acquirement

GEORGE FREDERIC WATTS

of wealth that England should find her gratification. But in this, that she should know herself the pioneer of the future.

"As a nation with many faults she is well constituted to take a foremost part, strong in her sense of justice and freedom. If not doing right, certainly uneasy under sense of doing wrong. On the whole, rather prompted to protect than oppress. The seeds of growth and decay are alike in the nation's core. No nation living nobly and greatly has ever suffered destruction. It is internal rottenness that prepares for its extinction. This should be watched, as it does not always show itself externally. When we have finished our appointed work, or have proved ourselves unfit for doing it, we shall follow the fate of all that has gone before, and, it may be added, of all that is to come after."

Signor put some of his thoughts together in a paper for the *Nineteenth Century and Afterwards*, entitled "Our Race as Pioneers," in which he enlarged upon the theme that great social and political movements are the outcome of circumstances over which individuals, and even communities, seem to have little control. They are only instrumental in shaping events.

While war in South Africa was still waged, General Baden-Powell was ordered home on sick-leave, and Signor was able to carry out his wish, to present to Charterhouse School a portrait of this distinguished Carthusian. The Head Master,

Dr. Rendall, wrote to General Baden-Powell to mention the matter, and accordingly the promise of a visit in October was made. A telegram one afternoon announced that he would arrive about three o'clock, and there was no time lost, Signor set to work at once with great earnestness, and went on till the light of an October day had failed. Next morning there was time for another sitting, and I heard General Baden-Powell say, when looking at his own likeness, "It has more in it than I know of in myself!" Unluckily for the painter the General's time in England was unexpectedly shortened and there were no more sittings.

The portrait was given to Charterhouse on February 23, 1902, and later I received a letter from General Baden-Powell at Johannesburg, to say he had heard from Dr. Rendall that the portrait was a success. He wrote: "Mr. Watts is indeed wonderful to have made so effective a likeness in so short a sitting. I feel most guilty of having failed to help him as I ought to have done. I had so fully intended coming again to Limnerslease to sit, before leaving England; but my release from sick-leave was unexpectedly ante-dated, and I rushed off by the first available ship the same week that I got the permission: and now here I am back at my work, which takes up every minute of my time, but at the same time is of absorbing interest, and shows progress every day. In the intervals between difficult questions or extra hard work, I relieve my mind by modelling in clay; it is a delightful relaxation. And then my mind often and often wanders back to the delightful peep I had of a beautiful home life, which I enjoyed at your house. How I envy every bit of it! But I suppose when one has work to do one must carry it through, though it takes one's best years." I wrote at the time that our delightful guest seemed perfectly happy among paints, gesso and clay. He left after exactly twenty-four hours, for Wales, and expected to pick up a post of seventy letters on his way through London. At that moment this was the average amount of letters received by him during a day.

Signor liked to speak of the pleasure that General Baden-Powell's earnestness, and the direction of his aims, had given to him. It is certain that had he lived to see the founding of the organisation of Boy Scouts with its ideals, by Sir Robert Baden-Powell, he would have welcomed it with enthusiasm, as probably the most hopeful movement of the century.

Meanwhile the work went on with the same enthusiasm and the same desire to do it well. "Mary and I find our days only look in upon us to nod and say good-bye," he wrote to Lady Burne-Jones. His birthday in 1902 was near. "Eighty-five," he said to me, with a bright look of surprise, "a wonder to myself who have always been so frail. Certainly these last years I have been better in health." To him for this birthday Lord Rosebery wrote: "Life with you mellows, does not decay, so I wish you a long lease."

The list of pictures begun and completed during these late years is a long one. Among these is one he named "The Sower of the Systems." It was an attempt made to paint an unpaintable subject. In a scheme of deep-blue colour, the vision is of a figure impelled rapidly forward, while stars, suns, and planets fly from hands that scatter them as seeds are scattered. With this picture perhaps more in his mind than any other, he wrote: "My attempts at giving utterance and form to my ideas, are like the child's design, who, being asked by his little sister to draw God, made a great number of circular scribbles, and putting his paper on a soft surface, struck his pencil through the centre, making a great void. This was utterly absurd as a picture, but there was a greater idea in it than in Michael Angelo's old man with a long beard."

He worked upon the "Court of Death," surprised that the difficulties which formerly made completion seem impossible had disappeared. "I suppose I am now learning to know how to use my colours," he said.

On the second of March 1902 that work, designed first in the 'sixties, was lowered down to the floor of the studio, the canvas was removed from the stretcher, and, rolled and packed, the picture went to its destination at the National Gallery of British Art. Sir Charles Holroyd came himself to watch the removal. Next morning I asked Signor how the emptied studio affected him, and he answered: "One would think after working so long upon a picture of some importance that one would feel the loss of it, but I really did not; I forgot all about it, to tell you the truth. I want my work to be of some use, and when it is done and gone I don't think any more about it." If he thought at all he was usually depressed. For instance, when the telegram came from Thompson to say that the "Physical Energy" had left the studio for Parlanti's foundry, his first words were, "I confess I am ashamed of having to let it go, it seems like presumption." Signor had now lived under five sovereigns, and all through the longest British reign on record. King Edward VII. desired to honour in a special manner some of the men of mark of the Victorian era, and created a select order to be called the Order of Merit, and this honour was conferred upon Signor. The members were invited to a dinner at the Athenæum; to this he went for a quarter of an hour before dinner, but he did not stay to dine.

Of this honour he wrote to Lady Burne-Jones: "Thanks, dearest Georgie. I am sure you are pleased by anything that seems to be good for Mary or me. I suppose I should be pleased by this thing, and as it does give pleasure to my friends of course I am."

In his country studio the large picture of "Progress" was placed in the space which had been framed in for the "Court of Death." "I am now beginning to understand how to paint," he said one day; "it is very sad, but at the end of my life I have overcome difficulties that have hitherto crippled me. If there was any secret known to the old masters, it was that they used their paints as stiffly ground as mine are now." A copyist at the National Gallery told him that the Christ with Mary Magdalene by Titian, which he had lately copied and inspected without the glass, had paint half an inch thick upon it. Signor found the stiff colour gave him the clean edge he knew was so important and the characteristic of all great art. I asked him if the old masters did not perhaps get that sharpness more easily because of their use of resins—Venetian turpentine, for instance. He thought not, as Boscini records that Titian abhorred varnishes with his whole soul.

Before the year was out, Signor had found a great alleviation to the deafness that had long been a trial to him. It was an early adaptation of the electrical instrument for improving the power of hearing, on a principle now much further developed. The improvement in his case was marvellous. I could now read to him without raising my voice; he even heard when I read in quite a low tone. One day some months later, with the windows closed, he said to me, "I hear a thrush singing." Before this, as we walked in our wood and garden, he had deplored that no

G. F. Watts at work upon the statue of Lord Tennyson. August 1903.

sound of the birds' song could reach his ear or ever would again.

The idea which had been present to his mind, even before our marriage in 1886, that it would be well for him to give up Little Holland House, was gaining more and more acceptance with him each year. Now that he required summer weather for the work on the Tennyson statue at Limnerslease, we went less and less to London. He therefore decided to build a small picture gallery there. For this purpose he bought some three acres of ground, that the building might not be attached to the house, though easily reached by a five minutes' walk through our garden. Mr. Christopher Turnor, who had become a neighbour of ours, with whom Signor liked much to exchange thoughts upon the many and wide subjects of interest they had in common, undertook to design a picture gallery, as well as a hostel for the young fellows who came to work at the pottery.

In 1903, on February 23, his eighty-seventh birthday, Signor placed the corner-stone of this building. His great object was now to complete the statue of Tennyson. The work had taken far longer than he anticipated, and he knew it was due to Lord Brownlow and his committee that he should give them a definite promise that by a certain date the model would be in the hands of the bronze-founders. The day at last came, and very reluctantly, having worked up to the last moment, he allowed the men sent from Frome to begin the work of removal. Very carefully and slowly the great figure was lowered upon its back, laid upon a stretcher, and carted away. Signor saw it go with real suffering: "I think what it ought to have been," he said. Had it been the work of another he would have seen that the sculptor had certainly grasped the whole, and had just marked in the details that were necessary for the presentation of the "monumental" aspect and large and reverent mind. He would have been satisfied with a certain cosmic dignity of line which put it into harmony with the background of either a great mountain, or that of a great cathedral. All this was felt to be true when, in 1905, it was unveiled at Lincoln. Most probably if he had seen the figure in bronze he would have found out this, but he never did see it; and during the ten months of life left to him he constantly reproached himself for having allowed it to go to the foundry. Mr. Christopher Turnor[1] made a fine photograph of the sculptor hard at work on the morning before the statue left. He also designed and made a small model of a base, which he brought to Signor for approval; and the whole work is now well set in the green space by the cathedral, where, from one point of view, the three towers rise behind it, and from another the trees of the Deanery garden. Some months later Mr. Turnor put into writing a few of his recollections of Signor's

[1] The author of *Land Problems*.

conversations, and from these notes, which he kindly gave to me, I am allowed to quote the following : " Whatever subject was occupying his attention he dealt with in that comprehensive and broad-minded way that was so striking ; his conclusions were so convincingly true ; conclusions arrived at not so much from knowing what the opinions of the respective experts were or what they were doing, but rather the conclusions of a great intellect marshalling facts for himself and weighing their merits.

" In discussing the great problem of education, not only had he arrived at the same conclusion as Fröbel, Spencer, and Pestalozzi, but he came out with scientific and modern details of the true art of teaching, that could not have been better put by Dewey, the talented author of *School and Society*, yet Mr. Watts had not heard of that book, which later I gave to him. A great painter ! and more than any one endowed with that intense feeling of poetry, and music, and yet with a mind keenly scientific. What an unusual combination !

" When I talked to him about up-to-date scientific methods of agriculture, I found him not only better versed in the principles involved, but even in minute details of execution, than almost any landlord, politician, or farmer I have talked to."

CHAPTER XX

THE FLIGHT OF THE ONE TO THE ONE

Calm be the body for her in that hour, and the tumult of the flesh.

Yea, all that is about her calm; calm be the earth, the sea, the air, and let Heaven itself be still.

Then let her feel how into that silent heaven the Great Soul floweth in.

And so may man's soul be sure of vision, when suddenly she is sure of light: for this light is from Him and is He; and then surely shall one know His presence when like a god of old time He entereth into the House of one that calleth Him, and maketh it full of light.

And how may this thing be for us? Let all else go.

PLOTINUS.
(Translated by F. W. H. Myers.)

CHAPTER XX

I FOUND among Signor's papers the following lines, evidently part of a letter—I do not know to whom written, but the words well express the general tone of his thought on art; characteristically in the minor key with regard to its present position—characteristically in the major key with regard to his belief in its true functions. He wrote: "Standing as one does at my age upon the brink of that dark abyss, deep, unmeasured, and unplumbed, the everyday becomes more and more attenuated in its interest, excepting, to my mind, in as much as it is laying the foundations of the future. My whole desire is to do something for that, in the only way possible to me. The activity of the human mind was never so great, or spread over such an extent, as at present; but it has learnt to draw its inspiration from literature and science (especially the latter) to the abandonment, if not extinction, of appeal to mind and action, by those sensibilities that come under the head of taste, the possession, as far as we know, of man alone. This certainly in the case of the

Fine Arts—of painting, sculpture, and architecture—which now only owe their existence to the reflux wave of the past. I am speaking only of the greater manifestations, when art was the language of the greater thoughts, inspired by what was highest and greatest in the spirit of the age, and inspiring what was noblest and greatest. An endeavour to inspire by the same means now is perhaps futile; as futile as would be an endeavour to fix a reflection! But even a reflection or an echo may be worth something; if the future should, by the weariness that its very activity may bring about, incline to crave relief from the turmoil of seeking only for material advantages. Already there are indications of this in the ardent will to work, actuating and employing many so sympathetically and so nobly. This is the spirit I wish to appeal to, and which I should like you and those who are dissatisfied with the ordinary conditions of modern society to understand and find in my very sincere efforts after what my limited powers enable me only indistinctly to grasp."

There was no abatement of the zeal for work during the last year (1903-4). He had said, "The desire in me to paint landscape grows, I want to paint landscape more and more"; and from his studio window he painted the picture which he afterwards called "Green Summer." He worked upon it from time to time, for five or six years, and as we breakfasted there one morning during the last months, I realised how that familiar scene revealed itself anew to me on the canvas. He answered my thought by saying: "That is the result of going all over it again and again. If it could be done all at once with a dexterous swish of colour, you would not have anything that was not apparent at once. You get the breathing quality into it, that quality which is in fact our atmosphere, for beyond it there is no such thing as living and breathing for us." The dream landscape — literally painted from his dream, and which he called "Two Paths"—and quite five others besides, belong to this time. One morning I went in to find that in the early hours of the day Signor had taken up the canvas upon which in the late 'sixties he had laid in an outline of his "Endymion." The small version, so well known by reproductions, being sculpturesque and definite, he had decided to make this larger picture visionary and mystic, the moon goddess only luminously visible. When first I saw it I exclaimed in surprise, "Oh, Signor, what a dream for him to have!" and he answered with a half-regretful smile, "Yes, but it was only moonshine after all." Then there was a new landscape, quite unlike his usual work, all sky and cloud and struggling sunlight; there was the glowing "Progress," and the blue and gold "Fugue"—a picture that may be said to have a likeness to his own habitual mood, both glad and serious.

About a year before he had begun a picture

for which Lily stood. She had for fun one evening put on her head a big laurel wreath that had been sent to him for his birthday, and his first idea was to paint a sort of dryad. This autumn, when I was in London for a day, he called to Lily to come to the studio, and began to work hard upon this picture. On my return he told me he had something to surprise me, and indeed when we went to the studio I was surprised. For suddenly, in these few hours, the picture had become a true portrait, the wreath was gone, and instead of it her light garden hat was blown into graceful lines and curves about her head, and the eyes that now looked at me were hers. I could only say, "You are a wizard." And Lily told me he had been at work "quite furiously" all day. The portrait, completed later, was in the Academy exhibition of 1904 with her name, "Lilian," as a title.

After the Tennyson statue had gone, he went up to Little Holland House to try and complete the "Physical Energy" that had returned from the foundry. He had also, during many years, put occasional work upon a figure of Dawn. Long ago in the old Little Holland House he had worked out the same subject, and it was eventually cast in plaster, but he never felt satisfied with it. Of this, many years before, he had written: "I have great hopes of making something really good of 'Aurora.' When I call it 'Aurora' I mean a good deal more by it; I want the form to be in harmony with, and so

G. F. Watts at Limnerslease
November 1903
an instantaneous photograph

far expressive of, the awakening and unveiling of all that is great in resolve and perfect in hope ; the idea carried out in all the directions you will be able to imagine. Of course all this cannot be expressed, but, as I say, the form, by its power and spring, may be in harmony with the idea." Latterly he had been trying for something far more archaic, straight and flat in line like a ray of sunlight, and friends who saw it in that stage were satisfied that he had achieved a unique and beautiful thing. But something he was trying for eluded him, and feeling unhappy he cut the figure to pieces. Talking of this at Limnerslease the following spring he deeply regretted it : " I was a fool to change it, I cannot think what I was about," were his words. " I thought it was wrong, but if it looked right what did it matter? We think now-a-days that we must get our work to be mechanically exact, but that has nothing to do with it ; the quality of exactness is quite another element."

Through the last months Signor went on working with the old zeal. In 1903, on the last 21st day of June of which he was conscious, he went downstairs cheerfully to greet the dawn, saying, " This is the longest day ; I mean to work through it. Another day for work, and yet," he added, " one seems to do little more than desire ! Well, perhaps that is of some use after all ; it may be that we have to go on desiring the good as a miser desires gold." He had spent much time during these last years on a picture of sunrise, with which he seemed to wrestle, but with which he was never satisfied. "Ah, me," he said, "I have only such dim glimmerings. Shall I ever see the opening eyelids of the morn?"

Amongst his earliest works the "Aurora" is notable for its accomplishment, and in his latest years, with his heart still intent on carrying out a great dawn, either in sculpture or in painting, he continued to struggle to give expression to the vision in his mind.

Very often through the years we were together he had spoken of death quite calmly, and in this way: "We must remember the great White Angel, but it need not make us sad." I find in my journal this entry: "He looked at me yesterday when we spoke of one who had planned to go to Egypt but who had died. I said, 'He took another journey.' 'Yes, and a much better one,' he answered; 'I want you not to mind when the day comes for me to take that journey—it leads to better things.'" And again, when the author in whose book we were reading had described the blessed forgetfulness of sleep, and the painful awaking to anxiety, and I had said, "Yes, and how one longs to sleep again and forever!"—"And that comes sure enough," he answered, "and there will be nothing to shrink from except the pain of leaving those we love, and who will miss us, and that is mitigated if we know they will go on living and working for the right." The beautiful idea in which human life was compared to a candle, and the soul to a flame, the material consumed by it till at last it disappears into air, made him say one day: "That is really the reason why I wish to be cremated, or one of these. It proves how little of us is really material : we go into flame and air, and what is left is but a handful of ashes. I like the thought that the material is compelled to follow the spiritual. The older I grow the more I am aware that the only real existence is the spiritual"; and his words made me realise what the loosening from earth would be to him. " Ah, but, Signor," I said, " you will soon ask for a paint-brush when you get to the new life." "That I am sure I shall," he said, smiling.

During the last weeks at Limnerslease he talked of plans for the future, and decided that the moment the " Physical Energy" was completed, he should return there and take up life for the remaining years.

It so happened that in the previous autumn a change had occurred which had confirmed in his mind the advisability of leaving Kensington as soon as possible. His assistant, Thompson, associated with the sculpture work for twenty-four years, recognised that his health was failing, so much so that he and Mrs. Thompson, for long Signor's valued housekeeper, found that they could no longer take charge of the house in our absence. They went to their own house at Wandsworth, and there the active little man occupied himself all winter making the home complete for his wife; painting, papering, and carpentering, as all came easy to him. When everything was finished and in order, he spent one day in cleaning up his tools and putting them away; and that night he went to sleep, never to wake again. The news was a great sorrow and shock to my husband. "Oh, I *have* lost a friend!" he exclaimed; for it had been quite understood that when we returned in summer, Thompson would come back to work: but his condition was far more serious than he knew, and without a moment's pain the brave heart had ceased that night to beat.

Some days after this, feeling uneasy about Signor, I wrote to Sir Clifford Allbutt to ask him if he would fulfil his promise and come to see what he thought of him. He came at once, arriving at midnight as he had an important engagement in London that evening. The next morning he was long with Signor in the studio, and talked over matters with the local doctor. When he found me in the drawing-room his first words were: "I can see no sign of failure; his mind is as vigorous as ever, and he took a piece of charcoal, and used it at arm's length, to show me that his hand was as steady as it had ever been." And it was so; the signs were slight indeed, and nothing of failure was to be found in the work. The little soul running from out of the eternal deep to the shore of life, that he had named "Whence? Whither?" was

By himself Emery Walker Ph.sc.

George Frederick Watts O.M., R.A.
1904
(unfinished)

entirely painted this winter. After his pictures went to the exhibitions in April, upon a seven-foot canvas he designed and almost completed the painting called " Destiny," where again the child is found, but a little further up upon the shore of life ; and the great angel waits behind with an open book ready for life's record. He had been discussing the use of tempera for ground work in oil-painting with Mr. Kerr Lawson, and to try this method he made a study of his own head with a monochrome tempera, and over this painted in oil-colour that portrait of himself which, as a likeness, is the most perfect that exists. At the same time he designed a picture which was to have for title his motto, " The utmost for the highest."

When writing to Lady Wemyss in March, I find he said : " I got wrong on my last visit to town and have never been at all well since : I sometimes think my lease is pretty nearly at its end, but I go on working.

" I have sent for fun five pictures to the New Gallery, all worked upon till the last moment, and one begun this year. Also a portrait to the Academy, so I still work."

His mind had not lost anything of its lighter charm, that quality of light spontaneity which this record, dwelling more on the serious aspect, has kept too much out of view. This perhaps intentionally, because the charm, robbed of the swift change of expression in look and in intonation, is not to be conveyed in words.

GEORGE FREDERIC WATTS

Perhaps one example may be allowed because it belongs to the time when the weight of his eighty-seven years was upon him. Mr. Walter Earle was sitting beside his sofa and happened to tell him that in a bookseller's shop he had overheard a customer ask for a reproduction of "Mr. Watts's painting of 'Lot's Wife,'" at the same time pointing out a photograph of the picture "She shall be called Woman." Laughing heartily, Signor exclaimed, "Well! I wanted her to have plenty of salt." And again, though more gravely, he replied with the same readiness, when a friend had described somebody as one "who gave herself airs,"—"Ah!" he answered, "airs which are never graces!"

I also remember the amused exclamation, "I would not take a hundred dollars for that!" made by an American lady, who had described to Signor some fine mural designs as being grand in scale and noble in line, but carried out in the palest washes of colour; and he had replied, "Ah dear! playing the Pastoral Symphony on a jews' harp!"

As the days lengthened he was as hard upon himself as ever, beginning his day at dawn, often when the flesh urged against the spirit. To a protest of mine he answered hotly, "You are quite wrong, I know I *must* live in the light." He had finished a small version of the picture named "The All-pervading" for the little chapel, and it was placed there in April, as now the covering of the walls with gesso had been completed. He had not walked as far as the chapel for many months, but one day early in May, when my sister-in-law and I had gone there, we looked round and found he had followed us. He had not before realised what I had aspired to in the matter of this glorified wall-paper, and now he saw and liked what had been done, and spoke with his usual too generous appreciation; but I am glad forever that he saw it.

A few days later we went to London. He was fairly well, and glad to see many friends who came. The Diamond Jubilee of Doctor Joachim was celebrated by a presentation to him of his portrait painted by Mr. Sargent. There was a great concert at the Queen's Hall, where the picture was made the centre-piece on the platform, and Signor was able to be present. During an interlude he rose from his seat in the first row and went a few steps nearer to get a better view of the portrait. Some one in the audience started applause, and it became general. Signor, thinking that Professor Joachim had returned to the platform (which was not the case), stepped quickly back to his seat. We could never persuade him that it was he to whom the audience gave their greeting. He met numbers of friends that night whom he never saw again. We went back to Limnerslease for another fortnight, where he seemed quite well, and was as full of work as usual. He had always dreaded that a time might come when he should do bad work and not know it; but he was spared that enfeeblement, of which most certainly he would have been aware.

He returned again to London on May 25, and set to work at once upon the "Physical Energy." One considerable change was being made; the head of the rider was thrown further back, and his outlook was therefore towards a higher point of view. We paid many visits to the Academy, partly that he might examine each time the group exhibited there in bronze, before its despatch to South Africa. As he saw it there in the quadrangle of Burlington House, he was better satisfied than he had expected to be, and said that he knew now that the work at Little Holland House would soon be completed.

He toiled on earnestly, but the short time he required was shortened beyond his expectations. On June 4 his physician—Doctor Archibald Keightley—happened to come to see how he was. Signor was at work in his studio and said he was well, but for a slight touch of soreness in his throat. He went to his room earlier than usual that night, and never entered his studio again.

A few years before, speaking of some slight failure, he had said smiling, "A sign of change!" The look of light in his face compelled the answer "going sun-wise!" "Yes, sun-wise!" he said.

"I am glad I painted Death with that white

robe," he told me not very long before the last illness, "it makes it an angel, and I often catch a glint of that white garment behind my shoulder, and it seems to me to say 'I am not far off.'"

Nevertheless, during the greater part of his illness he would have chosen to live, and he was hopeful, as we were hopeful, until within a few days of the last. Then he became glad to go. Though devoted doctors and nurses did all that skill and care could do, the walls of the Dwelling-House of that ardent spirit grew thin and more thin. One morning he beckoned to us [1] to come nearer, and he tried to put into words a state of vision he had been in when he appeared to be neither sleeping nor waking. He had looked into the Book of Creation, and understood that the whole could be comprehended—made plain from that other point of view which was not our earthly one. "A glorious state," he called it, and we looked on the face of one who had at last seen "true being" when he said, "Now I see that great Book—I see that great Light."

On Friday, the first day of July, his pilgrimage on earth ended.

After the last visit paid to Signor by Mr. F. W. H. Myers he wrote these words: "If it be true that there is a spiritual world, wherein, even while still on earth, we veritably are living; if it be true that with man's growing knowledge his conviction of that unseen environment must

[1] Geraldine Liddell and myself.

for ever deepen;—then types of character must needs arise responsive to that revelation; there must be saints of a universal religion who shall answer to the welcoming Infinite with simplicity and calm. No man, perhaps, has filled this type more perfectly than the great painter who must soon, from a life's work on earth, pass to continue, with all readiness, his task elsewhere.

"When last I saw Mr. Watts among the symbolic pictures of his later years, he seemed to me to have become himself a sacred symbol; and I should scarcely have wondered, as I gazed on him, if he had vanished into air. His look, his words were simple; he stood as it were unconcernedly in both worlds, the one as present to him as the other.

"To the child-like intuition of Watts the great secret was, as the French phrase goes, *simple comme bonjour*. For such a man what we call death is reduced to a mere formality and by an opening of inner vision the immanent becomes the manifest of heaven."

T. M. Rooke, R.W.S. pinx. *Emery Walker Ph. sc.*

The Studio at Little Holland House, Melbury Road

INDEX

Abbey, Mrs. Edwin, *see* Mead, Miss M. G.
Abbey Leix, ii. 261
Abel, i. 258, 259
Aberdare, Lord (Henry Bruce), i. 125, 126, 179; ii. 45-47, 219, 254
    Letters to Watts, i. 247, 248; ii. 4
Academy, The, *see* Royal Academy
Achilles, ii. 74, 199, 211
Acland, Sir Henry, i. 136, 138, 140, 141; ii. 237
Activities of the mind, On, ii. 276, 277, 311
Adelaide Art Gallery, ii. 164, 167 *note*
Ady, Mrs. Henry, ii. 279
Æneas, i. 225
Agamemnon, ii. 199
Age, Unsympathetic, i. 277
Agnew, Sir William, ii. 192, 220
    Letters to, and from, Watts, ii. 105-109
Agriculture, ii. 307
Aïdé, Hamilton, ii. 65, 72
Aird, Mr., ii. 15
Airlie, Lady, ii. 8, 260
Aitchison, George, ii. 9, 85
Aix-les-Bains, ii. 118, 120, 122, 123, 124, 125, 133
Ajax, ii. 74
Alcibiades, i. 149
Alexander, Henry, ii. 49
Alexandria, ii. 73
Alford, Lady Marion, ii. 6, 8
Alfred, King, i. 76, 78-81, 87-89, 151
Alison, Charles, i. 165
Allbutt, Sir Clifford, ii. 163, 177, 194, 318
    Letter to Mrs. Watts, ii. 178-188
Allegory, On, i. 228
Alps, ii. 114, 126
Amateur work, ii. 176, 177
America, ii. 25, 26, 29, 33, 34, 36, 215

American intellect, ii. 32
American Stranger, Loan from, i. 47
America's relations with England, ii. 33, 34
Ancestry, On, i. 4, 5
Anchises, i. 225
Anderson, Miss Mary, Portrait of, by Watts, ii. 131, 132
Andrews, Mr. and Mrs., ii. 159
Angelico, i. 95
Anglo-Saxon mind, i. 161
Apollo, i. 79
Architecture, i. 184, 213, 214, 215, 250; ii. 37, 79, 312
Ariosto, i. 64
Aristides, i. 77
Armenian peasants, ii. 75
Armitage, Edward, i. 42, 44, 45, 87, 231, 232
Armour, i. 53
Armstrong, Mr., ii. 48
Arno in flood, i. 52, 53
Arnold, Matthew, ii. 117, 118, 244, 278
Art, i. 91, 92, 99, 135, 236; ii. 311
    Ancient, i. 237
    Belonging to region of thought, ii. 262
    Carelessness about, ii. 8
    Celtic, ii. 278
    Contemplation of, i. 60
    Egyptian, ii. 66, 69, 94
    English, i. 6, 182, 184, 217
    Essentials of, i. 99, 315
    Fertilises the mind, i. 239
    French, ii. 31, 32
    French view of, i. 314, 315
    Functions of, ii. 36, 37, 311
    Future of, ii. 311, 312
    Gothic, ii. 278
    Great, Characteristics of, ii. 94
    Greatness of, ii. 248
    Greek, ii. 25, 79, 80, 81, 94, 138
    Highest expression in, ii. 174-176

Art (contd.)—
  Importance of, i. 135, 223, 224
  Influence of, i. 284
  Influence on children, ii. 230
    „   „   nation, ii. 69
  Intellectual intention of, ii. 31
  Interpreter of Nature, ii. 36, 44
  Italian, i. 113; *see also* Masters
  Language, A, i. 286; ii. 213
  Language of great thoughts, ii. 312
  Life of, ii. 6
  Limits of, ii. 175
  Living, ii. 2
  Love of, i. 120
  Material view of, ii. 36
  Mediæval, ii. 94
  Morals of, ii. 39-43
  Mission of, ii. 213
  Object to make men better, ii. 279
  Oneness of, ii. 80, 211
  Principles of, i. 239
  Professional, ii. 176
  Religious, i. 279, 307; ii. 174, 256
  Servant of religion, i. 194
  Standards of, ii. 186
  Symbolism of, ii. 130
  Training in, i. 18, 19, 99, 100, 137, 213-217, 239, 320, 321; ii. 40, 41
  Transmission of, i. 238
  Truthfulness of, i. 92-94
  Value of, i. 249
  Value in teaching, ii. 5, 263
  Value to a nation, ii. 215
  Venetian, i. 63, 144, 148; ii. 214
  Wide range of, ii. 32
Art Congress, ii. 151
Artevelde, Philip van, i. 205
Artist, The, a prophet, ii. 174
Artistic genius, i. 60
Artists' aims, influence, and work, i. 40, 84, 134, 204; ii. 44, 174-176, 214, 215, 235, 236
Artist's calling, Dignity of, ii. 276
Artists' Corps, i. 197
Artists' exclusiveness, i. 250
Artists' Orphan Fund, i. 297
Arts and Crafts Society, ii. 259, 285
Arundel Marbles, i. 237
Ashmolean Museum, i. 238
Asia Minor, i. 163
Aspirations, i. 312, 319
Assouan, ii. 68, 71
Assyria, i. 104
Athene, i. 15
Athens, i. 164; ii. 73, 78-82, 144

Athens, National Museum, ii. 78
Attila, ii. 171
Aumale, Duc d', i. 186, 189
  Letter, i. 189, 190
Austen, Jane, her influence on Watts, i. 15
Avignon, i. 45, 143, 274

Bach, ii. 56, 261
Bacon, Francis, Epigram by, ii. 52
Baden-Powell, General Sir Robert, ii. 299-301
  Letter to Watts, ii. 300, 301
  Portrait of, by Watts, ii. 299, 300
Bagshaw, Mr., Portrait of children, i. 35
Balfour, Right Hon. Arthur, ii. 250
Ball in Florence, i. 53, 69
Bargello, i. 55
Barlow, Thomas O., i. 199, 262
Barnett, Canon and Mrs., ii. 99
Baron, Villa, ii. 113, 117
Barrington, Mrs., i. 291, 329; ii. 28, 103, 106
Basaiti, ii. 105
Bath, Marchioness of, ii. 173
  Portrait of, by Watts, i. 236
Bautte, watchmaker, i. 57
Beadle, J. P., ii. 55
Beauty—
  And religion, i. 70, 240; ii. 225
  Conception of, i. 230, 240
  Discernment and appreciation of, i. 240; ii. 72, 177
  Greek idea of, ii. 282
  Indifference to, i. 240; ii. 8, 64
  Righteousness of, ii. 214
Beck, Mr., ii. 151
Beethoven, i. 186, 201, 303; ii. 56, 261, 265
Behnes, Charles, i. 20-22
Behnes, Henry, i. 19
Behnes, William, i. 19-23
  His studio, i. 21
Bell, John, and Co., i. 175
Benckendorff, Count, i. 162
Benedite, M. Léon, ii. 234
Bentham, Jeremy, i. 33, 34, 128
Benzoline, i. 174
Berbers, ii. 67, 68
Best, Mr., i. 128
Bethnal Green Museum, ii. 48
Betteshanger, i. 43
Bible reading, i. 16, 17
Billiards, ii. 154, 159
Biographie Universelle, i. 250

INDEX

Birds of Egypt, ii. 70, 71
Birmingham Art Gallery, ii. 37
Blackheath, i. 29, 30
Black Sea, ii. 75
Blake, William, i. 140; ii. 185
Blanc, Dr., ii. 120, 125
Blanc, Mont, ii. 126
Blanche, see Cocks, Mrs. H. S.
Blickling, i. 98, 210, 212, 280
Bloomfield Place, Pimlico, ii. 49, 55
Blundell Sands, i. 270
Boccaccio, i. 64, 107
Bodleian, i. 306
Boehm, Sir Edgar, i. 255 and *note*
Boers, ii. 296
Bojardo, i. 64
Bologna, i. 144
Bond, Dr. Thomas, i. 301; ii. 60, 191, 193, 194, 219
Bond Street, i. 106
Bond Street Galleries, ii. 192
Bonelli, i. 55
Book collecting, Tennyson's opinion of, ii. 86
Bosanquet, Bernard, i. 236
Boscini, ii. 304
Bosphorus, ii. 75, 76
Boston, ii. 34
Botticelli, Painting by, "The Virgins with Saints and Tobias," ii. 119
Boulak Museum, ii. 65
Boulogne, i. 45, 46
Bournemouth, i. 278
Bowman, Lady, ii. 264
Bowman, Sir William, i. 217, 218; ii. 167 *note*, 195, 196
  Letter to Watts, i. 217, 218
Bowood, i. 174, 195
Boy Scouts, ii. 301
Boyle, Miss Mary, i. 327
Bradford, Elizabeth, *aft.* Mrs. G. Watts, i. 5
Brewers, i. 282
Briary, Freshwater, i. 265, 278, 279, 292-294, 301, 303, 313, 320, 327; ii. 100, 155, 159, 160, 164, 165, 167
  Drain troubles, i. 292, 293
  Life at, i. 298-300
Bricklaying, ii. 28
Bridgewater House, ii. 87
Brighton, i. 221, 222, 266, 328, 329, 330; ii. 14, 16, 17, 39, 55, 135-137, 139, 140, 141, 144, 145, 274
Brighton Harriers, i. 266
Briseïs, ii. 199

Bristol Art Gallery, i. 283 *note*
British Museum, i. 100, 209, 256; ii. 45
Broadwood, Messrs., ii. 209
Brock, Mr., i. 20
Brougham, Lord, ii. 111
Brown, Madox, i. 244, 319
Browning, Miss, ii. 132, 152
Browning, Mrs. Barrett, i. 56; ii. 250
Browning, Robert, i. 56, 202; ii. 132, 152, 153, 156, 157, 177, 210
Brownlow, Countess (Lady Adelaide Talbot), i. 211; ii. 6, 58, 203, 209 *note*
Brownlow, Earl, ii. 58, 283, 305
Bruce, Henry, see Aberdare, Lord
Brunton, Miss, Portrait of, i. 34
Brushes, i. 122; ii. 90
Brussels, i. 112
Bryanston Square, i. 198
Budrum, i. 163
Bulawayo, ii. 272
Bulgarian peasants, ii. 75
Bull Hotel, Piccadilly, i. 95
Bunyan's *Pilgrim's Progress*, i. 16; ii. 181
Buonaparte, Prince Jerome, i. 162
Buonaparte, Princess Matilde, Portrait of, i. 66
Buondelmonti, i. 64
Burlington House, i. 94, 270; ii. 200, 201, 322; *see also* Royal Academy
Burne-Jones, Lady, i. 170; ii. 229, 274, 301
Burne-Jones, Sir Edward, i. 96, 160, 170, 171, 219, 237, 290, 302, 324, 325, 326; ii. 7, 98, 99, 145, 187, 230, 233, 260
  His ancestry, ii. 206
  His death, ii. 274
  His humour, ii. 229
  Letter to Watts, ii. 14, 15
Burne-Jones, Margaret, ii. 45
Burne-Jones, Sir Philip, i. 160; ii. 101, 102
Burton, Sir Frederick, i. 87 *note*, 291; ii. 156
Burton, Mr., i. 131
Butler, Edward, i. 259
Butler, Mrs. Josephine —
  Letter to Watts, ii. 251
  Portrait by Watts, ii. 250, 251
"Buzz," see Prinsep, Valentine
Byron, i. 109, 249

Cæsar Augustus, i. 225
Café Doney, Florence, i. 54

327

Caillard, Sir Vincent, ii. 78
Cain as subject for a cantata, etc., i. 258-260
Cairo, ii. 65, 72
Calderon, Philip, R.A., ii. 15, 200, 201
Camberwell, ii. 229, 230
Cambridge, Duke of, ii. 202
Cambridge Street, London, i. 86
Cambridge University, ii. 17, 18, 20
Camelford, Lord, i. 128
Cameron, Hardinge, i. 206, 300
Cameron, Mrs. (Julia Margaret), i. 123, 177, 204-209, 265, 288, 294, 300, 301; ii. 163
    Anecdotes of, i. 205, 206, 294
    Description of, i. 205
    Leaves Freshwater for Ceylon, i. 300, 301
    Photographs by, i. 206, 207, 288, 301
Campagna Romana, ii. 119
Campbell, Charles, ii. 31 *and note*
Campden Hill, i. 204
Canada, ii. 215
Canada, s.s., ii. 27
Candilli, ii. 75
Cannes, ii. 111
Canterbury, ii. 83
Canterbury, Archbishop of, ii. 284
"Cape to Cairo," ii. 268, 271
Careggi, i. 49, 54, 55, 61-63, 65, 75-77, 81, 82, 85, 98, 115, 190 *note*, 234; ii. 253
Carlisle, Earl of, i. 138; ii. 38, 265
Carlton House Terrace, i. 162, 174; ii. 104, 203
Carlyle, Thomas, i. 105, 190, 248-250; ii. 215
    Impatience and irritability, i. 248, 249
    Influence of, ii. 55
    Letter to Watts, i. 249
    Meredith's opinion of, ii. 231, 232
    Photograph of, i. 301
    Portraits by Watts, i. 248, 249
Carmen Sylva, ii. 132, 189, 190
Carmichael, Alexander, ii. 292
Carpaccio, i. 146
Carr, Comyns, ii. 258, 259
Cartoons, *see* Drawings
Casa Feroni, *see* Feroni
Casa Gordon, *see* Careggi
Casavetti, Madame (Euphrosyne Ionides), ii. 78 *and note*, 106 *note*
Cavafy, G. F., i. 32
Cavendish-Bentinck, Mrs. G., Portrait by Watts, i. 174

Cayley, Mr., i. 198
Ceiling, Design for, i. 101, 102
Cellini, Benvenuto, ii. 138
Celtic characteristics, ii. 277, 278, 280
Cemetery, Scheme for, i. 228
Ceylon, i. 206, 300
Chaldean symbolism, ii. 138
Chalk drawings, i. 131; ii. 192, 194
Chalons, i. 45, 143
Chambers's Journal, i. 130
Chandelier, ii. 104, 105
Channel, Crossing, i. 46
Character, Change of, i. 274
Charcoal drawings, i. 110, 126, 158; ii. 44
Charing Cross, ii. 127
Charlemagne, i. 151
Charles Street, Berkeley Square, i. 86, 106, 107, 110, 113, 114, 116, 121, 122, 131, 138, 139, 140; ii. 95
Charterhouse School, ii. 299, 300
Charteris, Lady Anne, i. 132
Charteris, Frank, i. 132
Chartres, Duc de, i. 189
Chaucer, i. 133; ii. 263
Chelsea, i. 250
Chester Street, ii. 63
Chesterfield Street, i. 121, 122, 129
Chesworth, Miss, i. 223, 303
Cheyne Walk, i. 267
Childe, Mrs. Baldwin, i. 241 *note*
Children, On, i. 110, 303, 304
Cholmondeley, Lady Alice, i. 241 *note*
Cholmondeley, Reginald, i. 85, 241
Cholmondeley, Thomas, i. 241
Choristers, i. 151, 152
Christ Church, Oxford, i. 136, 305, 307
Christianity, ii. 147, 222, 226, 243
Christie's, i. 270
Christmas tree, i. 304
Chuck-halfpenny, i. 129
Church Congress, ii. 40
Cimabue, ii. 198
Circles, i. 317
Civilisation, i. 103, 151; ii. 37, 43, 80, 268, 298
Civita Castellana, i. 72
Claremont, i. 188, 189
Clark, Sir Andrew, ii. 193
    Opinion on overwork, ii. 204, 205
    Portrait by Watts, ii. 204, 238
Clay modelling, i. 65, 244; ii. 301
Clipstone Street, i. 27
Cliveden, i. 256
Clothing, On, i. 149, 150

INDEX

Cockerell, Frederick, i. 279, 293; ii. 9
Cocks, Herbert Somers, ii. 117, 159
Cocks, Mrs. Herbert Somers, "Blanche," i. 266, 303, 304, 308, 309, 330; ii. 39, 117, 159, 254
Children of, Arthur and Verena, ii. 207, 208
Coleridge, i. 128
Colleoni, i. 146; ii. 135
Colonies, ii. 297
Colorossi, Italian model, ii. 45
Colour and colours, ii. 89, 97, 214
Colwell Bay, i. 319, 322
Comet, i. 203
Competition, On, ii. 91
Competition in art, ii. 3
Compliments to young ladies, i. 288
Compton, Surrey, i. 265
Compton Cemetery and Chapel, ii. 284
Compton Chapel, ii. 320
Compton Gallery, i. 21, 28, 67, 124, 212; ii. 45, 66, 250, 251 *note*
Condover Church, i. 241 *and note*, 251
Coniston, i. 95, 108; ii. 238
Conrad, i. 293
Conscience, ii. 151, 295
Conscientiousness, ii. 41
Constantinople, i. 32, 164, 165; ii. 72-78
Conversation, Sir C. Allbutt on, ii. 178-181
Convictions, ii. 225
Cook, E. T., i. 93
Cook, John, ii. 66, 151, 152
Cook, Messrs. Thomas, ii. 66
Cope, Charles West, R.A., i. 42, 134
Copsham, i. 190
Copyright, i. 275; ii. 34, 35
Coquelin, Monsieur, i. 313; ii. 235
Views on art, etc., i. 314
Coriolanus, i. 196
Cornice Road, i. 71
Coronio, Mrs. (Aglaia Ionides), i. 135
Corsica, ii. 83
Cosmopolitan Club, i. 107, 139, 140
Cosson, Baron de, ii. 197
Cotton, General Frederick, Portrait of, by Mrs. G. F. Watts, ii. 59
Cottrell, Count, i. 52, 55, 81
Portrait of, i. 66
Couzens, Charles, i. 44, 106
Coventry, Countess of, i. 50
Coxe, Rev. Henry O., Portrait by Watts, i. 306
Crane, Walter, ii. 58, 103, 200

Creation, ii. 166, 167
Creator, The, ii. 243, 245
Crèche, ii. 136, 137
Cremation, ii. 317
Crete, ii. 73
Cricketers, i. 28, 29
Crimea, i. 107
Critics and criticism, On, i. 227, 302; ii. 3-5
Cromwell, i. 128
Cross, J., Painting of Richard Cœur de Lion, i. 88
Crystal Palace, i. 105, 111, 256
Cuchulain Saga, ii. 292
Curragh Chase, i. 108, 110-112
Curves, Theory of, i. 316, 317; ii. 79, 184
Cust, Lionel, ii. 249, 271

Dalcrombie Lodge, ii. 289, 290
Dalrymple, Lady ("Sorella"), i. 155-157, 180; ii. 117
Dalrymple, Sir John, ii. 117
Dante, i. 64
Portrait by Giotto, i. 55
Darwin, Charles, i. 203; ii. 142
Darwin, Francis, ii. 142
Davey, Lord, i. 283
Dean Street, Soho, i. 20
Death, On, ii. 194, 254, 316, 317, 322-324
De Hooghe, i. 95
Deirdre, ii. 292
De Morgan, William, i. 65
Denmark Hill, i. 264
Derbyshire, i. 35
Deserts, ii. 70, 73
Detail, i. 92
De Vere, Aubrey, i. 108-110, 112, 113; ii. 227
Letters to Watts, i. 108, 109
Devonshire, Duke of, ii. 18
Dewey, *School and Society*, ii. 307
Diana of the Crossways, i. 190, 191
Dickinson, art dealer, i. 44
Dickinson, G. Lowes, *The Greek View of Life*, ii. 282 *note*
Diligence, Description of, i. 45, 46, 143
Dilke, Right Hon. Sir Charles, i. 273-275
Portrait by Watts, ii. 16
Dilke, Lady, i. 273
Dinner, Grosvenor Gallery, ii. 12-17, 39
Discharged prisoners, i. 130
Distemper, *see* Tempera colour
Distinctions, On, ii. 240, 241
Divine Intelligence, i. 317

GEORGE FREDERIC WATTS

Docking of horses, i. 186, 187
Donaldson, Rev. S. A., ii. 264
Donders, Professor, ii. 197, 198
Dorchester House, i. 85, 90, 96, 106, 131
Down, ii. 142
Doyle, Richard, i. 160, 204
Drains, i. 292
Drama, Italian, i. 69
Dramatic poem, i. 308
Drapery, i. 148, 149; ii. 82
Drawing, i. 137
Drawing from casts and models, i. 213
Drawing on metallic paper, i. 67
Drawings by Watts—
  Alfred, King, i. 78-81
  Caractacus led in triumph, i. 42-44, 77
  Cricketers, i. 28, 29
  Dalrymple, Lady, i. 157
  Death the Angel crowning Innocence, ii. 60
  Jackson, Mrs., i. 157
  Jackson, Adeline, i. 157
  Jackson, Julia, i. 157
  Jackson, Mary, i. 157
  Lion, i. 44
  O'Brien, Sir Lucius, i. 110
  "People which sat in darkness," i. 101
  Prinsep, family, i. 158
  Prinsep, Mrs., i. 157
  Prinsep, Arthur, i. 158
  Rossetti, Dante Gabriel, i. 267
  Sisyphus, i. 11
  Somers, Lady, i. 158
  St. George overcoming the dragon, i. 134
  Verdi, i. 69
  Preserved by Count Cottrell, i. 55, 81
Dreams, ii. 211
Dresden Gallery, i. 289
Dress, On, ii. 8
Dromoland, i. 110, 111
Drummond, Professor, *The Greatest Thing in the World*, ii. 157
Dryden, i. 133
Dual nature, ii. 221
Duckworth, Mrs. Herbert (*née* Prinsep), i. 298
Dudley, Countess of (Rachel), i. 330
Dudley Gallery, i. 283
Duff Gordon, *see* Gordon
Du Maurier, i. 171
Dunyardil, ii. 291, 292
Du Roveray, i. 32, 33
Dutch tiles, ii. 54
Duty, On, ii. 226
Dying rich, On, i. 319

Earle, Walter, ii. 320
Earthquake, i. 167
Eastlake, Sir Charles, i. 88, 89, 133, 158, 212, 231
Eastnor, Lord, *see* Somers, Lord
Eastnor Castle, i. 91, 125
Eaton Hall, i. 254, 256
Eccleston Square, ii. 55, 63
Eden, Miss Mabel, i. 173
Edinburgh, ii. 151
Edmonds, Richard, Portrait of, by Watts, i. 34
Education, On, ii. 307
Edward VII., King, creates the Order of Merit, ii. 303
  Portrait of, by Watts, i. 280, 281
Edwards, family name, i. 5
Edwards, Passmore, ii. 102, 230
Egypt, ii. 60, 62, 63, 66, 68, 69, 70, 71, 83, 86, 152, 244
Egyptians, i. 103; ii. 220
Elcho, Lord, i. 132, 214, 215, 216 (*see* Earl of Wemyss)
  Letter to Watts, i. 197
Elgin Marbles, i. 23, 68, 137, 141; ii. 183
  Carlyle's opinion of, i. 249, 250
Elijah, ii. 166
Eliot, George, *see* Lewes, Mrs. George
Elkington, silversmiths, i. 198
Ellice, General and Mrs., i. 47
Ellis, family, i. 33
Elysian fields, ii. 225
Emerson, ii. 207
Emmanuel Philibert of Savoy, Statue of, by Marochetti, ii. 119
Empire—
  Rhodes's ideal, ii. 269
  Watts's opinion, ii. 268
England as a nation, ii. 299
England's defences, ii. 297
English character, i. 217
English history, i. 42, 183, 185
Engravings by Watts, *see* Lithographs
Epigrams by Watts, i. 2, 40, 60, 70, 84, 120, 154, 230, 234, 286, 312; ii. 2, 24, 94, 130, 144, 170, 207, 218, 221-223, 248, 288
Epitaphs, Tennyson's examples, ii. 165
Esher, i. 176, 185, 186, 188, 190
Etching of portrait of Mill, i. 274, 275
Eton College Chapel, ii. 262, 264
Eugenie, Empress, ii. 65
Europe, Disturbed state, i. 106

INDEX

Euston Station, i. 132
Evangelical school, i. 16
Eve, i. 262; ii. 138, 141, 202
Evesham, i. 190
Exhibitions, On, i. 302, 325; ii. 3-5, 26, 29, 91
Eyes, Opinions of Carlyle and Watts, i. 250

Fairy tales, ii. 214
Faith, On, ii. 223
Falcon, i. 28
Fame, Mountain of, Dream, ii. 143, 144
Fane, Julian, i. 107
Farrar, Canon, ii. 224, 225
Farringford (*see also* Freshwater), i. 253, 265, 294, 320; ii. 159-161, 164, 167
Fastidiousness of modern taste, i. 308
Fates, The, ii. 166
Fawcett, Mr. and Mrs., i. 273, 274
Fawkes, Guy, i. 16
Felix, Nicholas, *see* Wanostrocht
Felix Holt, i. 224
Fellaheen, ii. 66, 67, 152
Feroni, Casa, i. 48, 50, 52, 54, 57, 61, 69, 70, 132
Feroni, family, i. 48
Ferrari, Gaudenzio, "St. Peter," ii. 119
Fine Art Institution, i. 214
Fine Arts, i. 181; ii. 213, 312
Fine Arts Commission, i. 78, 87-89, 132, 133
FitzGerald, Edward, i. 107
Flaxman, John, i. 110, 140, 141, 142, 214; ii. 43
Fleming, Mr., i. 121, 122
Flight of the one to the One (Plotinus), ii. 310
Floods in Florence, i. 52, 53
Florence, i. 47, 68, 69, 81, 85, 132, 144, 289; ii. 95; *see also* Feroni, Casa
  Bargello, i. 55
  Borgo San Frediano, i. 48
  Gallery, ii. 19
  Guelf and Ghibeline, i. 64
  Life in, i. 54
  Piazza del Carmine, i. 48
  Ponte Santa Trinità, i. 52
  Ponte Vecchio, i. 52
  Torrential rain, i. 52
  Via dei Serragli, i. 48
Floris, i. 5
Flowers, ii. 36
Flower-seller, i. 55

Foley, Mr., i. 20
Ford Castle, i. 98
Form, Principles of, ii. 97, 184, 213
Fortescue, Chichester, i. 107
Fortune, i. 109, 110
Fountains Abbey, ii. 133
Fox, Henry Edward, *see* Holland, Lord
Fox, Miss, i. 127, 128
Fox, Right Hon. Charles James, i. 128
France, i. 43-47
Francis I. of France, ii. 296
Francis Street, i. 49
Fraser-Tytler, family, i. 287, 288
Fraser-Tytler, Mr., brother of Mrs. Watts, ii. 228
Fraser-Tytler, Charles Edward, i. 298
Fraser-Tytler, Ethel, i. 298
Fraser-Tytler, Mary, *see* Watts, Mrs. G. F.
Fraudulent dealer, ii. 101
Frederick, Emperor, ii. 118
Frederick, Empress (Crown Princess of Germany), i. 294
French students, i. 44
French view of art, i. 314, 315
Frescoes and mural decoration, i. 52, 61, 78, 96, 101, 111 *note*, 132, 134, 143, 162, 163, 189, 195, 196, 209, 318; ii. 69
  Educational value, i. 214, 225, 226, 243
  Italian, i. 181, 182
  Lincoln's Inn Fresco, i. 136, 168, 176, 178-184; ii. 188, 189
  Little Holland House Frescoes, i. 290, 291, 293
  Watts's opinion of, i. 136, 179, 183, 184, 196, 214, 216
Freshwater, Isle of Wight (*see also* Briary and Farringford), i. 123, 205, 255, 265, 278, 288, 293, 295, 300, 301
Fröbel, ii. 307
Frome, ii. 306
Future life, ii. 118

Gaelic mind, i. 161
Gaelic prayer, ii. 292, 293
Gaelic proverb, i. 6
Gainsborough, Earl of, Children of, i. 34
Galenga, Miss, Portrait of, by Watts, i. 34
Games, i. 111, 139, 203; ii. 208, 227, 228
Garibaldi, General Ricciotti, i. 220
  Portrait of, by Watts, i. 220
Genesis, i. 262; ii. 202
Geneva, i. 57; ii. 125, 126, 127

331

Genghis Khan, ii. 171
Genius, On, i. 60
Genoa, i. 143
George, Ernest, A.R.A., ii. 158
German Count, i. 294
Gesso grosso, i. 244, 256
Giant stride, i. 139
Gifford Lectures, ii. 242
Gilbert, Alfred—
    Portrait Bust of Watts, ii. 133-135
    Portrait of, by Watts, ii. 252
Gin-shop, ii. 298
Giorgione, i. 86, 144, 147, 148, 209; ii. 80
Giotto, i. 55, 146, 147, 243
Gladstone, i. 236, 238; ii. 15, 207
    Death, ii. 273
    Letters to and from Watts, i. 236, 237, 306; ii. 38, 239-241
    Portrait by Watts, i. 176, 305, 306; ii. 273, 274
Gladstone, Mrs., i. 176
Glazing, ii. 90
Globe, The, ii. 3
God, Drawing of, ii. 302
Goderich, Lord, i. 107
Goethe, i. 249; ii. 182
Golden Age, i. 103
Golden Horn, ii. 75
Goldhawk Road, i. 241
Goodness, On, ii. 282, 283
Gordon, General, ii. 30 *note*
Gordon, Sir Alexander Duff, i. 190
Gordon, Lady Duff, i. 76, 85, 97, 99, 171, 191; ii. 253
Gordon, Miss Duff, i. 76, 78, 81, 99
Gordon, Alice Duff, i. 76
Gordon, Janet Duff, *see* Ross, Mrs.
Gordon, Lina Duff, ii. 253
Gordon, Lucie, Lady Duff, i. 190
Gorgon, H.M.S., i. 163; ii. 73, 75
Gothic Cathedral, ii. 277
Gouache, ii. 110, 111, 113, 125
Gow, James, crofter, ii. 291, 292, 294, 295
Gower, Lord Ronald Sutherland, i. 73, 74
Gozzoli, Benozzo, i. 62
Graham, William, ii. 10
Grail, ii. 221
Granby, Marchioness of (Miss Violet Lindsay), ii. 260, 267
Grant, Sir Francis, i. 231, 233
Grass of Parnassus, ii. 292
Graver, Emma, i. 304, 305
Greece, i. 76, 104, 105, 149; ii. 71, 73, 78, 83, 244

Greek civilisation, i. 142
Greek form, i. 316
Greek friends, i. 32, 33
Greek ideal, i. 238; ii. 282
Greek islands, i. 164; ii. 73, 290
Greeks, ii. 278, 279
Gregory, Sir William, ii. 131
Grenfell, Field-Marshal Lord, Sirdar of Egypt, ii. 65 *and note*
Grésy, ii. 124
Greuze, i. 10
Grey, Earl, ii. 267, 270, 271-273, 296, 297
Gros Veneur, *see* Lupus, Hugh
Grosvenor Gallery, i. 240; ii. 57, 100, 106, 257
    Exhibition, i. 323-328; ii. 5, 6, 10, 11, 14, 15, 16, 262
Grosvenor Street, London, i. 301
Guelfs and Ghibelines, i. 64
Guitar, i. 76
Guizot, i. 100, 250
Gulley, Dr., i. 125, 163
Gurney, Rev. Alfred, Portrait of, by Watts, ii. 252

Halicarnassus, i. 163
Hallé, Charles, i. 202; ii. 15, 88, 89, 145, 192, 258
Hallé, Miss Elinor, ii. 259, 260
Hamerton, P. G., Visit and letter to Watts, ii. 173
Hamilton, family, i. 35
Hamilton, Admiral, Portrait of, i. 34, 35
Hamilton, Sir Bruce, ii. 73
Hanbury, Charles, i. 282
Hanbury, Trueman, and Co., Messrs., i. 282
Handel, i. 183
Hanging pictures, On, i. 224, 225, 325; ii. 29
Hanson, Arthur, ii. 77
Hanson, Mrs. Arthur, ii. 75-77
Harcourt, Vernon, i. 107; ii. 15
Hardwicke, Philip, i. 107, 136, 168
Hardy, Thomas, ii. 194
Harris, Lord, i. 29
Harrogate, i. 308, 309; ii. 133
Haskett-Smith, Mr., i. 35
Haydon, Benjamin, i. 23, 68, 146; ii. 140
Helen, ii. 199
Helouan, ii. 73
Herbert, Hon. Auberon, ii. 132

INDEX

Hereford, i. 5, 10
Herkomer, Sir Hubert von, ii. 44
Hermes, ii. 81
Herne Hill, i. 219
Heroic self-sacrifice monument, ii. 102-104
Heron, i. 27, 28
Herschel, Sir John, i. 202, 203
Hervey, Hubert, ii. 297 *and note*
Heseltine, Evelyn, ii. 291
Hesiod, i. 140
Hibbert Lectures, ii. 242
Hichens, Andrew, i. 298; ii. 63, 109, 117, 123, 153-158, 173, 192, 242, 275, 276, 283
    Letter to Watts on his marriage, ii. 60-62
Hichens, Mrs. Andrew (May Prinsep), i. 124 *note*, 160, 276, 298; ii. 117, 153-158, 173, 260
Highlanders, ii. 294
Hill, Miss Octavia, ii. 102, 103
Hillyer, Mary, i. 301
Hilton, William, i. 26, 27
Hipkins, Mr., ii. 209 *and note*
Hodgson, Mr., ii. 151
Hogarth, i. 185
Holbein, i. 314; ii. 156
Holford, R. S., i. 85, 86
Holiday, Henry, ii. 136
Holiday, Mrs. Henry, i. 28; ii. 209 *and note*
Holl, Frank, i. 281; ii. 202
Holland, Elizabeth, Lady (wife of the 3rd Baron), i. 71, 72
Holland, Mary Augusta, Lady (wife of the 4th Baron), i. 74-76, 100, 114, 162, 191, 279
    At Careggi, i. 63
    At Florence, i. 47-54, 57
    Contemplates sale of Little Holland House Estate, i. 251-254
    Her brilliancy and fluent French and Italian, i. 51
    Her domestic training, i. 50
    Her kindness to Watts, i. 56, 57
    Letter to Watts, i. 53, 54
    Portraits of, by Watts, i. 50, 52, 66, 100
Holland, Lord (Henry Edward Fox, 4th Baron), i. 100, 252; ii. 278
    At Careggi, i. 63
    At Florence, i. 47-56
    At Villa Rochella, i. 70, 71
    Death, i. 191
    Minister to Court of Tuscany, 1839-1846, i. 61, 69

Holland, Lord (*contd.*)—
    Portrait of, damaged by fire and restored by Watts, i. 53, 54
    Travels with Watts, i. 71, 72, 75
Holland, Canon Scott, ii. 20
Holland House, i. 47, 53, 54, 56, 66, 71, 100, 109, 113, 121, 126, 127, 159, 191, 255; ii. 16
Holland House, Little, *see* Little Holland House
Holland House Little, Second, *see* Melbury Road
Holland Park Road, i. 200
Hollyer, Mr., i. 220; ii. 264
Holroyd, Sir Charles, ii. 302
Home Arts and Industries Association, ii. 58, 251
Homer (*Iliad*, etc.), i. 14, 15, 30, 100, 142; ii. 74, 75, 199
Hone, Nathaniel, Letter to Mrs. Watts, i. 162
Hood, Thomas, i. 126
Hopkins, Miss, Portrait of, i. 28
Hopkins, Miss Ellice, i. 299, 300
Horses, i. 186-188, 195, 256, 282, 287, 295
Horsley, Mr., i. 42, 43
    Paper on Art Schools, etc., ii. 40, 42
Houses of Parliament, *see* Parliament
Housing Question, i. 260
Hughes, Mrs., manager of Crèche, ii. 137
Hughes, Mrs., mother of Mrs. Senior, i. 319
Hughes, Gerard, i. 320, 321
Hughes, Thomas, i. 107, 160
Hullah's system of singing, i. 29
Human form, i. 317
Hunt, William Holman, i. 95, 167, 172, 212, 231
    "Christ among the Doctors," i. 158
    "The Shadow of Death," i. 278, 279
Hunting, i. 186, 188, 190, 266
Hyde Park, i. 128, 215, 276; ii. 149
Hypocrisy, On, ii. 43

Ida, Mount, ii. 73, 74
Ilchester, Earl of, i. 280
Ilissus, ii. 81
Imagination, On, ii. 31, 213, 276
Imaginative work, On, i. 27, 91
Imitation, On, i. 92, 239; ii. 69
Impressionist Art, ii. 235, 293
Indecision, On, i. 196
India, i. 104, 172
India Office, i. 123, 160

GEORGE FREDERIC WATTS

Indian Mutiny, i. 167, 172
Indian Princes, ii. 73
Ingestre, i. 212
Inverness-shire, i. 288 ; ii. 294
Ionides, family, i. 32
    Portrait of, by Watts, i. 34
Ionides, Madame, Portrait of, by Watts, i. 34
Ionides, Aglaia, *see* Coronio, Mrs.
Ionides, Aleco, ii. 81
Ionides, Constantine, i. 32, 76, 77, 116
Ireland, i. 108, 109, 111
Ireton, i. 128
Irishmen, i. 109
"Iron-pot," *see* "Tin-pot"
Irving, Edward, i. 10
Isaiah, i. 260
Italy, i. 36, 43, 44, 47-57, 65, 66, 81, 82, 106, 110, 143, 144, 181, 220 ; ii. 78 *note*, 83, 89, 118, 126
    Value of visiting, i. 68

Jackson, Mrs., i. 129, 130, 157
Jackson, Adeline, i. 157
Jackson, Julia, *see* Stephen, Mrs. Leslie
Jackson, Mary, i. 157
James, Sir Walter, *see* Northbourne, Lord
Janotha, Miss, ii. 131
Jardine, Miss, Portrait of, by Watts, i. 34
Jarvis, family, i. 34
Jarvis, Richard, Portrait of, by Watts, i. 34
Jaws, Carlyle's opinion of, i. 249
Jedburgh Abbey, i. 280
Jekyll and Hyde, ii. 221
Jenkinson, John, ii. 254
Jerusalem, i. 104
Jews, ii. 226
Joachim, Dr. Joseph, i. 201, 202 ; ii. 260
    Diamond Jubilee of, ii. 321
    Portrait of, by Watts, i. 202
Job, i. 103
Johnson, Richard, i. 261, 262, 275, 276, 303
Joinville, Prince de, i. 189
Joldwynds, ii. 196
Jones, Sir Edward Burne-, *see* Burne-Jones
Joseph, ii. 68
Jowett, Professor, ii. 97, 100, 179
    Portrait of, by Watts, i. 307 ; ii. 100, 132

Jubilee of Queen Victoria, ii. 85, 102
Julius II., Pope, i. 102
Justinian, i. 151

Kaïrus, Theophilus, Portrait of, by Watts, i. 134, 135
Karnac, ii. 69
Keble, i. 105
Keightley, Dr. Archibald, ii. 322
Kensington (*see also* Holland House ; Melbury Road ; etc.), i. 199, 252 ; ii. 97, 219
Kerr-Lawson, Mr., i. 146
Khartoum, ii. 30 *note*
Khedive, ii. 65
Kingsley, Charles, i. 105
Kirkup, William, i. 54, 55
Knell, W. A., "Battle of St. Vincent," i. 88
Knights Templars, i. 164
Knowles, Sir James, i. 316
    Letter to Mrs. Watts, ii. 238

Laburnum, ii. 162
Landor, Walter Savage, i. 56
Landscape painting, ii. 312
Landseer, Sir Edwin, i. 254
Lanini, Bernardino, "Descent from the Cross," ii. 119
Lansdowne, Marquis of, i. 195, 196
Laocoon, ii. 81
La Roche-sur-Foron, ii. 126
La Sizeranne, Robert de, ii. 48
Laws of nature, On, ii. 71, 166
Lawson, Kerr-, ii. 319
Layard, Lady, ii. 110
Layard, Sir Henry, i. 107, 164, 186 ; ii. 45, 46, 110, 254
    Letter to *Times* about Watts's fresco, i. 180-182
    Portrait by Watts, i. 114
Lear, Edward, ii. 162
Lecky, W. E. H., ii. 132
    History of England, ii. 154, 155
    Opinion on æsthetic genius, i. 6
Leda, yacht, ii. 291
Leeds, i. 328, 329
Leghorn, i. 47, 81, 144
Legros, i. 246
Leicester Art Gallery, i. 234 ; ii. 151, 152
Leighton, Lord, i. 20, 167, 198-200, 202, 231-233, 235 ; ii. 15, 25, 135, 154, 242, 249, 290
    Anti-suffragist, ii. 145, 146

334

INDEX

Leighton, Lord (*contd.*)—
  Business capacity, i. 280
  Death of, ii. 254, 255
  Friendship with Watts, i. 198-200 ; ii. 62, 254, 255
  Letters to Watts, i. 199, 200 ; ii. 200-202
  President of South London Fine Art Gallery, ii. 228-230
  Watts's opinion of, i. 199 ; ii. 254, 255
Leinster, Duchess of, Portrait begun by Watts, ii. 252
Lely, Sir Peter, i. 21
Leroux, Madame (afterwards Princesse de la Tour d'Auvergne), Portrait of, by Watts, i. 66
Leslie, Lady Constance, Letter to Mrs. Watts, i. 159, 160
Leslie-Melville, *see* Leven and Melville
Lestrange's Fables, i. 10
L'Étang, Madame de, i. 129
Leven and Melville, Earl and Countess (Mr. and Mrs. R. Leslie-Melville), ii. 152
Lewes, Mrs. George (" George Eliot "), i. 276, 277 ; ii. 179, 181, 232, 250
  Letter to Watts, i. 277
Leyland, Frederick, i. 269
  Collection of pictures, i. 270
Lichfield, Bishop of, *see* Lonsdale
Lichfield Cathedral, i. 243
Liddell, Dean, i. 305-307 ; ii. 18, 19
  Letters to Watts, i. 306 ; ii. 19
Liddell, Mrs. Edward, ii. 211
Liddell, Mrs. Frederick, ii. 261
Liddell, Geraldine, ii. 56, 57, 63, 161, 164, 209 *note*, 252, 259, 260, 323
Lieven, Princess, i. 162
Life, Watts's aspect of, i. 2 ; ii. 54, 95, 96, 170, 174, 177, 186, 207, 212, 213, 221, 222, 226, 245, 276, 277, 288, 317
Lighting of pictures, ii. 29
Lilford, Lady, i. 72
Lilford, Lady (Emma Brandling), i. 202
" Lily," ii. 208, 209, 293, 314
Limnerslease (*see also* Compton), i. 97 ; ii. 157, 158, 190, 192, 196-198, 207, 219, 228, 230, 250, 253, 261, 272, 294, 300, 305, 315, 317, 321
  Farm and garden, ii. 283, 284
  Picture Gallery, ii. 305
Lincoln, ii. 306
Lincoln's Inn, i. 135, 136, 150, 162, 168, 174, 178, 180, 181, 183, 184, 189, 195, 196, 225, 280, 281 ; ii. 188, 189, 238
Lindsay, Lady (Coutts), i. 323 ; ii. 4, 5
  Portrait by Watts, i. 325
Lindsay, Sir Coutts, i. 160, 323 ; ii. 4, 5, 10, 14, 15
Lindsay, Leonard, ii. 258
Lines, On, i. 265, 316, 317 ; ii. 184, 213
Lions' heads, i. 165, 166
Lips, On, i. 249
Literature, ii. 276
Lithographs by Watts—
  Cricketers, i. 28, 29
  Roebuck, Mr., i. 33
Little Holland House, i. 127, 128, 136, 138-140, 155, 156, 158-162, 167-171, 178, 185, 188, 200, 201, 204, 219, 221, 222, 236, 251-254, 256, 265, 266, 270, 271, 274, 276, 279, 281, 282, 288, 290, 304, 305, 309 ; ii. 96, 159, 219, 314
  Bad sanitation, i. 161
  Demolition, i. 290-293
  Drawings of, i. 304, 309
  Garden, i. 251, 288
Little Holland House, Second, *see* Melbury Road
Liverpool, i. 111, 328
Livre d'Or, ii. 285
Lockhart, Miss Marietta, Portrait of, i. 67
Loire, i. 143
London, *see* various districts, streets, etc.
London, fields in, i. 10
London and North-Western Railway, i. 132
London Scottish, i. 197
Longleat, i. 236
" Long Mary," ii. 44
Lonsdale, Dr., Bishop of Lichfield, Monument to, i. 241, 243, 255
Lonsdale, Miss, i. 243
Lords, House of (*see also* Parliament, Houses of, *for building*), ii. 255
Loseley, ii. 158, 230
Lothian, Marchioness of, i. 211, 212, 280 ; ii. 209 *note*
Lothian, Marquis of—
  Memorial to, by Watts, i. 251, 280
  Portrait of, by Watts, i. 210, 211, 306
Louvre, ii. 83, 127
Love, Religion of, i. 279 ; ii. 235
Lowe, Mr., i. 316
Lowell, James Russell, ii. 132
Lucca, i. 66
  Grand Duke of, i. 55

335

Luini, i. 95
Lupus, Hugh (Le Gros Veneur), i. 251, 254, 256, 280
Luxembourg, The, ii. 234
Luxmoore, H. E., ii. 262, 263
Luxor, ii. 68, 72
Lybian Range, ii. 66, 72
Lyons, Admiral Lord, i. 164
Lytton, Countess of, ii. 260
Lytton, Earl of, i. 327
    Letter to Watts, ii. 11, 12
    Portrait of, by Watts, ii. 57

Macaulay, i. 128
Machinery, On, ii. 6
Mackintosh, Sir James, i. 128
Macnamara, Mr. and Mrs. Charles, i. 301
Maddiston, Captain, i. 164
Magdalen, Master of (1899), ii. 199 *note*
Mahomet, i. 151, 250; ii. 171
Mahommedans, i. 166
Mainfroid, i. 198
Maitland, F. W., ii. 179
Maitland, Mr. Fuller, ii. 261
Malta, i. 167; ii. 63, 104, 105, 110, 113
Malvern, i. 125
Mammon-worship, i. 263; ii. 149, 299
Manchester, i. 130, 247, 261, 262, 276, 283, 284, 301, 319, 328; ii. 107-109
Manchester City News, i. 302
Manchester Institution, ii. 3, 5
Manchester School of Art, i. 226
Manchester Ship Canal, i. 319
Manchester Town Hall, i. 318
Mantelpiece, Melbury Road, ii. 54
Marcellus, i. 225
Marlborough House, i. 280
Marochetti, Statue of Emmanuel Philibert of Savoy, ii. 119
    Richard Cœur de Lion, ii. 120
Marseillaise, i. 46
Marseilles, i. 45, 47, 71, 143; ii. 111
Martineau, James, On power of a superior mind upon an inferior, ii. 53, 54
Martinengo Cesaresco, Countess, i. 220
Marylebone, i. 23
Marylebone Cricket Club, i. 29
Mason, George, i. 264, 265; ii. 119, 140
Masters, Old, i. 67, 76, 77, 113, 217, 239; ii. 89, 304
    Exhibition, i. 94
Material things, On, i. 2
Matoppo Hills, ii. 271 *and note*

Maurice, Rev. Frederick Denison, i. 105; ii. 99, 229
Mazzini, i. 131
Mead, Miss Mary Gertrude (Mrs. Edwin Abbey), arranges exhibition of Watts's paintings in New York, ii. 25-37, 106
Medici, Cosimo de', i. 61
Medici, Lorenzo de', i. 61-63
Medici, Piero de', i. 62
Mediterranean, i. 142; ii. 104, 112, 113
Medusa, i. 65, 66
Melbourne Gallery, i. 170; ii. 167 *note*
Melbury Road, "Paradise Row" (Little Holland House, Second), i. 291, 293, 304, 305, 326, 329; ii. 16, 25, 37, 54, 55, 57, 58, 95, 127, 133, 149, 156, 163 *note*, 193, 194, 209, 229, 254, 255, 258, 305, 317, 329
    Description, ii. 84-86
Men of science, i. 203
Mentone, ii. 106, 111, 112, 113, 118
Merchant Service, ii. 297
Meredith, George, i. 190, 191, 210; ii. 179
    Letter to Watts, ii. 233
    Outlook on life, ii. 231
    Portrait by Watts, ii. 230-233
Mesmeric influence, On, ii. 2
Messageries boats, ii. 83
Messina, ii. 83
Metternich, i. 162
Michael Angelo, i. 72, 73; ii. 80, 183, 302
    Influence of, ii. 214, 215
Michelozzi, Michelozzo, i. 62
Middle Ages, i. 181; ii. 214, 291, 296
Milan, i. 71
Mill, John Stuart, i. 273-276
    Letter to Sir Charles Dilke, i. 273
    Portrait of, by Watts, i. 273
Millais, Sir John, P.R.A., i. 167, 172, 174; ii. 15, 19, 140, 200
Millet, Jean François, i. 265
Milman, Dean, i. 209, 210
    Letter to Watts, i. 209
Milnes, Monckton, i. 107
Milo Venus, ii. 41
Miltiades, i. 77
Milton, i. 41, 133; ii. 139 *note*, 202, 275, 276
Mind power, ii. 223
Miracles, ii. 166
Misseri, i. 164
Mitylene, i. 142, 143

INDEX

Model, Drawing from, ii. 175, 185
Models, Professional, ii. 40-45
Money, Use of, ii. 147-149
Monkshatch, Guildford, ii. 61, 154-157, 190, 196
    Garden in winter, ii. 191, 192
Monnetier, Haute-Savoie, ii. 125
Monte Carlo, ii. 117
Morality, On, ii. 39-43
Morelli, Mr., i. 189
Morier, Sir Robert, i. 106, 107
Morley, John, ii. 232
Morris, William, ii. 7
Mortuary Chapel, i. 228
Mosaics, i. 145, 207, 209, 210
Moses, i. 151
Motley, J. L., as talker, i. 210
    Portrait of, by Watts, i. 210
Mountains, ii. 114, 115, 126
Mount-Temple, Lady, ii. 189
Mozart, ii. 265
Mud, Heap of, i. 94
Müller, Professor Max, ii. 190, 242, 244
    Portrait of, by Watts, ii. 252
Mural paintings, *see* Frescoes
Murray, G., *Rise of the Greek Epic*, ii. 276, 279
Music, i. 69, 70, 284, 315; ii. 36, 37, 56, 213, 307
Mycenæ, ii. 138
Myers, F. W. H., i. 222; ii. 179, 310, 323
    Poem by, ii. 20, 21
Myers, Mrs. F. W. H. (Eveleen Tennant), i. 313; ii. 20
"My Faithful Johnnie," song, ii. 56
Mynn, Alfred, i. 28, 29
Myrtle, ii. 133
Mysteries of being, i. 312
Mysterious, Love of the, ii. 177
Mythology, ii. 48, 49

Nantes, Edict of, ii. 227
Naples, i. 72, 74, 75; ii. 110, 111, 192
Napoleon I., i. 249, 250
National decay, ii. 299
National Gallery, i. 212, 291; ii. 131, 195
National Gallery of British Art, *see* Tate Gallery
National gratitude, On, ii. 49, 50
National Portrait Gallery, i. 101, 114, 131, 165, 176, 267, 270, 274, 276; ii. 46, 47, 49, 167 *note*, 249, 271, 274
National Rifle Association, i. 197, 198

Nation's misfortunes, ii. 30
Nature, On, i. 19, 96, 144, 149, 239, 286; ii. 36, 44, 70-72, 74, 80, 114, 115, 126, 155, 163, 175, 225, 274, 293
Nausicaa, i. 77
Navy, English, ii. 81, 296, 297
Needlework, ii. 6-8
Nelson, Mr., ii. 241
Neptune's horses, ii. 104
Ness, Loch, ii. 290-292
New Gallery, i. 90; ii. 123, 145, 151, 192, 233, 285, 319
    Exhibition of Watts's pictures 1896-1897, ii. 256-258, 263, 264, 267
    Presentation of address, ii. 258, 259
Newman, i. 105
New Testament, ii. 221
Newton, Sir Charles, i. 126, 136, 209, 237; ii. 75, 78
    Excavations at Halicarnassus, i. 163-166
    Letter to Watts, i. 142
Newton, Sir Isaac, i. 161, 162
New York, ii. 25, 27, 33, 37
Nightingale, Florence, ii. 100
    Portrait by Watts, ii. 250, 251
Nile, ii. 67-72
Nineteenth Century and After, i. 137 *note*, 312, 315, 316; ii. 6-8, 299
Normanby, Marquis and Marchioness of, i. 69
Normandy, i. 256
Northbourne, Lord, i. 43
Norton, Mrs., i. 190 *and note*, 191, 202
Nottingham Art Gallery, ii. 37
Nude, The, i. 261; ii. 43

Oblivion, Tennyson's, and Watts's opinion of, i. 3
O'Brien, Mrs., i. 110
O'Brien, Sir Lucius, i. 110
O'Brien, Mary, i. 110-113
Observation, Power of, ii. 6
Old age, Definition of, ii. 238
"Old Maid," ii. 208
Olympia, ii. 78
Olympus, i. 15
Omnium, Jacob, i. 160
Orleans, family, i. 188-191
Orme Square, i. 199
Orsini, i. 189
Osnaburgh, Street, i. 20 22
Ossian, i. 22
Ossulton, Lord, i. 86

VOL. II   337   Z

"Our wooden house," ii. 72 *and note*
Oxford, i. 140, 141, 237, 306
Oxford Union, i. 171
Oxford University, ii. 18-20

Padua, i. 144-147, 243
Painting, On (*see also* Art), i. 314, 315; ii. 31, 37
Painting materials, ii. 87-91; *see also* Brushes *and* Varnish
Paintings by Watts (*see also* Portraits)—
Division *of*, i. 307
Achilles watching Briseïs, i. 195
Alfred inciting the English to resist the Danes by sea, i. 76, 78-80, 81, 87-89, 150
"All the air a solemn silence holds," i. 219 *note*
All-pervading, The, ii. 105, 173, 320
Alps behind Mentone, ii. 113
"And the Lord said unto Satan, Whence comest thou?" i. 97
Angel of Death, *see* Court of Death, *below*
Ariadne in Naxos, i. 236, 283
Aspiration, i. 158
Aurora, ii. 316
Bayard and Aristides, i. 131
Boccaccio, Story from, i. 64
Britomart, i. 328
Buondelmonti, i. 64
Caractacus, i. 44
Chaos, i. 102, 105, 275, 301, 302; ii. 105
Childhood of Zeus, ii. 45
Copy of painting by Sir P. Lely, i. 21
Coriolanus, i. 196
Court of Death, The (The Angel of Death), i. 219, 228, 235, 262, 284, 307, 308, 319; ii. 58, 101, 135, 265, 289, 302, 304
Creation, The, i. 235
Daphne, i. 236; ii. 45
Dawn, ii. 45, 57
Dead Heron, *see* Wounded Heron
Death crowning Innocence, ii. 123
Death of Cain, i. 259, 260; ii. 57
Deluge, The, ii. 57, 192
Denunciation of Cain, The ("My punishment is greater than I can bear"), i. 235, 257
Destiny, ii. 319
Dweller in the Innermost (Soul's Prism), ii. 57, 180
Early Study (Arcadian), i. 107, 108

Paintings by Watts (*contd.*)—
Echo, i. 64, 65, 107, 108
Elements, i. 163
Endymion, ii. 313
Eve Trilogy (*see also* "She shall be called Woman"), i. 262; ii. 45, 138-141, 183
Eve of Peace, i. 287, 289
Faith, ii. 234
Fata Morgana, i. 64, 234; ii. 145, 151
First Whisper of Love, i. 69
"For he had great possessions," ii. 182
Found Drowned, i. 126
Fugue, ii. 313
Galahad, Sir, i. 158, 188, 228, 328; ii. 262-264
Genius of Greek Poetry, i. 235; ii. 74
George (St.) overcoming the Dragon, i. 134, 143, 150
Good Luck to your Fishing, ii. 104
Good Samaritan, i. 130
Green Summer, ii. 312
Habit does not make the Monk, ii. 141
Happy Warrior, The, ii. 244
Hemicycle of Lawgivers, *see* Frescoes, Lincoln's Inn
Heron, *see* Wounded Heron
Holland House decorations, i. 100
Hope, ii. 57, 106 *and note*, 150, 163, 270
Hyperion, i. 158
In the Highlands, ii. 293
In the Land of Weiss-nicht-wo, ii. 220
Iris, ii. 220
Irish Eviction (Irish Famine), i. 109, 126
Island of Cos, The, i. 235, 236
John, Saint, i. 52, 207, 210
Judgment of Paris, ii. 45
Justice, i. 150
Life of Unrequited Toil (Old Horse), ii. 155, 156
Life's Illusions, i. 90, 101, 107
Lot's Wife, ii. 320
Love and Death, i. 283 *and note*, 284, 314, 324; ii. 49, 86, 87, 105-109
Love and Life, ii. 49, 150, 215, 234, 235
Love defending the Door of Life, i. 27
Love Triumphant, ii. 256, 265, 289
Man of Sorrows, i. 31
Mary, Saint, i. 52
Messenger of Death, ii. 254, 257

INDEX

Paintings by Watts (*contd.*)—
  Michael the Archangel contending with Satan for the Body of Moses, ii. 96
  Mid-day Rest, The, i. 236, 282
  Mischief, i. 328
  "Muffin Pictures," i. 172
  "My punishment is greater than I can bear," *see* Denunciation, *above*
  Naples, ii. 192
  Off Corsica, ii. 83
  Olympus on Ida, ii. 45, 57
  Open Door, The, ii. 113
  Ophelia, i. 328
  Panthea, i. 77, 126
  Peace and Goodwill, ii. 124, 125
  Progress, ii. 303, 313
  Red Cross Knight with Una, i. 158
  Saxon Sentinels, The, i. 131
  Scene after Death of Lorenzo de' Medici, i. 61
  Sea Ghost, The, ii. 83
  Sea Shore, i. 127
  Seamstress, The, i. 126
  "She shall be called Woman" (*see also* Eve), i. 261; ii. 138, 139, 200-203, 320
  "Sic Transit," ii. 197, 199
  Soul's Prism, *see* Dweller in the Innermost
  Sower of the Systems, ii. 105, 302
  Sphinx, ii. 66, 269
  Spirit of Christianity, i. 279, 281, 282
  Sunset on the Alps, ii. 126
  Thetis, i. 236
  Time and Oblivion, i. 90, 91, 93, 97, 101, 131; ii. 264
  Time, Death, and Judgment, i. 228, 235, 307, 319, 327; ii. 86, 215
  Titans, The, *see* Chaos, *above*
  Tragedy of the Lovers, i. 64
  Two Paths, ii. 313
  Under a Dry Arch, i. 126
  "Utmost, The, for the Highest," ii. 319
  "What I spent I had, etc.," ii. 190
  Whence? Whither? ii. 318
  Wife of Midas, The, ii. 45
  Wife of Pygmalion (Galatea), i. 236, 238
  Witch pursuing the Knight, i. 64
  Wounded Heron (*first Academy picture*), i. 27, 28 *and note*; ii. 145, 180

Paintings contemplated by Watts—
  Adam and Eve in Paradise, i. 319
  Charity giving the Water of Life to thirsty souls, i. 101
  Cosmos, *see* House of Life, *below*
  Death and Resurrection, i. 101
  House of Life, i. 101-105, 110, 132, 258, 262; ii. 203
  Lincoln's Inn Decoration, i. 184, 185
  Procession of Life, ii. 212, 213
  Satan calling up his Legions, i. 101
  Satan, Sin, and Death, i. 101
  Temptation of Eve, i. 101
  Wellington, Duke of, i. 113
Paintings in gouache, ii. 110, 111, 113, 125
Palazzo Amerighi, *see* Feroni, Casa
Palazzo Torre Arsa, i. 55
Palestine, i. 104
Palgrave, Francis, i. 107
Pallas Athene, Statue of, ii. 81
Palmer, General and Mrs., ii. 230
Panathenaic procession, i. 147
Panizzi, Anthony, i. 100, 189
  Portrait of, i. 66
Paris, i. 44, 45, 161, 189; ii. 41, 83, 125, 127
  International Exhibition, ii. 25
Parisienne, song, i. 46
Park Street, 1. 90
Parlanti's foundry, ii. 303
Parliament, Houses of (Westminster Palace), frescoes in, i. 41, 85, 87-89, 93, 111 *note*, 133, 143
Parliament, Members of, ii. 109
Parliamentary Reports, i. 42
Parma, Duke of, i. 66
Parthenon, i. 146, 148, 250; ii. 21, 73, 74, 79, 80, 144, 244, 276
Party politics, ii. 146-148
Pastel painting, ii. 113 *and note*
Pastor Fido, Il, i. 30
Pastoral symphony, ii. 320
Patriotism, ii. 147
Patroclus, ii. 74
Pattle, Miss Virginia, *see* Somers, Countess
Paul Veronese, i. 50, 173
  "Queen of Sheba before Solomon," ii. 119
Pavia, Battle of, ii. 296
Peace, Universal, ii. 298
Peasantry of Savoy, ii. 116, 117, 119, 123

339

Pembroke, Countess of (Lady Gertrude Talbot), i. 211 ; ii. 203, 207, 209 note
Penelope, ii. 7
Penrose, Professor, ii. 79
People's Palace, ii. 88
People's Play Ground, i. 297
Pera, ii. 75, 77
Percheron, i. 256
Persia, i. 104
Perugia, i. 72
Pestalozzi, ii. 307
Peter the Hermit, i. 104
Peter Martyr, i. 146
Pheidias, i. 26, 73, 74, 86, 90, 99, 100, 142, 146-149, 238, 243, 249, 317 ; ii. 78, 80, 82
Phillips, Henry, i. 107, 139
Phœnix Park, ii. 18
Photographs of Watts's paintings, ii. 26
Photography, i. 206-208
Pickersgill, F. R., "Burial of Harold," i. 87, 88
Pilch, Fuller, i. 28
Pilgrims' Way, ii. 219, 220
Piræus, ii. 73
Pisa, i. 47, 144
Plato, i. 62 ; ii. 21, 138 note, 220
Plotinus, quotation from, ii. 310
Po, ii. 118
Poetic genius, On, i. 60
Poetry, On, i. 284 ; ii. 31, 36, 37, 44, 130, 174, 175, 185, 211, 213, 225, 307
Poet's mind and function, On, ii. 174, 175, 177
Political parties, On, i. 247
Pollaiuolo, "Tobias," ii. 119
Pollution of streams, i. 260
Polycrates, ii. 105
Pompeii, i. 74, 75
Pompey, i. 225
Pope, Alexander, i. 133
Porpoises, ii. 112
Portrait painting, On, i. 33, 34, 76, 77, 174, 175, 208, 226, 243, 245, 247, 255, 266 ; ii. 164
Portraits by Watts—
　Characteristics of, i. 66, 67
　Earliest, i. 34
　Object of, ii. 267
　Anderson, Miss Mary, ii. 131, 132
　Arnold, Matthew, ii. 118
　Baden-Powell, General Sir Robert, ii. 299, 300

Portraits by Watts (contd.)—
　Bagshaw, Mr., Children of, i. 35
　Barnett, Canon, ii. 99
　Bath, Marchioness of, i. 236
　Bentham, J., i. 33, 34
　Brunton, Miss, i. 34
　Buonaparte, Prince Jerome, i. 162
　Buonaparte, Princess Matilde, i. 66
　Burne-Jones, Sir Edward, i. 325
　Butler, Mrs. Josephine, ii. 250
　Caillard, Sir Vincent, Son of, ii. 78
　Carlyle, i. 248, 249 ; ii. 232
　Cavendish-Bentinck, Mrs. G., i. 174
　Clark, Sir Andrew, ii. 104, 238
　Cottrell, 2nd Count, i. 66
　Coxe, Rev. Henry O., i. 306
　De Vesci, Viscount, ii. 261, 262
　Dilke, Sir Charles, ii. 16
　Eden, Miss Mabel, i. 173
　Edmonds, Richard, i. 34
　Edward VII. (Prince of Wales), ii. 280, 281
　Friends of Lord and Lady Holland, i. 54
　Gainsborough, Earl of, Children of, i. 34
　Galenga, Miss, i. 34
　Garibaldi, i. 220
　Gilbert, Alfred, ii. 252
　Gladstone, i. 176, 305, 306 ; ii. 273, 274
　Guizot, i. 100
　Gurney, Rev. Alfred, ii. 252
　Hamilton, Admiral, i. 34, 35
　Holland, Lady, i. 50, 52, 66, 100
　Holland, Lord, i. 53
　Hopkins, Miss, i. 28
　Ionides, family, i. 34
　Ionides, Madame, i. 34
　Jackson, Miss, i. 130
　Jackson, Mrs., i. 130
　Jardine, Miss, i. 34
　Jarvis, Richard, i. 34
　Joachim, i. 202
　Jowett, Professor, i. 307 ; ii. 100, 132
　Kaïrus, Theophilus, i. 134, 135
　Layard, Sir Henry, i. 114
　Leinster, Duchess of, ii. 252
　Leroux, Madame (afterwards Princess de la Tour d'Auvergne), i. 66
　Lieven, Princess, i. 162
　Lilford, Lady, i. 202
　Lilian, ii. 314
　Lindsay, Lady (Coutts), i. 325
　Little Girl, i. 32
　Lockhart, Miss Marietta, i. 67

INDEX

Portraits by Watts (*contd.*)—
  Lothian, Marchioness of, and her sisters, i. 211
  Lothian, Marquis of, i. 210, 211, 306
  Lytton, Earl of, ii. 57
  Meredith, ii. 230-233
  Mill, John Stuart, i. 273
  Motley, John Lothrop, i. 210
  Müller, Professor Max, ii. 252
  Panizzi, A., i. 66, 100
  Pattle, Miss Virginia, *see* Somers, Lady, *below*
  Prinsep, Thoby, i. 124
  Rhodes, Cecil, ii. 267-271
  Rice, Miss A. S., i. 34
  Rickards, Charles H., i. 222-225
  Ristori, Madame, i. 66, 69
  Roebuck, Mr., i. 33
  Rogers, Mrs. Charles Coltham, ii. 252
  Rossetti, Dante Gabriel, ii. 267-271
  Russell, Lord John, i. 114
  Salisbury, Marquis of, ii. 57
  Selborne, Earl of, ii. 238
  Senior, Miss, i. 174
  Senior, Mrs. Nassau, i. 174, 175
  Senior, Walter, i. 296, 297
  Shrewsbury, Earl of, i. 211
  Somers, Countess (Miss Virginia Pattle), i. 122, 123, 126, 158, 174, 235
  Spedding, James, i. 114
  Spence, William, i. 66
  Stanley, Dean, i. 306
  Stratford de Redcliffe, Lord, i. 165
  Talbot, Sir R., i. 211
  Tennant, The Misses, i. 313
  Tennyson, Lord, ii. 158-167, 169, 170, 192, 217, 218, 232
  Thiers, M., i. 161
  Thynne, Lady Katherine, ii. 173, 193
  Tricoupi, Mr., ii. 81, 82
  Valeska, Countess, i. 66
  Verdi, i. 69
  Waterford, Marchioness of, i. 97, 98
  Watts, George, father, i. 9
  Watts, G. F., i. 34, 53, 287; ii. 196
  Wellsted, Rev. A. O., i. 34
  Wright, Thomas, i. 131
  Wyndham, Hon. Mrs. Percy, i. 239, 240, 325
  Young Lady, i. 28
Port Said, ii. 63
Poverty, On, ii. 147, 148
Powers, Hiram, i. 54
Poynter Sir Edward, ii. 15, 265

Praxiteles, ii. 82
Prayer, ii. 223
Prayer Book, i. 7, 16
Pre-Raphaelites, i. 105, 172, 215, 216
Press, American, ii. 27
Priam, ii. 199
Prince of Wales, *see* Edward VII.
Prinsep, Miss, ii. 110
Prinsep, Mrs. (Granny), ii. 61 *and note*
Prinsep, Alice, i. 174
Prinsep, Anne, i. 299
Prinsep, General Arthur, i. 125 *note*, 139, 158, 161, 167, 172, 228
Prinsep, Harry, i. 156, 200, 201
Prinsep, Henry, i. 56, 139, 143, 167, 172
Prinsep, Sir Henry Thoby, i. 158
Prinsep, May, *see* Hichens, Mrs. Andrew
Prinsep, Mr. Thoby, i. 121-129, 138, 143, 156, 159, 160, 190, 200, 234, 251, 252, 254, 255, 266, 276, 278, 279, 298, 309 ; ii. 125
  Character and death, i. 327
  Description of, i. 123
  "Greatest Indian legislator," i. 294
  Portraits by Watts, i. 124, 158
  Watts's opinion of, i. 327
Prinsep, Mrs. Thoby, i. 138, 143, 157, 159, 172, 173, 190, 200, 203, 266, 276, 278, 279, 288, 298, 327, 329, 330
  Her care of Watts, i. 125, 304, 305
  Her death, ii. 109
  Her grandchildren, i. 304, 330
Prinsep, Valentine ("Buzz"), i. 160, 161, 166, 171-174, 279, 328 ; ii. 127
  Paints the Durbar, i. 327
Probyn, Miss, i. 188 *and note*
Proportion, Sense of, ii. 42
Psychical Phenomena, i. 115-117
Pugh, family name, i. 5
Puritans, ii. 227
Pyramids, i. 103 ; ii. 65, 66, 70

Queen's Hall, ii. 321

Rajon, etcher, i. 274
Ramadan, i. 166
Rameses, ii. 68
Raphael, i. 148, 181 ; ii. 80
Rawlinson, Sir Henry, ii. 254
Rawnsley, Canon, ii. 283
Realism, ii. 94
Red Cross Hall, Southwark, ii. 103
Reason, ii. 212, 223, 224
Rebirth of the Soul, ii. 277
Reeve, Henry, i. 107

Religion and beauty, i. 240
Religion and religious beliefs (*see also* Art, Religious), i. 15-17, 70, 194, 260, 281; ii. 71, 157, 165-167, 170, 174, 207, 218, 221-227, 243, 244, 245, 277, 298
Rembrandt, i. 10, 314
Renaissance, ii. 89
Rendall, Dr., ii. 300
Repression of thought, ii. 226, 227
Revue des deux Mondes, ii. 48
Reynolds, i. 95; ii. 19
Rhodes, Cecil—
  Conversations, ii. 268-271
  Death, ii. 271-273
  Letter to Mrs. Watts, ii. 271
  Memorial, ii. 271
  Portrait by Watts, ii. 267
Rhodes, Island, i. 166, 167
Riccardi Palace, i. 62
Rice, Miss Alice Spring, i. 108
  Portrait of, by Watts, i. 34
Riches, *see* Mammon-worship
Richmond, George, Letter to Watts, i. 242, 243
Richmond, Sir William, ii. 238
  Portrait of Florence Nightingale, ii. 100
Richmond Terrace, ii. 168
Rickards, Charles H., i. 222-228, 243-247, 261, 275, 278, 283, 287, 302-305, 307, 308, 322, 326, 328; ii. 3-5, 220 *note*
  His collection of Watts's paintings, ii. 3, 4
  Honoured by Manchester, i. 247
  Portrait by Watts, i. 222-225
  Praised by Watts, i. 246, 247
  Troubled with cataract, i. 303
Rifle shooting, i. 197
Riley, E., i. 32
Ripon, Marquis and Marchioness, ii. 133
Ristori, Madame, i. 66, 69, 70
Ritual, ii. 225
Riviera, ii. 159
Riviere, Briton, ii. 149, 150
Roberts Road, Hampstead Road, i. 23
Rochella Villa, Naples, i. 72, 74
Rodin, ii. 135
Roebuck, Mr., i. 33
Rogers, Mrs. Charles Coltham, Portrait of, by Watts, ii. 252
Rogers, Samuel, i. 176
Roman history, as subject for fresco, i. 225
Roman Road, Careggi, i. 62

Rome, i. 45, 72, 81, 85, 104, 198, 209, 220, 225, 289
Rosebery, Earl of, ii. 175
  Letter to Watts, ii. 301
Ross, Mrs. Henry (Janet Duff Gordon), i. 44, 125 *note*, 190 *and note*
Rossetti, Dante Gabriel, i. 73, 160, 170-174, 267-273, 277, 280
  Anecdote of elderly artist, i. 272, 273
  Drawing by, i. 267
  Letters, i. 179, 180, 267, 268, 273
  Memorial Exhibition, i. 270
  Oxford Union frescoes, i. 171
  Painting of Two Lovers, ii. 244
  Poems, i. 267, 271
  Portrait of, by Watts, i. 267-271
  Religion, ii. 166
  Watts's opinion of, i. 173, 267
Rossetti, Mrs. (Miss Siddall), Ruskin's opinion of, i. 272
Rossetti, William, i. 269, 270
Rossiter, William, ii. 229
Rothschilds, i. 33
Royal Academy, i. 22, 25, 26, 28, 68, 91, 130, 141, 158, 167, 173, 175, 184, 185, 198, 212-216, 231-233, 236, 240, 242, 250, 265, 281, 324, 328; ii. 4, 44, 96, 113, 193, 200, 233, 319, 322
  Diploma Gallery, i. 73, 257
  Watts's opinion on, i. 212-216, 231, 232
Royal Academy Commission, i. 67, 212-216, 231, 250
Royal Albert, H.M.S., i. 164
Royal Commission, 1863, *see* Royal Academy Commission
Royal Commission on Fine Arts, *see* Fine Arts Commission
Royal Commission on Westminster Palace, *see* Parliament, Houses of
Rugby School, ii. 37
Ruskin, John, i. 56, 90-97, 105, 107, 114, 144, 170-173, 212, 272, 325; ii. 7, 184, 190, 209 *note*, 237, 295
  Criticism of "The Spirit of Christianity," i. 282 *and note*
  Differences of opinion with Watts, i. 93, 94, 325
  Letters, i. 93, 95, 96, 172, 174, 218, 219, 264, 272
  "Notes on Pictures," i. 93
  Opinion of Old Masters, i. 94
  Opinion of Watts, i. 93

INDEX

Ruskin, John (*contd.*)—
  St. George's Guild, i. 263, 264
  Teachings, i. 93, 94
  Watts's opinion of Ruskin, i. 91-94
Russell, Lord Arthur, i. 107
Russell, Lord John, i. 114
Russia, ii. 77
Russo-Turkish War, ii. 75, 77, 100

Sacred Books of the East, ii. 242
St. Anne's Hill, i. 254
St. Botolph's Churchyard, ii. 103
St. George's League, i. 263, 264
St. Jude's School, Whitechapel, ii. 58
St. Paul's Cathedral, i. 207, 209 ; ii. 124 *note*
Salamis, Bay of, ii. 74
Salisbury, Marquis of, ii. 273
  Portrait of, by Watts, ii. 57
Salisbury treatment, ii. 191
Salon, Paris, ii. 83, 127
Salvation Army, ii. 224
Samothrace, ii. 74
Samson, i. 263
Sandeman, Mrs., i. 185
Sandown House, i. 176, 185
San Remo, ii. 118
San Spirito, Church of, Florence, i. 48
Sant Agnese, *convent*, ii. 114
Saône, i. 45, 143
Saracen Power, i. 104
Sargent, Portrait of Dr. Joachim, ii. 321
Sartoris, Mrs. Adelaide, *née* Kemble, i. 160, 202
Saturn, i. 204
Savonarola, i. 63
Savoy, i. 93
Savoyards, ii. 121-123
Schott, Cecil, ii. 106 *note*
Scopas, i. 164
Scotland, i. 249 ; ii. 59, 60, 264, 289-291
Scott, Sir George Gilbert, Letter to Watts, i. 242, 243
Scott, Sir Walter, his influence on Watts, i. 15
Sculpture, On, i. 141, 142, 147-150, 237 ; ii. 31, 37, 81
  Coloured, i. 149, 165, 166
  Greek (*see also* Pheidias), i. 238, 243, 316, 317 ; ii. 80-82, 183, 184
Sculptures by Watts—
  Aurora, ii. 314, 315
  Cholmondeley, T., Memorial to (Condover memorial), i. 241, 251

Sculptures by Watts (*contd.*)—
  Clytie, i. 237, 241, 277 ; ii. 45
  Dawn, ii. 45
  Hugh Lupus, i. 251, 254-256, 280, 326 ; ii. 10
  Lichfield, Bishop of (Doctor Lonsdale), i. 241-244, 255
  Lothian, Marquis of, Memorial to, i. 251, 280
  Medusa, i. 65, 66
  Physical energy, i. 256, 257, 318, 328; ii. 85, 136, 150, 171, 172, 186, 235-237, 265, 270, 271-273, 303, 314, 317, 322
  Tennyson, statue to, ii. 283, 284, 305, 306, 314
Sculptures contemplated by Watts—
  Monument to the faithful who are not famous, i. 224
  Monument to heroic self-sacrifice, ii. 102, 103
Seal (engraved), i. 9
  Motto for, ii. 137, 138
Segré, Professor, i. 61
Selborne, Earl of, portrait of, by Watts, ii. 238
Self, The, ii. 244
Selfishness, On, i. 258, 259 *note*, 260
Self-portraiture, i. 245
Senior, Miss, Portrait of, by Watts, i. 174
Senior, Mrs. Nassau (Jeanie Hughes), i. 160, 161, 167, 170, 178, 295, 296, 319-322
  Death, i. 322
  Inspector of workhouses, i. 322
  Letter to Watts, i. 296-298
  Portrait of, by Watts, i. 174, 175
  Watts's opinion of, i. 322, 323
Senior, Walter, Portrait of, by Watts, i. 296, 297
Sermon on the Mount, ii. 218
Seven Champions of Christendom, i. 10
Severn, Mrs., i. 97 ; ii. 237
Seward, Edwin, i. 42
Seymour, Danby, i. 107
Shadouf, ii. 67, 68
Shaftesbury, Lord, i. 130
Shakespeare, i. 22, 41, 73, 133, 238 ; ii. 80, 199
Shee, Sir M. A.
  Opinion of Watts's drawings, i. 22
  President of the Royal Academy, i. 26
Shelley, i. 142 ; ii. 69

Shenstone, Verse by, i. 56
Sheridan, Thomas, i. 190 note
Shield, Design for, i. 197, 198
Shields, Frederick, i. 271; ii. 58
Shore, Offley, i. 35
Shrewsbury, Earl of, Portrait of, by Watts, i. 211
Siddall, Miss, see Rossetti, Mrs.
Sidgwick, ii. 179
Simons, Governor and Lady, ii. 63
Sinaitic Range, ii. 64
Singing, i. 22, 29, 30
Sistine Chapel, i. 72, 74, 103
Sliema, ii. 104
Smith, Mr., agent, i. 329
Smith, Frederic, i. 7
Smith, Harriet, see Watts, Mrs. G.
Smith, Mr. James, i. 270
Smoking, i. 162, 166
Smyrna, i. 163, 167; ii. 75
Snaffle-bit, i. 186
Soames, Mr., i. 62, 63
Social Reformation, i. 274
Socialism, ii. 147
Sodom and Gomorrah, ii. 70
Somers, Countess (Miss Virginia Pattle), i. 121-123, 125, 126, 160, 195, 202; ii. 124, 140, 261
 Portraits of, by Watts, i. 122, 123, 126, 158, 174, 235
Somers, Earl, i. 91, 125, 163
Somers-Cocks, see Cocks
Somerset, Lady Henry, i. 170
"Sorella," see Dalrymple, Mrs.
South, Sir James, i. 204
South African War, ii. 294-300
Southampton, i. 301
South Kensington Museum, ii. 46-48; ii. 131, 197
South London Fine Art Gallery, ii. 228, 229
Sparrow, tame, i. 13
Spectator, ii. 102
Spedding, James, i. 107, 114
Spence, William, i. 54, 69
 Letter to Watts, i. 55
 Portrait of, by Watts, i. 66
Spencer, Herbert, ii. 307
Spencer, Lord, ii. 46
 Letters to Watts, ii. 46-48
Spencer-Stanhope, Roddam, see Stanhope, R. S.
Spenser, Edmund, i. 41, 133, 134; ii. 182
Sphinx, ii. 65, 66

Spielmann, Marion, i. 131; ii. 259
Spiritualism, i. 54
Stafford House, i. 220
Stamboul, ii. 75
Stanhope, Lord, i. 215
Stanhope, Lady Elizabeth, i. 139
Stanhope, Roddam Spencer, i. 56, 136-138, 143, 166, 171, 320
Stanhope Street, i. 71
Stanley, Dean, Portrait of, by Watts, i. 306
Stanley, Lady (Dorothy Tennant), i. 313, 314, 316; ii. 167, 168, 267
Star Street, Marylebone, i. 23
Stars, i. 36, 37; ii. 212
Steaming of drawings, i. 42, 43
Stephen, Mrs. Leslie (Julia Jackson), i. 157; ii. 60 and note, 132, 205, 232, 254
Stephen, Sir Leslie, ii. 60, 179
Stephens, Mr., i. 275
Stevenson, R. L., ii. 221
Stirling, Colonel, i. 107
Stirling, Mrs., i. 137 note
Stokes, ii. 180, 181
Stone, Marcus, i. 329
Stratford de Redcliffe, Lord, i. 164
Streatham, ii. 203
Strettell, Miss Alma, ii. 190
Studios used by Watts, i. 23, 27, 32, 50, 53, 63-65, 86, 106-108, 116, 121, 139, 140, 161, 200, 241, 250, 251, 253, 279-281, 284, 290, 292, 293, 299; ii. 9, 49, 54, 104, 135, 136, 139, 303
Studley Royal, ii. 133
Suez Canal, ii. 63, 64
Sullivan, Sir Arthur, ii. 162
Sun, i. 48
Sundays, way spent in childhood, i. 15-17
Surrey, ii. 153, 203, 220, 232, 261
Surrey Union Foxhounds, i. 186
Sussex, i. 11
Sutherland, Duchess of, i. 220
Swallow, H.M.S., i. 164, 165; ii. 73
Swinburne, Sonnet by, ii. 259
Switzerland, i. 250; ii. 125-127
Symbolism, ii. 130, 138, 139, 243
Symonds, John Addington, ii. 137
Sympathy, On, i. 260
Synnot, Miss, i. 296, 297

Talbot, Lady Adelaide, see Brownlow, Countess

INDEX

Talbot, Lady Gertrude, *see* Pembroke, Countess of
Talbot, Sir Reginald, i. 211
Tate, Sir Henry, ii. 49, 203, 265
Tate Gallery (National Gallery of British Art), i. 64, 102, 108 ; ii. 49, 203, 264, 265, 302
Taylor, Lady, i. 205
Taylor, Miss Helen, i. 273, 275
Taylor, Sir Henry, i. 108, 176, 205 ; ii. 208
Taylor, J. E., i. 222, 223
Taylor, Mr. Scott, ii. 90
Taylor, Tom, i. 107, 160, 186, 222, 223
Taylor, Mrs. Tom, i. 169, 186
Tempera colour, i. 64, 65 ; ii. 319
Temperament, On, ii. 280, 281
Tennant, Mrs., i. 313
Tennant, Dorothy, *see* Stanley, Lady
Tennant, Eveleen,*see* Myers,Mrs.F.W.H.
Tennyson, Lady, i. 186 ; ii. 160, 210
Tennyson, Lord, i. 3, 109, 160; ii. 177, 232
  Annoyed by strangers, ii. 160
  Appearance, ii. 165
  Death, ii. 210
  "Leg of mutton" anecdote, i. 204
  Life at Freshwater, i. 294, 295
  Love of chaff, i. 205
  "Northern Farmer," i. 208
  On Arthur, i. 169
  On his poems, ii. 162, 163
  Watts's opinion of, ii. 210, 211
  Opinion of Thoby Prinsep, i. 123
  Photograph of, i. 208
  Portraits by Watts, i. 169, 170, 217, 218 ; ii. 158-167, 192
  Proud of his garden, ii. 162
  Scorn of book-collecting, ii. 86
  Statue by Watts, ii. 283, 284, 305, 306, 314
Tennyson, Hallam (2nd Baron), ii. 158-162, 164, 210
Terra-cotta modelling, ii. 284
Teucer, ii. 199
Thackeray, Miss (*Old Kensington*), i. 4
Thackeray, W. M., i. 106, 160
Thames, s.s., ii. 64
Thames Ditton, i. 256
Therapia, ii. 77
Theseus, ii. 41, 81, 265
Thiers, M., Portrait of, by Watts, i. 161, 162
Thompson (Watts's assistant), ii. 237, 265-267, 303, 317, 318
Thornycroft, Mr. and Mrs., i. 329

Thornycroft, Hamo, ii. 134
Thornycroft, Thomas, ii. 39, 40
Thunderstorm, i. 46
Thynne, Lady Katherine, Portrait by Watts, ii. 173, 193
Time lost through illness, i. 308
Times, The, i. 180, 185 ; ii. 19, 102
Timon the Tartar, ii. 171
"Tin-pot" (or "Iron-pot") studio, i. 290, 293 ; ii. 9
Tintoretto, i. 95 ; ii. 80
  "Miracle of St. Mark," i. 67
Titian, i. 67, 144, 146-148, 162, 209, 210, 219, 291, 314; ii. 80, 87, 140, 304
Titles, On, ii. 38, 39
Tolstoi, ii. 144
"Tom Bowling," i. 163
Towsey, Captain, i. 163
Toynbee Hall, ii. 99
Travel, Value of, i. 68
Treasury, i. 88, 89
Trees, i. 278, 304 ; ii. 156
Tricoupi, Mr., ii. 81, 82
  Portrait by Watts, ii. 81
Trinity College, Cambridge, ii. 158, 164, 167 *note*
Trinity Lodge, Bournemouth, i. 278
Troubridge, Lady (Laura), ii. 330
Troy, i. 15 ; ii. 74, 199, 273
Truth, On, i. 92-94 ; ii. 72, 94, 222
Tulse Hill, i. 116
Tupper, Mr., i. 292
Turf, The, ii. 298
Turin, i. 173 ; ii. 118, 119
Turkish apathy, ii. 167
Turks, i. 165, 166
Turner, i. 209
Turnor, Christopher, ii. 305-307
Tuscany, i. 47
Tuscany, Court of, i. 61
Tweed, ii. 289
Twickenham, i. 188, 189
"Twilight of the Gods," ii. 293
Tytler, Fraser-, family, *see* Fraser-Tytler
Tytler, Miss Fraser-, *see* Watts, Mrs. G. F.

Undine, horse, i. 195
Usnach, Sons of, ii. 292

Val d'Arno, i. 61
Valeska, Countess, Portrait of, i. 66
Valetta, ii. 105
Van Dyck, i. 22, 23
Varnishes, i. 174, 234 ; ii. 29, 304

GEORGE FREDERIC WATTS

Vatican, i. 181
Velasquez, i. 314
Venetian Art, *see* Art
Venice, i. 144, 289
  Accademia, i. 146
  St. Mark's, i. 144, 145
Verdi, i. 69
Verestchagin, ii. 100, 101, 266, 279
Verner, Miss Ida, ii. 110, 127
Vesci, Viscountess de, ii. 209 *note*, 260, 263
Vesci, Viscount de, Portrait by Watts, ii. 261
Vesuvius, i. 75; ii. 111
Victoria, Queen, Sculpture by W. Behnes, i. 19, 20
Victorian Exhibition, i. 270
Villa Medicae di Careggi, *see* Careggi
Village life, Rhodes's opinion of, ii. 269
Vinci, Leonardo da, i. 71; ii. 183
Vines, i. 47
Violin, i. 201, 202
Viper, i. 64
Virgil, i. 22, 225
Virgin of the Waters, ii. 120
Vision, ii. 323
Vittoria, dahabeah, ii. 66, 72
Volunteers, i. 196, 197

Wagner, i. 258
Walker, Frederick, Headmaster of St. Paul's School, Letter on Watts's portrait of Rickards, i. 225, 226
Walker, Frederick, Painter, i. 265, 320
Walpole, Lord, i. 75
Wandsworth, ii. 317
Wanostrocht, Nicholas, "Nicholas Felix," i. 28-30
War, Watts's and Ruskin's attitude towards, ii. 295-298
Wars of the Roses, ii. 276
Watch, given by Lady Holland, i. 57
Water-colour drawings by Watts—
  Caractacus, i. 44
  Tintoretto's Miracle of St. Mark, i. 67
  Titian's Battle of Cadore, i. 67
  Trees, i. 33
  Preserved by Count Cottrell, i. 55
Water Colour School, i. 215
Waterford, (Louisa) Marchioness of, i. 97 *and note*, 98, 211, 212; ii. 203
Waterglass, i. 318
Waterhouse, Alfred, i. 318
Waterloo, Battle of, i. 6
Watts, Surname, i. 4

Watts, George, grandfather of G. F. Watts, i. 5, 7
Watts, George, father of G. F. Watts, i. 5, 7, 9, 10, 12, 14, 22, 23, 25
  His affection for G. F. Watts, i. 12, 86
  His association with Behnes, i. 19
  His books, i. 10
  His character and refinement, i. 9, 10, 32
  His death, i. 75
  His desk, i. 9
  His inventions, i. 9, 87
  His religion, i. 15, 16
  His seal, i. 9
Watts, Mrs. George, mother of G. F. Watts (*née* Harriet Smith), i. 5, 7, 8, 23
  Her sister's photograph, i. 8
Watts, George Frederic—
  Ambitions and aims, i. 4, 6, 7, 30, 31, 87, 89-92, 104, 176, 177, 194, 226, 241, 248, 252, 262, 277, 281, 284, 307, 312; ii. 13, 14, 31, 33, 114, 115, 143, 144, 172, 187, 193, 195, 196, 204, 207, 214, 215, 236, 257, 258, 262, 265, 279, 315
  Desire to write poetry, ii. 210-212
  Ancestors, i. 5-7
  Appearance, i. 51, 69, 289, 300; ii. 152, 153
  Articles and lectures—
    "Dress," ii. 8, 9
    Needlework, ii. 6-8
    "Our Race as Pioneers," ii. 299
    "The position that Art is worthy to hold amongst us," ii. 151
    "Preface to New Gallery Catalogue," ii. 257
    "Present Conditions of Art," i. 313, 316
  Benefactions to the nation, etc. (Offers and Gifts), i. 88, 113, 200, 226, 262, 267, 274, 276, 284; ii. 45-50, 58, 85, 106, 107, 123, 195, 203, 204, 215, 234, 249, 250, 265, 272
  Brothers of, i. 8
  Career (*arranged chronologically*)—
    Birth and Baptism (1817), i. 7
    Early Life, i. 3, 7-18
    Drew from earliest childhood, i. 11, 18
    Visits to his godfather's farm, i. 11
    Education, i. 14, 31
    Visits to studio of W. Behnes, i. 20-22

INDEX

Watts, George Frederic (*contd.*)—
Career (*contd.*)—
  Encouraged by B. Haydon, i. 23
  Plays trick on W. Behnes, i. 23
  Early art studies, i. 24
  First commissions, i. 24, 25
  Self-supporting, i. 25
  Admitted to R.A. Schools (1835), i. 25, 26
  Influenced by Pheidias, i. 26
  Advised by W. Hilton, i. 27
  Presents drawing of cricketers to Marylebone C.C., i. 29
  Studies French, Italian, and Greek, i. 30
  Studies Art, i. 31, 32
  Visits to West End Lane, i. 33
  Goes to Derbyshire to paint, i. 35
  Competition for cartoons for Westminster Palace, i. 41-43
  Visit to France and Italy, i. 43-57
  Florence (1843), i. 47-49
  Stays with Lord and Lady Holland in Florence, i. 48-57
  At Careggi, i. 61-65
  Nearly stung by viper, i. 63
  Visits Lucca, i. 66
  Influence of Italy, i. 66, 68
  Gives evidence before Royal Commission on the Royal Academy, i. 68
  Social pleasures, i. 68, 69
  Fancy-dress ball, i. 69
  Visit to Holland House, i. 71
  Visit to Italy with Lord Holland, i. 71, 72
  Visit to Rome, i. 72
  Visit to Pompeii, i. 74, 75
  Returns to Careggi, i. 75, 81
  Leaves Italy, i. 81, 82
  Enters competition for prizes offered by Royal Commission, i. 78, 87, 88
  Friction with stepsisters, i. 87
  Difference of opinion with Ruskin, i. 93-96
  Contemplated visit to Greece (1848), i. 105
  Visits Ireland (1851), i. 109-111
  Psychical phenomena, i. 115-117
  Meeting with Mrs. Prinsep and Miss Pattle, i. 121, 122
  Resides at Little Holland House, i. 128, 129
  Teacher, i. 138, 139
  Visits Italy (1853), i. 55, 56, 143

Watts, George Frederic (*contd.*)—
Career (*contd.*)—
  Kissed by flower-seller in Florence, i. 56
  Works on Lincoln's Inn fresco, i. 150
  In Paris (1855-56), i. 161
  Visit to Constantinople and Asia Minor (Halicarnassus, etc.) (1856-1857), i. 163-167
  Visits Esher, i. 176, 185-190
  Honoured by Benchers of Lincoln's Inn (1860), i. 185
  Volunteer, i. 197
  Scheme for decoration of St. Paul's, i. 207, 209
  Visit to Blickling (1862), i. 210-212
  Suggestions to Royal Academy Commission, i. 212-216
  Marriage (1864), i. 221
  Works on monumental statue (1866), i. 224
  Associate of the Royal Academy, i. 231
  Academician (1867), i. 232
  Member of Hanging Committee of Royal Academy (1869), i. 233
  Commissions refused, i. 242, 248
  Devotes himself to sculpture (1867, etc.), i. 250, 251
  Friction with Lady Holland (1871), 251-254
  Paints diploma picture, i. 257
  Disappointed at lack of general sympathy, i. 262, 263
  Offer to help Ruskin, i. 263, 264
  Builds the Briary, i. 265, 278
  Guardian of orphan girl, i. 266
  Riding, i. 276
  First met Mrs. Watts (1870), i. 287-289
  Leaves Little Holland House for Melbury Road (1876), i. 304
  Appreciation from strangers, i. 324
  At Brighton (1876), i. 330
  Works exhibited at Manchester (1880), ii. 3-5
  Builds gallery (1881), ii. 9
  Appreciation from strangers, ii. 10
  Declines Grosvenor Gallery dinner (1882), ii. 12-17, 39
  American Exhibition, ii. 26-37
  Declines baronetcy (1885), ii. 38, 39

GEORGE FREDERIC WATTS

Watts, George Frederic (*contd.*)—
  Career (*contd.*).—
    Marriage (1886), ii. 59, 60, 63
    Voyage and travels in Egypt, Turkey, and Greece, ii. 63-83
    Work at Melbury Road studio, ii. 84, etc.
    At work on "Physical Energy," ii. 85, 171, 172, 235, 236
    Erection of cloister in St. Botolph's churchyard (1899), ii. 103
    Winters in Malta, ii. 104-110
    Naples, ii. 110
    Mentone, ii. 111-118
    Aix-les-Bains, ii. 118-125
    Switzerland, ii. 125-127
    Home life, ii. 132
    In Brighton, ii. 135-145
    Winter at Monkshatch, Surrey, ii. 154-158
    In the Isle of Wight, ii. 159-167
    Visited by Queen of Roumania, ii. 189-190
    Purchases Limnerslease, ii. 192
    At Limnerslease, ii. 198
    Grief at Tennyson's death, ii. 210
    Honoured by Cambridge and Oxford, ii. 217-220
    Takes to riding again, ii. 219, 220
    Lays foundation stone, ii. 228
    Declines second offer of baronetcy, ii. 239-242
    Trustee of National Portrait Gallery, ii. 250
    Raises funds for Home Arts Association, ii. 251, 252
    Eightieth birthday celebrations, ii. 258-262
    Pictures taken to Tate Gallery, ii. 265
    Paints portrait of Cecil Rhodes, ii. 267-270
    Home life at Limnerslease, ii. 274
    Undertakes statue to Tennyson, ii. 283, 305
    Classes held at Compton, ii. 284, 305
    Visits Scotland, ii. 289-295
    Order of Merit, ii. 303
    Builds a gallery at Limnerslease, ii. 305
    At Queen's Hall, ii. 321
    Death (1904), ii. 323
  Characteristics—
    Affable, i. 162

Watts, George Frederic (*contd.*)—
  Characteristics (*contd.*)—
    Affection for father, i. 32, 86, 87
    Allowances for temperament, etc., ii. 280, 281
    Ambitious, i. 176
    Analytic and creative, ii. 183
    Anxiety, ii. 205-207
    Anxious to satisfy, i. 244
    Appreciative of sympathy and praise, i. 245, 246; ii. 17, 145, 193, 258, 263
    Ascetic habits, i. 51
    Beautiful, Lover of the, i. 5, 240
    Calmness, ii. 205
    Charm of personality, i. 115
    Children, Fondness for, i. 299, 303, 304, 330; ii. 207, 208
    Courteous, i. 299, 300; ii. 132, 183, 187, 255
    Criticism, Dislike of, i. 176, 242, 245, 281
    Desire and power to paint the best in people, i. 114
    Determination to do his best, i. 17
    Dread of deceiving, ii. 13
    Dread of defrauding, i. 227, 244, 255
    Early riser, i. 24, 256, 299, 326, 328; ii. 84-86, 227, 237, 275, 315, 320
    Faculty for taking pains, i. 18
    Fascinated by armour, i. 53
    Finds out excellencies, i. 171
    Forgiving, ii. 280
    Friend, Constant, i. 51
    Games, Love of, ii. 208, 227, 228
    Gardening, Fondness for, ii. 198
    Generosity, i. 242, 243, 263, 267, 297; ii. 108, 137, 152, 206
    Generosity towards brother artists, ii. 187
    Gift of revealing nobler undertones, ii. 55
    Gratitude, i. 56
    Hard to coax, ii. 267
    High spiritual plane, ii. 221
    Horses, Fondness for, i. 186-188, 295
    Humility, ii. 207
    Imaginative work, Preference for, i. 27, 35
    Independent views in childhood, i. 16

INDEX

Watts, George Frederic (*contd.*)—
  Characteristics (*contd.*)—
    Indignation at indifference to advantages, i. 15
    Jonah-like, ii. 149
    Lenient, i. 171
    Letter-writing, Dislike of, i. 176
    Liberally minded, i. 5 ; ii. 146, 224, 225, 227
    Liked by his playmates, i. 10
    Memory for form, etc., ii. 183
    Musical, i. 186, 201, 258 ; ii. 56, 57, 209, 211
      Singing, i. 22, 30, 46, 76, 163
    Mystic, ii. 180, 181
    Name, Dislike of, i. 4
    Nervous temperament, i. 12, 17
    Never desultory, i. 24
    Never repeated evil of any one, ii. 280
    Objection to daubs, i. 49
    Orderly and careful, i. 50; ii. 281, 282
    Over-estimation, Dislike of, i. 177, 178
    Pathos, i. 27
    Patience and persistency, ii. 278, 279
    Patience with amateur work, i. 289; ii. 98, 177
    Patriotism, i. 89, 90 ; ii. 14, 33, 295
    Portrait painting, Dislike of, i. 266; ii. 161
    "Professional element," Dislike of, ii. 56
    Proportion, Love of, ii. 96
    Public dinners, Dislike of, ii. 13-17
    Publicity, Dislike of, ii. 18, 38, 39
    Ready to praise, i. 51 ; ii. 98
    Realist, ii. 185
    Rebellious against unnecessary discomforts, ii. 113
    Resolute character, i. 24
    Roman virtue, i. 233
    Sadness, i. 221
    Says the right thing, ii. 54
    Self-confidence, lack of, i. 13, 14
    Self-control, i. 17 ; ii. 182, 185
    Self-depreciation, ii. 257, 258
    Sense of humour, ii. 181
    Sensitiveness, ii. 39
    Sensitive to pain, i. 245 ; ii. 183
    Shrewdness, ii. 181
    Simplicity in speaking, ii. 178, 324

Watts, George Frederic (*contd.*)—
  Characteristics (*contd.*)—
    Singleness of heart, i. 177
    Spontaneity, ii. 319
    Steadiness of purpose, i. 18
    Symbolist, ii. 138, 139
    Sympathetic, ii. 54, 60, 227
    Tenderness, ii. 227
    Trees, Fondness for, i. 304
    Troubled by business affairs, i. 280
    Wholeness of ideas, ii. 187
    Work, Capacity and fondness for, i. 68, 299 ; ii. 254, 275
    Youthfulness in old age, ii. 238, 239
  Conversational powers, ii. 177-188, 305-307; Italian, i. 47
  Dignities and honours—
    Baronetcy offered and declined, ii. 38, 39, 239-242
    Cambridge and Oxford degrees, ii. 217-220
    Order of Merit, ii. 303
    Order of San Lodovico, i. 66
  Drawings by Watts, *see* Drawings, *as separate heading*
  Estimates and appreciations of, by—
    Airlie, Countess of, ii. 8, 9
    Alford, Lady Marion, ii. 8
    Allbutt, Sir Clifford, ii. 178-188
    Anonymous, ii. 282
    Arts and Crafts Society, ii. 259, 260
    Baden-Powell, General, ii. 300
    Bosanquet, B., i. 236
    Bowman, Sir William, ii. 196
    Brown, Madox, ii. 244
    Burne-Jones, Sir Edward, i. 171
    Burne-Jones, Sir Philip, ii. 101
    Carlyle, i. 249
    Child, A, ii. 208
    Coquelin, M., i. 314 ; ii. 235
    Crane, Walter, ii. 200
    De Vere, Aubrey, i. 113
    Fawcett, Mrs., i. 274
    Graham, William, ii. 11
    Hamerton, P. G., ii. 173
    Hanson, Mrs. Arthur, ii. 77
    Hichens, Andrew, ii. 61, 123
    Hilton, W. (R.A.), i. 26, 27
    Hone, Nathaniel, i. 162
    Hopkins, Miss Ellice, i. 299, 300
    La Sizeranne, Robert de, ii. 48, 49
    Layard, Sir Henry, i. 180-182
    Leighton, Lord, i. 199; ii. 201, 202

Watts, George Frederic (*contd.*)—
  Estimates, etc. (*contd.*) by—
    Lewes, Mrs. George, i. 277
    Lytton, Earl of, ii. 11, 12
    Martinengo Cesaresco, Countess, i. 220
    Mazzini, i. 132
    Mead, Miss, ii. 26
    Meredith, i. 210
    Millais, ii. 172, 200
    Myers, F. W. H., i. 222; ii. 20, 21, 323, 324
    Rhodes, Cecil, ii. 271
    Richmond, George, i. 242, 243
    Rossetti, D. G., i. 170, 179, 180
    Rossetti, William, i. 269, 270
    Ruskin, i. 93-96, 114, 127, 282
    Shee, Sir M. A. (P.R.A.), i. 22
    Somers, Countess, i. 122
    Spencer, Earl, ii. 48
    Stanhope, R. S., i. 138, 139
    Stanley, Lady (Miss Tennant), i. 316
    Thompson, Watts's assistant, ii. 266, 267
    Thornycroft, Thomas, ii. 40
    Turnor, C., ii. 307
    Walker, Frederick, i. 225
    Watts, G. F., criticisms of himself, i. 79, 80, 89, 90, 91, 92, 127, 134, 141, 175, 177, 178, 208, 209, 226, 227, 228, 236, 239, 241, 243, 244, 247, 248, 250, 252, 253, 255, 264, 271, 275, 277, 279, 283, 284, 307, 308; ii. 6, 7, 13, 27, 28, 30, 31, 32, 34, 50, 85, 214, 215, 234, 235, 262, 263, 302, 304, 306, 313, 315, 322
    Watts, Mrs. G. F., i. 289; ii. 54, 177, 178, 227
    Wells, H. T., ii. 16
    Wemyss, Earl of, ii. 253
    Z——, Mr., ii. 35
  Health, i. 8, 11-13, 18, 19, 24, 31, 50, 110, 163, 168, 177, 178, 181, 232, 233, 240, 244, 252, 277, 305, 308, 318; ii. 5, 30, 63, 72, 78, 109, 110, 112, 125, 133, 172, 182, 190, 196, 210, 212, 237, 274, 301, 318, 322, 323
    Cough, ii. 67
    Depression, i. 126, 161
    Gout, ii. 120
    Headache and nausea, i. 12, 124, 125
    Influence of sorrow, ii. 210

Watts, George Frederic (*contd.*)—
  Health (*contd.*)—
    Influenza, ii. 193, 194
    Kick on shin, i. 266
    Measles, i. 8
    Nerves, ii. 205
    Nervous fever, i. 125
    Pneumonia, ii. 142, 143, 294
    Salisbury treatment, ii. 191
    Sight, i. 217
    Surgical treatment, i. 301
  Letters, i. 3; ii. 20
    to
    Aberdare, Lord (Henry Bruce), i. 248; ii. 45, 46
    Acland, Sir Henry, i. 140, 141
    Agnew, William, ii. 106-108
    American Exhibition, ii. 33
    Anonymous, i. 146-150, 182-185, 187, 281, 283; ii. 311
    Armitage, Edward, i. 45, 46
    Burne-Jones, Lady, ii. 301, 303
    Butler, Edward, i. 259, 260
    Cameron, Mrs., i. 207-209
    Carlisle, Earl of, ii. 38
    Dilke, Right Hon. Sir Charles, i. 274, 275
    Elcho, Lord, i. 214, 216, 217
    Gladstone, i. 236, 237, 305; ii. 38, 240, 241
    Gordon, Lady Duff, i. 171, 172
    Gordon, Miss Duff, i. 78-82, 99, 100
    Gower, Lord, i. 73, 74
    Grey, Earl, ii. 272, 273, 296
    Holland, Lady, i. 252, 253
    Horsley, Mr., ii. 40
    Ionides, Mr., i. 76
    Lewes, Mrs. George, i. 277
    Liddell, Mrs. Edward, ii. 211, 212
    Lincoln's Inn Architect, i. 178, 179
    Lincoln's Inn Benchers, ii. 135, 136
    Luxembourg Authorities, ii. 234
    Luxmoore, H. E., ii. 262-264
    Lytton, Earl of, ii. 13, 14
    Mead, Miss (Mrs. E. Abbey), ii. 27-37
    Newton, Sir Charles, i. 143
    O'Brien, Mary, i. 110-112
    Rickards, C. H., i. 225-228, 243, 247, 254, 255, 261, 275, 276, 279, 295, 302, 307, 308, 322, 323, 326, 328; ii. 3-5, 10
    Riviere, Briton, ii. 150
    Rossetti, Dante Gabriel, i. 268, 269, 271

INDEX

Watts, George Frederic (*contd.*)—
  Letters (*contd.*)—
    Ruskin, i. 91, 92, 93, 144
    Senior, Mrs. Nassau, i. 167, 170, 171, 178, 320, 321
    Somers, Countess, i. 195
    Stanley, Lady (Dorothy Tennant), i. 314, 315
    Stuart, Sir John, i. 168, 169
    Taylor, Sir Henry, i. 176-178
    Watts, Mrs. G. F., ii. 58, 59, 60
    Wells, H. T., ii. 17
    Wemyss, Countess of, ii. 319
    Westminster, Marquis of, i. 254
    Westminster Hall Commissioners, i. 88, 89
    Wylie, Mrs., i. 275, 292, 293
    Wyndham, Hon. Mrs. Percy, i. 240, 241, 325, 326 ; ii. 6, 7
  Method of work : painting, i. 65, 174, 175, 211, 234, 328 ; ii. 44, 45, 77, 84, 85, 87-91, 107, 114, 115, 124, 125, 197
    Sculpture, i. 256 ; ii. 45, 85, 236, 237
  "Mistakes," ii. 33, 35
  Money matters, i. 195, 252, 253, 255, 292 ; ii. 34, 206, 207
    Payments, i. 25, 35, 77, 88, 89, 195, 218, 227, 242, 263, 264 ; ii. 107
    Refusal of, i. 228, 242, 281, 296
  Moral influence, i. 35, 36, 222, 324, 325 ; ii. 55, 56, 270
  Nicknames and pseudonyms—
    "Divine Watts," i. 300
    Fra Paolo, i. 50
    George, F. W., i. 175, 176
    Lamb, i. 156
    Mr. Royal, i. 4
    "Pynter to the Nytion," ii. 50
    Saint George, ii. 40
    Signor, i. 155
    Titian of Limnerslease, ii. 233, 259
  Opinions by Watts, *see various subjects throughout the Index*
  Paintings by Watts, *see* Paintings, *as separate heading*
  Political views, ii. 146-148
  Portraits by, *see* Portraits, *as separate heading*
  Portraits of, by himself, i. 34, 53, 245 ; ii. 196, 319
    Photograph by C. Turnor, ii. 306
    Portrait bust by Gilbert, ii. 133-135
  Prizes gained, i. 42, 87

Watts, George Frederic (*contd.*)—
  Stepsisters, i. 8, 9, 85-87
  Style of writing, i. 316
  Verse by, i. 69
Watts, Mrs. G. F. (Mary Fraser-Tytler), i. 49, 74, 159, 191, 197, 329 ; ii. 53, 109, 178, 194, 200, 204, 205, 206, 238, 243, 264, 301, 303, 318, 323
  Accident to her nephew, ii. 59
  Andrew Hichens' opinion of, ii. 61, 62
  At the Briary, i. 298, 299
  Childhood, i. 288
  Clay-modelling class for boys, ii. 57
  Collects for Home Arts Association, ii. 251, 252
  Conversations with Rhodes, ii. 268, 269
  Daily life at Melbury Road, ii. 84-87
  First meeting with Watts, i. 287-289
  Impressions of G. F. Watts, ii. 53, 54, 205, 206
  Marriage, ii. 63
  Meets G. F. Watts at Bournemouth, i. 278
  Old home, ii. 289
  Painting, i. 289, 298 ; ii. 55
  Reading to Watts, i. 93, 271
Watts Collection, *see* Compton Gallery
Watts-Dunton, i. 271
Wax modelling, i. 65, 74
Weekes, Henry, his opinion of W. Behnes, i. 20
Wellington, Duke of, i. 113
  Statue of, i. 215
Wells, H. T., i. 248
  Letters to and from Watts, ii. 15-17
Wellsted, Rev. A. O., Portrait of, by Watts, i. 34
Welsh pony, ii. 219
Wemyss, Countess of, ii. 319
Wemyss, Earl of, ii. 95, 209 *note*, 253
  Letter to Mrs. G. F. Watts, i. 198
Wemyss, Mrs. Erskine, i. 122
Wenlock, Lady (Lady Constance Lascelles), ii. 260, 285
West, Sir Algernon, i. 107
West End Lane, i. 33
Westminster Abbey, ii. 156, 157
Westminster, City of, i. 274
Westminster, Duke of [Marquis of], i. 251, 254, 256, 280
Westminster Hall, *see* Parliament, Houses of

351

Whitechapel, ii. 57, 99
Whitman, Walt, i. 239
Wight, Isle of (*see also* Freshwater), i. 253, 266, 329; ii. 159, 161
Downs, i. 295, 299
Wilson's force, Memorial to, ii. 270
Wiltshire Downs, i. 195
Window, Painted, i. 170
Winsor and Newton, Messrs., i. 151; ii. 90
Wint, Peter de, i. 26
Womanhood, ii. 139
Woman Suffrage, ii. 145, 146
Woods, Mr., auctioneer, i. 270
Wordsworth, ii. 179, 180; ii. 244
Work, On, i. 326; ii. 177, 275
Workhouses, i. 322 *note*
Working Man's Club, ii. 99, 229

Wright, Thomas, i. 130, 131
Wylie, Mrs. Charles, i. 290, 291, 293; ii. 98, 104
Wyndham, Hon. Mrs. Percy, i. 138; ii. 6, 7, 260
Portrait by Watts, i. 239, 325

X——, Mr., ii. 28
Xenophon, i. 77, 126

York, i. 131
Yorke, Lady Lilian, ii. 157

Z——, Mr., ii. 35
Zimmermann, Mrs. Agnes, ii. 261
Zola, ii. 121
Zoological Gardens, i. 44
Zoroastrian writing, ii. 243

END OF VOL. II

Printed by R. & R. CLARK, LIMITED, *Edinburgh.*

In thanking Mrs. EDWARD LIDDELL for a letter he had received from her, in which a description of village life had much pleased him, G. F. WATTS said :—

"But the poet turns everything to poetry. Why do you never write? you to whom the gift of words has been given; a gift I envy more than I can say. . . . I think it is too bad of you, who have these obedient to your command, to keep them eating their heads off doing nothing; if I had these at all tractable, I would make them do something, if only in a carrier's cart."—[See page 211, vol. ii. of " George Frederic Watts."]

SONGS IN MINOR KEYS

BY

C. C. FRASER-TYTLER

(MRS. EDWARD LIDDELL)

Fcap. 8vo.   6s.

Spectator.—"Very simple and charming songs, with the genuine lyrical spirit in almost all, and considerable power of vivid imagination in many. . . . It is very rarely indeed of late years that we have read religious poetry so genuine, so attractive, and so simple."

Academy.—"Mrs. Liddell has produced a book that displays feeling and thought no less conspicuously than music and beauty —a book distinguished by a varied tone and temper, full of sunshine and shadow, and wholly free from alloy of unworthy matter."

LONDON: MACMILLAN AND CO., LTD.

DATE DUE